GOD'S
BATTALIONS

GOD'S
BATTALIONS

The Case for the Crusades

RODNEY STARK

HarperOne
An Imprint of HarperCollins*Publishers*

HarperOne

GOD'S BATTALIONS: *The Case for the Crusades.* Copyright © 2009 by Rodney Stark. All rights reserved. Printed in the United States of America. No part of this book may be used or reproduced in any manner whatsoever without written permission except in the case of brief quotations embodied in critical articles and reviews. For information address HarperCollins Publishers, 10 East 53rd Street, New York, NY 10022.

HarperCollins books may be purchased for educational, business, or sales promotional use. For information please write: Special Markets Department, HarperCollins Publishers, 10 East 53rd Street, New York, NY 10022.

HarperCollins Web site: http://www.harpercollins.com

HarperCollins®, ♦®, and HarperOne™ are trademarks of HarperCollins Publishers

Title page image © Réunion des Musées Nationaux Art Resource, NY
Maps by Topaz Maps Inc.
Book design by Ralph Fowler / rlf design

FIRST EDITION

Library of Congress Cataloging-in-Publication Data
   Stark, Rodney.
   God's battalions : the case for the Crusades / Rodney Stark. — 1st ed.
      p.   cm.
   Includes bibliographical references.
   ISBN 978-0-06-158261-5
      1. Crusades—History.   2. Christianity and other religions—Islam.
   3. Islam—Relations—Christianity.   4. Religion and civilization.   5. Civilization,
   Medieval.   I. Title.
   D157.S736   2009
   909.07—dc22   2008051976

09 10 11 12 13   RRD(H)   10 9 8 7 6 5 4 3 2

CONTENTS

GOD'S
BATTALIONS

GREEDY BARBARIANS IN ARMOR?

Pope Urban II asks a gathering of bishops and clergy during the
Council at Clermont to help him preach the First Crusade. The next
day he preached the Crusade to a huge crowd in a meadow.
© Bridgeman-Giraudon / Art Resource, NY

On NOVEMBER 27, 1095, Pope Urban II mounted a platform set up in a meadow outside the French city of Clermont, surrounded in all directions by an immense crowd. A vigorous man of fifty-three, Urban was blessed with an unusually powerful and expressive voice that made it possible for him to be heard at a great distance. On this memorable occasion, addressing a multitude that included poor peasants as well as nobility and clergy, the pope gave a speech that changed history.

Urban had arranged the gathering in response to a letter from Alexius Comnenus, emperor of Byzantium, who had written from his embattled capital of Constantinople to the Count of Flanders requesting that he and his fellow Christians send forces to help the Byzantines repel the Seljuk Turks, recent converts to Islam who had invaded the Middle East, captured Jerusalem, and driven to within one hundred miles of Constantinople. In his letter, the emperor detailed gruesome tortures of Christian pilgrims to the Holy Land and vile desecrations of churches, altars, and baptismal fonts. Should Constantinople fall to the Turks, not only would thousands more Christians be murdered, tortured, and raped, but also "the most holy relics of the Saviour," gathered over the centuries, would be lost. "Therefore in the name of God . . . we implore you to bring this city all the faithful soldiers of Christ . . . [I]n your coming you will find your reward in heaven, and if you do not come, God will condemn you."[1]

There were many reasons that Europeans might have ignored any plea for help from Byzantium. For one thing, their cultural

heritage as well as their Christianity was Roman, while the Byzantines were Greeks, whose lifestyle seemed decadent to Europeans
and whose "Orthodox" Christianity held Latin Catholicism in
contempt—often persecuting its priests and practitioners. Nevertheless, when Pope Urban II read this letter he was determined
that it be answered by worthy deeds, and he arranged for a church
council at Clermont, which he followed with his famous speech.[2]

Speaking in French, the pope began by graphically detail-
ing the torture, rape, and murder of Christian pilgrims and the
defilement of churches and holy places committed by the Turks
(he called them Persians): "They destroy the altars, after having
defiled them with their uncleanness. They circumcise the Christians, and the blood of the circumcision they either pour on the
altars or pour into the vases of the baptismal font. When they wish
to torture people by a base death, they perforate their navels, and
dragging forth the extremity of the intestines, bind it to a stake;
then with flogging they lead the victim around until the viscera
having gushed forth the victim falls prostrate on the ground . . .
What shall I say about the abominable rape of women? To speak
of it is worse than to be silent. On whom therefore is the labor of
avenging these wrongs and recovering this territory incumbent, if
not upon you?"[3]

At this point Pope Urban raised a second issue to which he and
his illustrious predecessor Gregory VII had devoted years of effort—the chronic warfare of medieval times. The popes had been
attempting to achieve a "truce of God" among the feudal nobility, many of whom seemed inclined to make war, even on their
friends, just for the sake of a good fight. After all, it was what they
had trained to do every day since early childhood. Here was their
chance! "Christian warriors, who continually and vainly seek pre-
texts for war, rejoice, for you have today found a true pretext . . .
If you are conquered, you will have the glory of dying in the very

same place as Jesus Christ, and God will never forget that he found you in the holy battalions . . . Soldiers of Hell, become soldiers of the living God!"[4]

Now, shouts of *"Dieu li volt!"* (God wills it!) began to spread through the crowd, and men began to cut up cloaks and other pieces of cloth to make crosses and sew them against their chests. Everyone agreed that the next year they would set out for the Holy Land. And they did.

That is the traditional explanation of how and why the First Crusade began. But in recent times a far more cynical and sinister explanation of the Crusades has gained popularity. Thus, in the immediate aftermath of the destruction of the World Trade Center by Muslim terrorists, frequent mention was made of the Crusades as a basis for Islamic fury. It was argued that Muslim bitterness over their mistreatment by the Christian West can be dated back to the First Crusade. Far from being motivated by piety or by concern for the safety of pilgrims and the holy places in Jerusalem, the Crusades were but the first extremely bloody chapter in a long history of brutal European colonialism.[5]

More specifically, it is charged that the crusaders marched east not out of idealism, but in pursuit of lands and loot; that the Crusades were promoted by power-mad popes seeking to greatly expand Christianity through conversion of the Muslim masses;[6] and that the knights of Europe were barbarians who brutalized everyone in their path, leaving "the enlightened Muslim culture . . . in ruins."[7] As Akbar Ahmed, chair of Islamic studies at American University in Washington, D.C., has suggested, "the Crusades created a historical memory which is with us today—the memory of a long European onslaught."[8]

Two months after the attack of September 11, 2001, on New York City, former president Bill Clinton informed an audience at Georgetown University that "[t]hose of us who come from various

European lineages are not blameless" vis-à-vis the Crusades as a crime against Islam, and then summarized a medieval account about all the blood that was shed when Godfrey of Bouillon and his forces conquered Jerusalem in 1099.

That the Crusades were a terrible crime in great need of atonement was a popular theme even before the Islamic terrorists crashed their hijacked airliners. In 1999, the *New York Times* had solemnly proposed that the Crusades were comparable to Hitler's atrocities or to the ethnic cleansing in Kosovo.[9] That same year, to mark the nine hundredth anniversary of the crusader conquest of Jerusalem, hundreds of devout Protestants took part in a "reconciliation walk" that began in Germany and ended in the Holy Land. Along the way the walkers wore T-shirts bearing the message "I apologize" in Arabic. Their official statement explained the need for a Christian apology:

> *Nine hundred years ago, our forefathers carried the name of Jesus Christ in battle across the Middle East. Fueled by fear, greed, and hatred . . . the Crusaders lifted the banner of the Cross above your people . . . On the anniversary of the First Crusade . . . we wish to retrace the footsteps of the Crusaders in apology for their deeds . . . We deeply regret the atrocities committed in the name of Christ by our predecessors. We renounce greed, hatred and fear, and condemn all violence done in the name of Jesus Christ.[10]*

Also in 1999, Karen Armstrong, a former nun and a popular writer on religious themes, proposed that "crusading answered a deep need in the Christians of Europe. Yet today most of us would unhesitantly condemn the Crusades as unchristian. After all, Jesus told his followers to love their enemies, not to exterminate them. He was a pacifist and had more in common with Gandhi, perhaps, than with Pope Urban." Armstrong went on to propose that, in fact, "holy war is a deeply Christian act," since Christianity has "an inherent leaning toward violence, despite the pacifism of Jesus."[11] And a prominent former priest, James Carroll, agreed, charging that the Crusades left a "trail of violence [that] scars the earth and human memory even to this day."[12]

These are not new charges. Western condemnations of the Crusades were widespread during the "Enlightenment," that utterly misnamed era during which French and British intellectuals invented the "Dark Ages" in order to glorify themselves and vilify the Catholic Church (see chapter 3). Hence, Voltaire (1694–1778) called the Crusades an "epidemic of fury which lasted for two hundred years and which was always marked by every cruelty, every perfidy, every debauchery, and every folly of which human nature is capable."[13] According to David Hume (1711–1776), the Crusades were "the most signal and most durable monument to human folly that has yet appeared in any age or nation."[14] Denis Diderot (1713–1784) characterized the Crusades as "a time of the deepest darkness and of the greatest folly . . . to drag a significant part of the world into an unhappy little country in order to cut the inhabitants' throats and seize a rocky peak which was not worth one drop of blood."[15] These attacks also reinforced the widespread "Protestant conviction that crusading was yet another expression of Catholic bigotry and cruelty."[16] Thus the English historian Thomas Fuller (1608–1661) claimed that the Crusades were all the pope's doing and that this "war would be the sewer of Christendom" in that it attempted to deprive the Muslims of their lawful possession of Palestine.[17]

However, the notion that the crusaders were early Western imperialists who used a religious excuse to seek land and loot probably was originated by the German Lutheran church historian Johann Lorenz von Mosheim (1693–1755), who wrote: "The Roman pontiffs and the European princes were engaged at first in these crusades by a principle of superstition only, but when in the process of time they learnt by experience that these holy wars contributed much to increase their opulence and to extend their authority . . . [then] ambition and avarice seconded and enforced the dictates of fanaticism and superstition."[18] Mosheim's views were echoed by Edward Gibbon (1737–1794), who claimed that the crusaders really went in pursuit of "mines of treasures, of gold and diamonds, of palaces of marble and jasper, and of odoriferous groves of cinnamon and frankincense."[19]

During the twentieth century, this self-interest thesis was developed into an elaborate "materialist" account of why the Crusades took place.[20] The prolific Geoffrey Barraclough (1908–1984) wrote: "[O]ur verdict on the Crusades [is that it amounted to] colonial exploitation."[21] Or, as Karen Armstrong confided, these "were our first colonies."[22] A more extensive and sophisticated material explanation of why the knights went east was formulated by Hans Eberhard Mayer, who proposed that the Crusades alleviated a severe financial squeeze on Europe's "knightly class." According to Mayer and others who share his views, at this time there was a substantial and rapidly growing number of "surplus" sons, members of noble families who would not inherit and whom the heirs found it increasingly difficult to provide with even modest incomes. Hence, as Mayer put it, "the Crusade a[...] kind of safety valve for the knightly class . . . a class wh[...]d upon the Crusade as a way of solving its material probl[...] deed, a group of American economists recently proposed [...] rusaders hoped to get rich from the flow of pilgrims [...]g the shrines in Jerusalem with modern amusement p[...] that the pope sent the crusaders east in pursuit of "new [...]" for the church, presumably to be gained by converting [...] way from Islam.[24] It is thus no surprise that a leading col[...]book on Western civilization informs students: "From the perspective of the pope and European monarchs, the crusades offered a way to rid Europe of contentious young nobles . . . [who] saw an opportunity to gain territory, riches, status, possibly a title, and even salvation."[25]

To sum up the prevailing wisdom: *during the Crusades, an expansionist, imperialistic Christendom brutalized, looted, and colonized a tolerant and peaceful Islam.*

Not so. As will be seen, the Crusades were precipitated by Islamic provocations: by centuries of bloody attempts to colonize the West and by sudden new attacks on Christian pilgrims and holy places. Although the Crusades were initiated by a plea from the pope, this had nothing to do with hopes of converting Islam. Nor were the Crusades organized and led by surplus sons, but by the heads of great families who were fully aware that the costs of crusading would far exceed the very modest material rewards that could be expected; most went at immense personal cost, some of them knowingly bankrupting themselves to go. Moreover, the crusader kingdoms that they established in the Holy Land, and that stood for nearly two centuries, were not colonies sustained by local exactions; rather, they required immense subsidies from Europe.

In addition, it is utterly unreasonable to impose modern notions about proper military conduct on medieval warfare; both Christians and Muslims observed quite different rules of war. Unfortunately, even many of the most sympathetic and otherwise sensible historians of the Crusades are unable to accept that fact and are given to agonizing over the very idea that war can ever be "just," revealing the pacifism that has become so widespread among academics. Finally, claims that Muslims have been harboring bitter resentments about the Crusades for a millennium are nonsense: Muslim antagonism about the Crusades did not appear until about 1900, in reaction against the decline of the Ottoman Empire and the onset of actual

European colonialism in the Middle East. And anti-crusader feelings did not become intense until after the founding of the state of Israel. These are principal themes of the chapters that follow.

Historians disagree about which events were Crusades and therefore about when they occurred.[26] I exclude the "crusades" against heretics in Europe and accept the conventional definition: that the Crusades involved conflicts between Christendom and Islam for control of the Holy Land, campaigns that occurred between 1095 and 1291. However, unlike most conventional Crusade historians, I shall not begin with the pope's appeal at Clermont, but with the rise of Islam and the onset of the Muslim invasions of Christendom. That's when it all started—in the seventh century, when Islamic armies swept over the larger portion of what was then Christian territory: the Middle East, Egypt and all of North Africa, and then Spain and southern Italy, as well as many major Mediterranean islands including Sicily, Corsica, Cyprus, Rhodes, Crete, Malta, and Sardinia. It also is important to examine the Christian counterattacks that began in the eighth century and soon "liberated" many of the occupied areas, for these were previews of the military confrontations that eventually took place in the Holy Land. Nor shall I merely recount the crusader battles, for they are comprehensible only in light of the superior culture and technology that made it possible for European knights to march more than twenty-five hundred miles, to suffer great losses along the way, and then to rout far larger Muslim forces.

Many superb historians have devoted their careers to studying aspects of the Crusades.[27] I am not one of them. What I have done is synthesize the work of these specialists into a more comprehensive perspective, written in prose that is accessible to the general reader. However, I have been careful to fully acknowledge the contributions of the many experts on whom I have depended, some in the text and the rest in the endnotes.

Chapter One

MUSLIM INVADERS

The history of the Crusades really began in the seventh century when armies of
Arabs, newly converted to Islam, seized huge areas that had been Christian.
© *Werner Forman / Art Resource, NY*

IN WHAT CAME TO BE KNOWN as his farewell address, Muhammad is said to have told his followers: "I was ordered to fight all men until they say 'There is no god but Allah.'"[1] This is entirely consistent with the Qur'an (9:5): "[S]lay the idolaters wherever ye find them, and take them [captive], and besiege them, and prepare for them each ambush." In this spirit, Muhammad's heirs set out to conquer the world.

In 570, when Muhammad was born, Christendom stretched from the Middle East all along North Africa, and embraced much of Europe (see map 1.1). But only eighty years after Muhammad's death in 632, a new Muslim empire had displaced Christians from most of the Middle East, all of North Africa, Cyprus, and most of Spain (see map 1.2).

In another century Sicily, Sardinia, Corsica, Crete, and southern Italy also came under Muslim rule. How was this accomplished? How were the conquered societies ruled? What happened to the millions of Christians and Jews?

THE CONQUESTS

Before he died, Muhammad had gathered a military force sufficient for him to contemplate expansion beyond Arabia. Foreign incursions had become increasingly attractive because Muhammad's uniting the desert Bedouin tribes into an Arab state eliminated their long tradition of imposing protection payments on the Arab towns and villages as well as ending their freedom to rob caravans.

So, attention turned to the north and east, where "rich spoils were to be won, and warriors could find glory and profit without risk to the peace and internal security of Arabia."[2] Raids by Muhammad's forces into Byzantine Syria and Persia began during the last several years of the Prophet's life, and serious efforts ensued soon after his death.

In typical fashion, many historians have urged entirely material, secular explanations for the early Muslim conquests. Thus, the prominent Carl Heinrich Becker (1876–1933) explained that the "bursting of the Arabs beyond their native peninsula was . . . [entirely] due to economic necessities."[3] Specifically, it is said that a population explosion in Arabia and a sudden decline in caravan trade were the principal forces that drove the Arabs to suddenly begin a series of invasions and conquests at this time. But the

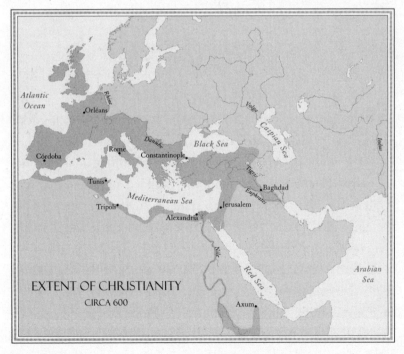

EXTENT OF CHRISTIANITY

CIRCA 600

MAP I.I

— 13 —

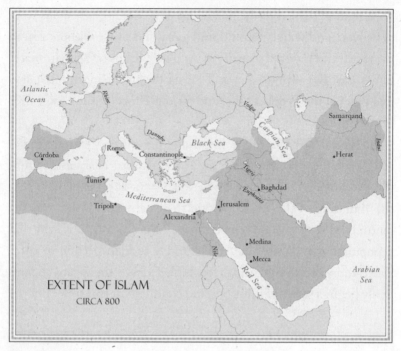

MAP I.2

population explosion never happened; it was invented by authors who assumed that it would have taken barbarian "Arab hordes"[4] to overwhelm the civilized Byzantines and Persians. The truth is quite the contrary. As will be seen, the Muslim invasions were accomplished by remarkably small, very well led and well organized Arab armies. As for the caravan trade, if anything it increased in the early days of the Arab state, probably because the caravans were now far more secure.

A fundamental reason that the Arabs attacked their neighbors at this particular time was that they finally had the power to do so. For one thing, both Byzantium and Persia were exhausted by many decades of fighting one another, during which each side had suffered many bloody defeats. Equally important is that, having become a unified state rather than a collection of uncooperative tribes, the Arabs now had the ability to sustain military campaigns rather than the hit-and-run raids they had conducted for centuries. As for more specific motivations, Muhammad had seen expansion as a means to sustain Arab unity by providing new opportunities, in the form of booty and tributes, for the desert tribes. But most important of all, the Arab invasions were planned and led by those committed to the spread of Islam. As Hugh Kennedy summed up, Muslims "fought for their religion, the prospect of booty and because their friends and fellow tribesmen were doing it."[5]

All attempts to reconstruct the Muslim invasions are limited by the unreliability of the sources. As the authoritative Fred Donner explained, early Muslim chroniclers "assembled fragmentary accounts in different ways, resulting in several contradictory sequential schemes," and it is impossible to determine which, if any, is more accurate.[6] Furthermore, both Christian and Muslim chronicles often make absurdly exaggerated claims about the size of armies—often inflating the numbers involved by a factor of ten or more. Fortunately, generations of resourceful scholars have provided more plausible statistics and an adequate overall view of the major campaigns. The following survey of Muslim conquests is, of course, limited to those prior to the First Crusade.

Syria

The first conquest was Syria, then a province of the Byzantine Empire (Eastern Roman Empire). Syria presented many attractions. Not only was it close; it was the most familiar foreign land. Arab merchants had regularly dealt with Syrian merchants, some of whom came to the regular trade fairs that had been held in Mecca for generations. Then, too, Syria was a far more fertile region than Arabia and had larger, more impressive cities, including Damascus. Syria also presented a target of opportunity because of its unsettled political situation and the presence of many somewhat disaffected groups. After centuries of Byzantine rule, Syria had fallen to the Persians in about 611, only to be retaken by Byzantium in about 630 (two years before Muhammad's death). During their rule the Persians destroyed the institutional basis of Byzantine rule, and when they were driven out a leadership vacuum developed. Moreover, Arabs had been migrating into Syria for centuries and had long been a primary source of recruits for the Byzantine forces. In addition, some Arab border tribes had long served as mercenaries to guard against their raiding kinsmen from the south. However, when Byzantium regained control of Syria, the emperor Heraclius, burdened with enormous debts, refused to reinstate the subsidies paid to these border tribes—an action that alienated them at this strategic moment.[7] The many Arab residents of Syria had little love for their Roman rulers, either. Hence, when the Islamic Arab invaders came, many Arab defenders switched sides during the fighting. Worse yet, even among the non-Arabs in Syria, "the Byzantine rule was so deeply hated that the Arabs were welcomed as deliverers."[8] And no one hated and feared the Greeks more than the many large Christian groups such as the Nestorians, who had long been persecuted as heretics by the Orthodox bishops of Byzantium.

The first Muslim forces entered Syria in 633 and took an area in the south without a major encounter with Byzantine forces. A second phase began the next year and met more determined resistance, but the Muslims won a series of battles, taking Damascus and some other cities in 635. This set the stage for the epic Battle of Yarmūk, which took place in August 636 and lasted for six days. The two sides seem to have possessed about equal numbers, which favored the Muslim forces since they were drawn up in a defensive position, forcing the Greeks to attack. Eventually the Byzantine heavy cavalry did manage to breach the Arab front line, but they were unable to exploit their advantage because the Muslims withdrew behind barriers composed of hobbled camels. When the Byzantines attacked this new line of defense they left their flanks exposed to a lethal attack by Muslim cavalry. At this point, instead of holding fast, the Greek infantry mutinied and then panicked and fled toward a ravine, whereupon thousands fell to their deaths below. Shortly thereafter, the shattered Byzantine army abandoned Syria.[9] Soon the Muslim caliph established Damascus as the capital of the growing Islamic empire (the word *caliph* means "successor," and the title *caliph* meant "successor to Muhammad").

Persia

Meanwhile, other Arab forces had moved against the Persian area of Mesopotamia, known today as Iraq. The problem of unreliable Arab troops also beset the Persians just as it had the Byzantines: in several key battles whole units of Persian cavalry, which consisted exclusively of Arab mercenaries, joined the Muslim side, leading to an overwhelming defeat of the Persians in the Battle of al-Qādisyyah in 636.

The Persians had assembled an army of perhaps thirty thousand, including a number of war elephants. The Muslim force was smaller and not as well armed but had a distinct positional advantage: a branch of the Euphrates River across their front, a swamp on their right, and a lake on their left. Behind them was the desert. The fighting on the first day was quite exploratory, although a probing advance by the war elephants was repulsed by Arab archers. The second day was more of the same. But on the third day the Persians mounted an all-out offensive behind their elephant combat teams. Again they were met with a shower of arrows, and the two leading elephants were wounded. As a result, they stampeded back through the other elephants, which followed suit, and the whole herd stomped their way back through the Persian ranks. As chaos broke out, the Arab cavalry charged and the battle was won—with immense Persian losses.[10]

Subsequently, after a brief siege the Muslim forces took the capital city of Ctesiphon. Thus was the area that today constitutes Iraq conquered by the Muslims, reducing Persia to what now is known as Iran. Soon it, too, was conquered by Muslim invaders, but not without fierce resistance, and Persians continued to erupt in rebellion against Muslim rule for the next century. Once Persia was sufficiently pacified, Caliph al-Mansūr moved the capital of the Muslim empire from Damascus to a new city he built on the Tigris River in Iraq. Its official name was Madina al-Salam ("City of Peace"), but everyone called it Baghdad ("Gift of God").

Having conquered Persia, Muslim forces ventured north to conquer Armenia and also moved east, eventually occupying the Indus Valley (modern Pakistan). From this base, over many centuries the Muslims eventually expanded far into India.

The Holy Land

Palestine was part of Byzantine Syria, and the crushing defeat of Greek forces at the Battle of Yarmūk left the Holy Land protected only by local forces. At this time, even though Palestine was administered by Greek Christians, the population was mostly Jewish. Apparently, the Muslim victories over the Byzantines had been interpreted by many Jews as signs that the Messiah was about to appear, and this may account for the reports that Jews welcomed invading Muslim forces.[11] Muslim units entered Palestine in 636, and after a long siege, Jerusalem surrendered in 638 to the caliph 'Umar, who rode into the city on a splendid horse, leading a camel. 'Umar allowed Byzantine Christians to continue to live in Jerusalem but prohibited all Jews from doing so,[12] continuing the policy Byzantine governors had imposed for centuries.[13] However, several years later the prohibition against Jews was lifted.

Egypt

Egypt was also a Byzantine province; hence its security was undermined by the defeats suffered by Greek forces to the northeast. In 639 Caliph 'Umar sent a small invasion force of about four thousand men to the Nile Delta area. In response, the Byzantine defensive forces withdrew into the walled towns, where they were quite secure against the small force of invaders. So, in 640 another twelve thousand Muslim troops arrived, and the two groups established themselves at Heliopolis. Having failed to attack either Muslim body when they were still separated, a Byzantine force now decided to march out and give battle. During the night the Arab commander managed to hide two detachments, one on each flank of the battlefield. After the main Arab force engaged the Greeks, these flanking units emerged from ambush, whereupon the Byzantine lines broke and "great numbers were cut down and slaughtered by the exultant Muslims."[14]

Next, in an effort to lure other Byzantine garrisons into coming out to engage in battle, the Muslims stormed the undefended city of Nikiou and massacred the inhabitants, and then did the same to a number of the surrounding villages.[15] At this point, most of the remaining Byzantine garrisons withdrew "in good order into the defences of Alexandria."[16] The Arabs followed and made an ill-advised assault against the walls, suffering a very bloody defeat. Withdrawing out of range of arrows and of catapult shots from the defensive walls, the Arabs set up camp.

What followed ought to have been a hopeless siege, since Alexandria was a port and the Byzantine navy, which then had complete control of the seas, could easily supply and reinforce the city for as long as necessary. Being the second largest city in the whole Christian world,[17] Alexandria "was surrounded by massive walls and towers, against which such missiles as the Arabs possessed were utterly ineffectual . . . Such a city could have held out for years."[18] But, for reasons that will never be known, in 641, a month after he had arrived by sea to become the new governor of Egypt, Cyrus went out to meet the Muslim commander and surrendered Alexandria and all of Egypt.

But this wasn't the end. Four years later a Byzantine fleet of about three hundred vessels suddenly arrived in the harbor at Alexandria and disembarked a substantial army that quickly dispatched the Muslim garrison of about one thousand. Once again the Greeks had an impregnable position behind the great walls of the city, but their arrogant and foolish commander led his forces out to meet the Arabs and was routed. Even so, enough Byzantine troops made it back to Alexandria to adequately man the fortifications, and once again they were secure against attack—but for the treachery of an officer who opened a gate to the Arabs. Some reports say he was bribed; others claim he was a Coptic Christian who was getting even with the Greeks for having persecuted people of his faith. In any event, having burst into the city, the Muslims engaged in "massacre, plunder, and arson . . . [until] half the city was destroyed."[19] They also tore down the city walls to prevent any repetition of the problem.

The need to take Alexandria twice made the Muslims fully aware of the need to offset Byzantine sea power. Turning to the still-functioning Egyptian shipyards, they commissioned the construction of a fleet and then hired Coptic and Greek mercenaries to do the navigation and sailing. In 649 this new fleet was adequate to sustain an invasion of Cypress; Sicily and Rhodes were pillaged soon after. A major Muslim empire now ruled most of the Middle East and was free to continue spreading along the North African coast.

But at this moment the Muslim conquests halted because a brutal civil war broke out within Islam and lasted for years. At issue were conflicting claims to be the true successor to Muhammad, which pitted Muhammad's cousin and son-in-law Ali against Muawiyah, cousin of the murdered caliph Uthman. After much bloodshed,

Ali was also murdered and Muawiyah became caliph, with the result that Islam was forever divided into the Sunnis and the Shiites (who had backed Ali). It was not until 670 that a Muslim army advanced further along the North African coast.

North Africa

As Egypt had been, the entire north coast of Africa also was under Byzantine rule. Since all the major cities were ports and well garrisoned, the Arab commander moved west over desert routes, established an inland base, and built a huge mosque in what became the city of Kairouan—now regarded as the third holiest Muslim city (after Mecca and Medina).[20] From this base in the Maghreb (as the Arabs called North Africa), the Muslim force first made war on the desert-dwelling Berbers, many of whom had long ago converted to Judaism.[21] Despite bitter resistance, especially by tribes from the Atlas Mountain area led by a charismatic Jewish woman named Kahina, the Muslims eventually prevailed and then succeeded in enlisting the Berbers as allies.[22] Meanwhile, a new Muslim army of perhaps forty thousand swept over the coastal cities, taking Carthage in 698. But, as had happened with Alexandria, the Greeks managed to land troops in the Carthage harbor and retake the city. In response, the Muslims assembled a fleet and another army, including large numbers of Berbers, and in 705 Carthage was "razed to the ground and most of its inhabitants killed."[23] Possession of an adequate fleet by the Muslims sealed the fate of all the remaining Byzantine coastal towns.[24]

Spain

In 711 an army of seven to ten thousand Muslims from Morocco crossed the Mediterranean at its narrowest western point and landed on the coast of Spain at the foot of a mountain jutting out into the sea. Later this mountain was named after the Muslim commander, the Berber Tariq ibn-Ziyad, as the Rock of Tariq, hence *Jabal Tariq* or Gibraltar.[25] The Muslim landing took everyone in Spain by surprise. King Rodrigo hastily assembled an army and marched south from his capital in Toledo, only to be routed in a battle at the river Guadalete; Rodrigo drowned while fleeing the carnage. This was the first time that Muslim forces engaged Christians who were not Byzantines, but were, in this instance, Visigoths who had conquered Roman Spain in about 500. As usual, contemporary figures as to the numbers involved and the extent of casualties are useless. Gibbon cited them to assign Rodrigo an army of one hundred thousand men and claimed that although the Muslims won, they suffered sixteen thousand killed in action. Rodrigo's force probably numbered fewer than ten thousand. What is certain is that Rodrigo lost and that Tariq sent what he believed to be Rodrigo's head (soaked in brine) to the caliph in Damascus.[26]

Then followed a seven-year campaign that brought the rest of Al-Andalus, as the Muslims called Spain, under their control, except for a small area in the north from which the Christians could never be ousted. Almost nothing is known of this campaign to conquer most of Spain except for the fact that there was no popular resistance to the Muslims because the corrupt and rather brutal Visigoth regime was widely hated by the indigenous population. This same population called the Muslim invaders Moors, or people from Morocco, and the name stuck. Immediately upon having located their capital in the city of Córdoba, the Moors built a great mosque on the site of a former Christian cathedral. Initially, Al-Andalus was part of the Muslim empire, but in 756 it was established as an independent emirate.

Sicily and Southern Italy

The first Muslim invasion of Sicily took place in 652 and failed. So did attacks in 667 and 720. Further attempts were delayed by civil wars in North Africa involving the Berbers and Arabs. The Muslims came again in 827 and landed about ten thousand troops. The local Byzantine commanders fought back furiously, and it took more than seventy years for the Muslims to succeed, only after "much fighting and many massacres."[27] Thus, although Palermo fell after a long siege in 831, Syracuse did not fall until 878, and Taormina, the last Byzantine stronghold, held out until 902.

From their initial foothold in Sicily the Muslims crossed into southern Italy, and in 840 Taranto and Bari were taken, Capua was razed, and Benevento was occupied. Rome was pillaged in 843 and again in 846, when all the famous churches were looted and the pope was forced to pay a huge tribute. Withdrawing to the south, the Muslim commanders divided portions of southern Italy into independent emirates.

The occupation of Sicily and southern Italy lasted for more than two centuries.

Major Islands

Little has been written about the Muslim conquests of major Mediterranean islands; perhaps historians have considered them too insignificant to matter much. However, possession of islands such as Crete and Sardinia were of considerable strategic importance to Muslim fleets. Hence, the fall of Cyprus (653), Rhodes (672), Sardinia (809), Majorca (818), Crete (824), and Malta (835) were significant losses for the West.

MUSLIM WARFARE

How did the Arabs triumph so quickly and seemingly so easily? Many historians unfamiliar with military arts have found this inexplicable. They ask: how could a bunch of desert barbarians roll over the large, trained armies of the "civilized" empires?

As noted, many have attributed the Muslim conquests to an immense superiority of numbers, to hordes of Arabs riding out of the desert to overwhelm far smaller Byzantine and Persian forces. But desert tribes are never very large, and, in fact, the conquering Muslim armies usually were substantially smaller than the "civilized" armies they defeated. Consequently, many historians have fallen back on the thesis that the Muslims won because "the Byzantines failed to appreciate the new power that Muslim religious fervor gave to Arab armies."[28] This suggests onslaughts by wave after wave of fanatics charging the enemy, screaming, "Death to the unbelievers." Finally, some historians have blamed the Byzantine and Persian losses on their being too civilized in contrast to fearless Islamic savages. Indeed, this explanation even was proposed by the famous Muslim thinker Ibn Khaldūn (1332–1406), who wrote, "It should be known that . . . savage people are undoubtedly braver than others."[29]

In truth, Muslim troops were as apt as Byzantines or Persians to break and run when the tide of battle went against them. Their victories are easily comprehended on the basis of ordinary military techniques and technology.

The first thing to recognize is that the more "civilized" empires did not possess any superior military hardware, with the exception of siege engines, which were of no use in repelling attacks. *Everyone* depended on swords, lances, axes, and bows; everyone carried a shield, and those who could afford it wore some armor, albeit the "civilized" forces wore more.[30] However, by this era there no longer were dedicated and highly disciplined "citizen soldiers" in the imperial forces of either Byzantium or Persia. Instead, these forces were recruited from hither and yon, and mostly drew "foreigners" who served mainly for pay, which placed limits on their loyalty and their mettle. Indeed, as mentioned earlier, many of the rank and file in the Byzantine and Persian forces were Arabs, large numbers of whom ended up deserting to the Muslim side.

Nor were the "professional" armies of Persia and Byzantium better trained. To the contrary, they mainly were "fortress" troops used primarily for static defense of strong points such as walled garrisons or cities, and they were poorly suited to battles of maneuver.[31] Worse yet, a chronic shortage of troops resulted in an inability to maintain a network of garrisons sufficiently dense to prevent an enemy from mounting surprise attacks. Nor did either the Persians or the Byzantines possess sufficient cavalry to make up for this lack of density by scouting enemy routes and strength; indeed, as noted earlier, what cavalry units they had consisted mostly of hired Arabs, who tended to desert at critical moments. Moreover, in contrast to the Persian and Greek soldiers, who came mostly from peasant backgrounds, the desert Arabs devoted themselves to arms from an early age, and when they went into battle, the individual Muslim fighters were part of a close-knit, small unit of men from the same tribe, who fought alongside their relatives and lifelong friends—a situation that placed each individual under extreme social pressure to be brave and aggressive.

Perhaps the most important advantage of the Muslim invaders was that they all traveled by camel; even the cavalry rode from place to place on camels, leading their horses. The use of camels made the Arabs the equivalent of a "mechanized force," in that they so greatly outpaced the Persian and Byzantine armies traveling on foot.[32] This superior mobility allowed the Arabs to find and attack the most weakly held places and avoid the main Persian and Byzantine forces until they had them at a great disadvantage. In addition, the "only means of locomotion across the desert was the camel, of which the Arabs held a monopoly. Thus neither the Byzantine nor Persian armies could cross the desert."[33] Hence, given the geography of the area, the Muslims could always outflank the imperial forces by using desert routes, and, should it be necessary, they could always withdraw into the desert to avoid battle. This ability not only gave the Arabs an immense edge in the Middle East, but was equally significant in the conquest of North Africa. Just as Erwin Rommel, Germany's "Desert Fox," frequently sent his tanks looping into the desert and thereby outflanked British forces attempting to prevent him from invading Egypt, so the Arabs used their camels to go around Byzantine forces attempting to defend the coastal settlements.

Contrary to what many would suppose, a very significant Arab advantage lay in the *small* size of their field armies; they seldom gathered more than ten thousand men and often campaigned with armies of two to four thousand.[34] Their successes against the far larger imperial forces were similar to those often enjoyed by small, well-led, aggressive forces in the face of lumbering enemy hosts; consider how often in ancient history tiny Greek armies routed immense Persian forces. Ironically, due to their smaller numbers the Arab invading forces often were able to far outnumber their opponents on a given battlefield because their much greater mobility allowed them to attack an inferior enemy force and destroy it before reinforcements could arrive. The imperial forces either wore themselves out marching in fruitless pursuit of a battle or made themselves vulnerable by spreading out and trying to defend everywhere at once. Nor was this merely a tactical problem facing Byzantine forces in a specific area; it was a more general strategic problem, in that the Byzantine forces were stretched very thin by the immensity of their empire. As a result, while the Arabs concentrated their forces to attack a specific area such as Syria or Egypt, tens of thousands of Greek troops sat idle, far from the battlefield, serving as garrisons in such places as southern Italy or Armenia.[35]

As should be clear, the Arab forces also were very well led. Not by their tribal leaders, but by officers selected from "the new Islamic ruling elite of settled people from Mecca, Medina or al-Tā'if."[36] All of the middle to higher ranks were staffed from the elite by men who clearly understood administration, including the chain of command, and who were able to keep the larger strategic goals in mind while embroiled in tactical engagements. Finally, promotion and appointment of officers in the early Muslim armies was based primarily on merit, while the Byzantine and Persian commanders often were unqualified other than by their bloodlines.

GOVERNANCE

Initially, the conquered societies were considered provinces of the Muslim state and were ruled by governors appointed by the caliph. Eventually, central control broke down, and, as already noted, many provinces became independent Muslim states "whose rulers commonly recognized the Caliph as Imam or chief of Islam but allowed him no power in their dominions."[37] Hence, when the West began its counterattacks, their opposition was limited to the troops available to a particular ruler; reinforcements usually were not sent from other Muslim states.

In the beginning, the conquering Arabs constituted a small elite who ruled over large populations of non-Muslims, most of whom remained unconverted for centuries, as will be seen. Indeed, the ruling Muslim elites were required by the caliphs to settle in their own garrison cities. "This would enable them to maintain their military control and discourage them from becoming assimilated and losing their religious and ethnic identity."[38] This was, of course, a two-way street, and Muslim isolation put a damper on conversion. Thus, relations with the subject people were limited to imposing restrictions on such activities as, for example, building churches or riding horses, and to collecting the substantial taxes always imposed on non-Muslims.

CONQUERED SUBJECTS

A great deal of nonsense has been written about Muslim tolerance—that, in contrast to Christian brutality against Jews and
heretics, Islam showed remarkable tolerance for conquered people,
treated them with respect, and allowed them to pursue their faiths
without interference. This claim probably began with Voltaire,
Gibbon, and other eighteenth-century writers who used it to cast
the Catholic Church in the worst possible light. The truth about
life under Muslim rule is quite different.

It is true that the Qur'an forbids forced conversions. However,
that recedes to an empty legalism given that many subject peoples
were "free to choose" conversion as an alternative to death or enslavement. That was the usual choice presented to pagans, and
often Jews and Christians also were faced with that option or with
one only somewhat less extreme.[39] In principle, as "People of the
Book," Jews and Christians were supposed to be tolerated and
permitted to follow their faiths. But only under quite repressive
conditions: death was (and remains) the fate of anyone who converted to either faith. Nor could any new churches or synagogues
be built. Jews and Christians also were prohibited from praying
or reading their scriptures aloud—not even in their homes or in
churches or synagogues—lest Muslims accidentally hear them.
And, as the remarkable historian of Islam Marshall G. S. Hodgson
(1922–1968) pointed out, from very early times Muslim authorities
often went to great lengths to humiliate and punish *dhimmis*—
Jews and Christians who refused to convert to Islam. It was official policy that *dhimmis* should "feel inferior and . . . know 'their
place' . . . [imposing laws such as] that Christians and Jews should
not ride horses, for instance, but at most mules, or even that they
should wear certain marks of their religion on their costume when
among Muslims."[40] In some places non-Muslims were prohibited

from wearing clothing similar to that of Muslims, nor could they be armed.[41] In addition, non-Muslims were invariably severely taxed compared with Muslims.[42]

These were the normal circumstances of Jewish and Christian subjects of Muslim states, but conditions often were far worse. In 705 the Muslim conquerors of Armenia assembled all the Christian nobles in a church and burned them to death.[43] There were many similar episodes in addition to the indiscriminate slaughters of Christians noted earlier in discussions of the Muslim conquests. The first Muslim massacre of Jews occurred in Medina when Muhammad had all the local adult Jewish males (about seven hundred of them) beheaded after forcing them to dig their own graves.[44] Unfortunately, massacres of Jews and Christians became increasingly common with the passage of time. For example, in the eleventh century there were many mass killings of Jews—more than six thousand in Morocco in 1032–1033, and at least that many murdered during two outbursts in Grenada.[45] In 1570 Muslim invaders murdered tens of thousands of Christian civilians on Cyprus.[46]

This is *not* to say that the Muslims were more brutal or less tolerant than were Christians or Jews, for it was a brutal and intolerant age. It *is* to say that efforts to portray Muslims as enlightened supporters of multiculturalism are at best ignorant.

CONVERSION

It was a very long time before the conquered areas were truly Muslim in anything but name. The reality was that very small Muslim elites long ruled over non-Muslim (mostly Christian) populations in the conquered areas. This runs contrary to the widespread belief that Muslim conquests were quickly followed by mass conversions to Islam.

In part this belief in rapid mass conversions is rooted in the failure to distinguish "conversions by treaty" from changes in individual beliefs and practices. Tribes that took arms for Muhammad often did so on the basis of a treaty that expressed acceptance of Muhammad's religious claims, but these pacts had no individual religious implications—as demonstrated by the many defections of these tribes following the prophet's death. Similar conversions by treaty continued during the Muslim conquests, the Berbers being a notable case. When attacked by the Muslim invaders of North Africa, some of the Berber tribes were pagans, some were Jews, and some were Christians. But after the defeat of Kahina and her forces, the Berbers signed a treaty declaring themselves to be Muslim. Perhaps some of them were. But even though Marshall Hodgson wrote that the Berbers "converted en masse,"[47] theirs was mainly a conversion by treaty that qualified them to participate in subsequent campaigns of conquest and share in the booty and tribute that resulted. The actual conversion of the Berbers in terms of individual beliefs was a slow process that took many centuries.

Aside from confusing conversion by treaty with the real thing, historians also have erred by assuming that once a people came under Muslim occupation, mass conversions "must have" occurred. But *must have* is one of the most untrustworthy phrases in the scholarly vocabulary. In this case, social scientists who have studied conversion would respond that there "must not" have been mass conversions, since it is very doubtful that a mass conversion has ever occurred anywhere! All observed instances of conversion have revealed them to be individual acts that occurred relatively gradually as people were drawn to a particular faith by a network of family and friends who already had converted.[48] In the instances at hand, the network model gains credibility from the fact that it took centuries for as many as half of the population of conquered societies to become Muslims.

Richard W. Bulliet has provided superb data on conversion to Islam in the various conquered regions.[49] For whatever reason, from earliest times Muslims produced large numbers of very extensive biographical dictionaries listing all of the better-known people in a specific area, and new editions appeared for centuries. Eventually Bulliet was able to assemble data on more than a million people. The value of these data lies in the fact that Bulliet was able to distinguish Muslims from non-Muslims on the basis of their names. Then, by merging many dictionaries for a given area and sorting the tens of thousands of people listed by their year of birth, Bulliet was able to calculate the proportion of Muslims in the population at various dates and thus create curves of the progress of conversion in five major areas. Because only somewhat prominent people were included in the dictionaries, these results overestimate both the extent and the speed of conversions vis-à-vis the general populations in that elites began with a higher proportion of Muslims and Muslims would have continued to dominate. Consequently, Bulliet devised a very convincing procedure to convert these data into conversion curves for whole populations.

Table 1.1 shows the number of years required to convert 50 percent of the population to Islam in five major areas. In Iran it took 200 years from the date of the initial conquest by Muslim forces to the time when half of Iranians were Muslims. In the other four areas it took from 252 years in Syria to 264 years in Egypt and North Africa. As to why things happened somewhat more rapidly in Iran, two things set it apart from the other areas. Probably the most important is that for more than a century after falling to Islamic invaders, the Iranians frequently revolted again Muslim rule and did so with sufficient success so that many very bloody battles ensued, as did brutal repressions. These conflicts would have resulted in substantial declines in the non-Muslim population, having nothing to do with conversion. Second, the climate of fear that must have accompanied the defeats of these rebellions likely would have prompted some Iranians to convert for safety's sake and probably caused others to flee.

In any event, despite the onerous conditions of dhimmitude imposed upon them, the conquered peoples only slowly converted to Islam. Even as late as the thirteenth century, very substantial segments of the populations of the Muslim empire outside of Arabia (where non-Muslims were not permitted) were Christians or Jews. Moreover, most of what has been regarded as Muslim culture and said to have been superior to that of Christian Europe was in fact the persistence of preconquest Judeo-Christian-Greek culture that Muslim elites only slowly assimilated, and very imperfectly (see chapter 3).

CONCLUSION

Many critics of the Crusades would seem to suppose that after the Muslims had overrun a major portion of Christendom, they should have been ignored or forgiven; suggestions have been made about

TABLE 1.1 *Number of Years Required to Convert 50 Percent of the Population to Islam in Five Major Areas*

AREA	YEARS REQUIRED FOR CONVERSION
Syria	252
Western Persia (Iraq)	253
Eastern Persia (Iran)	200
Egypt and North Africa	264
Spain	247

Source: Calculated from Bulliet, 1979a, 1979b.

turning the other cheek.[50] This outlook is certainly unrealistic and probably insincere. Not only had the Byzantines lost most of their empire; the enemy was at their gates. And the loss of Spain, Sicily, and southern Italy, as well as a host of Mediterranean islands, was bitterly resented in Europe. Hence, as British historian Derek Lomax (1933–1992) explained, "The popes, like most Christians, believed war against the Muslims to be justified partly because the latter had usurped by force lands which once belonged to Christians and partly because they abused the Christians over whom they ruled and such Christian lands as they could raid for slaves, plunder and the joys of destruction."[51] It was time to strike back.

Chapter Two

CHRISTENDOM STRIKES BACK

In 732, a large Muslim army from Spain pushed far north into France, there to be overwhelmed by Frankish troops led by Charles Martel. From then on, the Muslim invaders slowly began to be driven out of Europe.

© Réunion des Musées Nationaux / Art Resource, NY

D ESPITE HAVING SO QUICKLY assembled a large empire out of areas conquered from the Persians, Byzantines, and Visigoths, the Muslim armies were not invincible. When they abandoned their camels and ventured far from the deserts to face loyal and determined Christian forces, the "fierce" and "irresistible" Islamic invaders proved to be quite vulnerable and perhaps deficient in both arms and tactics. The first major Muslim defeat occurred at Constantinople, and then they were routed in Gaul. Soon after that, the Muslim tide began to ebb in Spain, and then they were driven out of Sicily and southern Italy.

DEFEATS AT CONSTANTINOPLE

Having defeated Byzantine armies in Syria and Egypt, and having begun a successful campaign to conquer the entire north coast of Africa from Byzantium, in 672 the caliph Muawiyah decided to strike directly at his enemy. From his new capital in Damascus, the caliph directed his fleet to transport an army through the Dardanelles (the narrow strait linking the Mediterranean with the Sea of Marmara). Numbering about fifty thousand men, the caliph's troops captured the peninsula of Cyzicus, across the water from Constantinople, and fortified it as their principle base, from where they began a siege of Constantinople.

Had the Muslims taken the city, the way would have been open to invading Europe through the Balkans. But Constantinople easily withstood the siege and inflicted a huge naval defeat on the Muslims.

With their fleet destroyed, it was the Arabs who were, in effect, under siege and starving. Soon dysentery became epidemic, and thousands of Muslim soldiers died. Worse yet, few Muslims had ever seen snow or ice, and when winter came they were entirely unprepared. Having no warm clothing, many froze to death. Even so, the Muslims hung on for several years, their ranks continuing to thin while well-fed Byzantines taunted them from the walls of Constantinople. Finally, with his army marooned, "discouraged and demoralized," Muawiyah accepted Byzantium's "offer of peace—under terms which, a few years before, he would have considered ignoble: the evacuation of the Aegean islands he had so recently conquered, plus an annual tribute to the Emperor [of Byzantium] of fifty slaves, fifty horses, and 3,000 pounds of gold."[1] A year later Muawiyah died, and the new caliph soon reneged on the annual tribute payments.

Western historians have long hailed this as "a turning point in the history of mankind."[2] The Russian-born Byzantine scholar George Ostrogorsky (1902–1976) characterized the attack on Constantinople as "the fiercest which had ever been launched by the infidels against a Christian stronghold, and the Byzantine capital was the last dam left to withstand the rising Muslim tide. The fact that it held saved not only the Byzantine Empire, but the whole of European civilization."[3] Or as the distinguished historian of Byzantium Viscount John Julius Norwich put it: "Had they captured Constantinople in the seventh century rather than the fifteenth, all Europe—and America—might be Muslim today."[4]

How was this Byzantine victory achieved? Unfortunately, Arab sources are "so confused as to be valueless."[5] Hence, we know little from the Muslim side, and the Greeks observed Muslim forces only from a distance, safe behind their battlements. That may not be very important since, perhaps surprisingly, there wasn't all that much fighting, victory being a triumph of Western technology—of impenetrable fortifications[6] and a secret offensive weapon.[7]

The walls of the city not only defended Constantinople on the land side but enclosed the three seaward sides of the city as well, even including the harbor, which could be entered only through a massive gate. These were not merely walls; they were an engineering marvel: a massive outer wall with towers and superb battlements and behind it an even stronger inner wall, forty feet high and fifteen feet thick, having even more elaborate battlements and towers. If that weren't enough, on the landward side there was a huge moat, and, of course, on the other three sides attackers could reach the walls only by boat. Against these extraordinary fortifications, the Arabs brought siege engines that were quite primitive, even for the times, and able to inflict nothing more than small gouges and scratches on the walls. Until attacked by heavy artillery in the fifteenth century, the walls of Constantinople could only be scaled, not shattered.

Of course, the Muslims might have been able to starve the city into surrender had they retained their control of the seas. But that's where the secret weapon came in.

Tradition has it that in about 670 a Greek architect or engineer named Kallinikos of Heliopolis invented something that has come to be called "Greek fire" and took it to Constantinople. Greek fire was a highly flammable liquid, somewhat akin to napalm, that burst into flames and could not be extinguished by water; it may have burned even more intensely when it came in contact with water. The story of its invention seems a folktale; more likely it was developed by "chemists in Constantinople who had inherited the discoveries of the Alexandrian chemical school."[8] In any event, the formula was a very closely held secret that eventually was lost when the Fourth Crusade caused many untimely deaths among the ruling elite in Constantinople,[9] and modern scientists have never been able to fully duplicate the effect.[10]

Possession of Greek fire allowed the Byzantines to destroy opposing fleets as well as terrorize opposing armies. It was delivered in several ways, but most often by catapult or by a pumping device. A glass or pottery container of Greek fire was loaded onto a catapult and then hurled toward a target as distant as four or five hundred yards. When it struck, it shattered and burst into flames, splashing its blazing liquid over a considerable area—perhaps as far as seventy-five feet in diameter. This was immensely effective when hurled from the battlements of Constantinople and soon discouraged the Muslims from approaching the city. However, catapults are not well suited for use from boats. So the Byzantine engineers invented a primitive flamethrower—a pump that discharged a stream of flaming liquid through a tube projecting from the bow of a galley. (These tubes often had animal heads.) This system had quite limited range but was more than adequate for the close-quarters action of galley warfare. Armed with pumps spewing Greek fire, the Byzantines rowed out and burned the Muslim navy to a cinder—several times.[11]

In 717 the Muslims tried once more. This time they came in even greater numbers aboard as many as eighteen hundred galleys. The Greeks lured them into the Bosporus by removing the huge chain used to block entry, and when the Muslim fleet was packed together in these narrow waters out came the Byzantines with their Greek-fire pumps and destroyed most of the fleet, killing or drowning most of the troops aboard. The Muslims tried again the next spring with a new fleet. The Byzantines came out spouting Greek fire again. Some Muslim galleys managed to flee, only to be caught in a devastating storm. In the end, only five Muslim galleys managed to survive.[12]

THE BATTLE OF TOURS/POITIERS

As they so often have throughout history, the Pyrenees Mountains served as a barrier that contained the Muslim advance in northern Spain—for a few years. But in 721, Al-Samh ibn Malik al-Khawlani, the Muslim governor of Spain, led his troops north, intent on annexing the duchy of Aquitaine in southern Gaul (now France). His first step was to lay siege to the city of Toulouse. After three months, with the city on the brink of surrender, Duke Odo of Aquitaine arrived with an army of Franks. While Odo had been away gathering his forces, lack of opposition had encouraged Muslim arrogance, setting them up for a devastating defeat. They had constructed no defenses around their camp, had sent out no scouts to warn of an approaching threat, and may not even have posted sentries. Taken completely by surprise when the Franks attacked, the Muslims fled, many without their weapons or armor, and most of them were slaughtered by Frankish cavalry as they ran away. Al-Samh ibn Malik al-Khawlani was mortally wounded.

In 732, led by 'Abd-al-Rahmân, the Muslims tried again, this time with a far larger force. Muslim sources claim it was an army of hundreds of thousands, and the Christian *Chronicle of St Denis* recorded that three hundred thousand Muslims died in the battle! More realistic is Paul K. Davis's estimate of an army of eighty thousand Muslims,[13] while Victor Davis Hanson thinks there were only about thirty thousand.[14] In any event, contrary to some historians who want to minimize the importance of the engagement,[15] this was no mere raid or exploratory expedition. The Muslims came with a large army and drove deep into Gaul: the battle occurred only about 150 miles south of Paris, although it is uncertain precisely where it was fought. The best that can be done is to place it near where the rivers Clain and Vienne join, between Tours and Poitiers. Thus some historians refer to it as the Battle of Tours, while others call it the Battle of Poitiers.

As they moved north from Spain, everything went very well for the Muslims. A company of Franks attempting to defend Bordeaux was defeated, and the city was plundered. Then another small Christian army was slaughtered at the Battle of the River Garonne. Along the way, the Muslim army laid waste to the countryside, and soon they were heavily burdened with booty and plunder.

At this point, according to Isidore of Beja's contemporary account, the Muslim commander "burned churches, and imagined he could pillage the basilica of St. Martin of Tours."[16] But first he paused to regroup. Once again the Muslims were brimming with confidence. According to an anonymous Arab chronicler, "The hearts of 'Abd-al-Rahmân, his captains and his men were filled with wrath and pride."[17] Hence, they sent out no scouts and failed to detect the approach of Charles Martel, de facto ruler of Gaul, leading an army of battle-hardened Franks.

Martel was an unusually tall and powerfully built man, the bastard son of King Pippin and famous for his military exploits. Even had he not confronted Muslim invaders, Martel would have been a major historical figure for having founded the Carolingian Empire (named for him) by winning many battles against the Bavarians, the Alemanni, the Frisians, and the Saxons—an empire later perfected by his grandson Charlemagne. Now, after gathering his troops, Martel marched south to meet the Muslim threat.

Taking the Muslims completely by surprise, Martel was able to choose a battleground to his liking, and he positioned his dense lines of well-armored infantry on a crest, with trees to the flanks, thus forcing the Muslims to charge uphill or refuse to give battle. And charge they did. Again and again.

It is axiomatic in military science that cavalry cannot succeed against well-armed and well-disciplined infantry formations unless they greatly outnumber them.[18] The effective role of cavalry is to ride down infantry fleeing the battlefield, once their lines have given way. But when determined infantry hold their ranks, standing shoulder to shoulder to present a wall of shields from which they project a thicket of long spears butted in the ground, cavalry charges are easily turned away; the horses often rear out of control and refuse to meet the spears. In this instance, the Muslim force consisted entirely of light cavalry "carrying lances and swords, largely without shields, wearing very little armor." Opposing them was an army "almost entirely composed of foot soldiers, wearing mail [armor] and carrying shields."[19] It was a very uneven match. As Isidore of Beja reported in his chronicle, the veteran Frankish infantry could not be moved by Arab cavalry: "Firmly they stood, one close to another, forming as it were a bulwark of ice."[20] The Muslim cavalry repeatedly rushed at the Frankish line, and each time they fell back after suffering severe casualties, with increasingly large numbers of bleeding and riderless horses adding to the confusion on the battlefield.

Then, late in the afternoon, as the Arab chronicler reported, many Muslims became "fearful for the safety of the spoil which they had stored in their tents, and a false cry arose in their ranks that some of the enemy were plundering the camp; whereupon several squadrons of the Muslim horsemen rode off to protect their tents."[21] To other units this appeared to be a retreat, and it soon became one, during which the Franks unleashed their own heavily armored cavalry[22] to inflict severe casualties on the fleeing Muslims; at least ten thousand of them died that afternoon, including 'Abd-al-Rahmân, who was run through repeatedly by Frankish lancers.[23]

Even during the rout, the Frankish infantry left the pursuit to their cavalry and maintained their discipline, remaining firmly in position, finally spending the night lying in their ranks. In the morning no Muslim forces reappeared. After very carefully scouting the Muslim camp, the Franks learned that during the night the Muslims had fled, leaving empty tents behind them.

Many historians have regarded the victory at Tours/Poitiers as crucial to the survival of Western civilization. Edward Gibbon supposed that, had the Muslims won at Tours, they would soon have occupied "the confines of Poland and the Highlands of Scotland . . . and the Arabian fleet might have sailed without a naval combat into the mouth of the Thames. Perhaps interpretation of the Koran would now be taught in the schools of Oxford, and her pulpits might demonstrate to a circumcised people the sanctity and truth of the revelation of Mahomet."[24] Subsequently, many Western historians have taken a similar view of the battle as a major historical turning point; indeed, the German military historian Hans Delbrück (1848–1929) wrote that there was "no more important battle in world history."[25]

As would be expected, some more recent historians have been quick to claim that the Battle of Tours was of little or no significance. According to Philip Hitti, "[N]othing was decided on the battlefield at Tours. The Muslim wave . . . had already spent itself and reached a natural limit."[26] And Franco Cardini wrote that the whole thing was nothing but "propaganda put about by the Franks and the papacy."[27] This is said to be consistent with evidence that the battle made no impression on the Muslims, at least not on those back in Damascus. Bernard Lewis claimed that few Arab historians make any mention of this battle at all, and those who do present it "as a comparatively minor engagement."[28]

Given the remarkable intensity of Muslim provincialism, and their willful ignorance of other societies,[29] the defeat at Tours/Poitiers probably was regarded as a minor matter as seen from Damascus. But that's not how the battle was seen from Spain. Indeed, unlike Muslim leaders elsewhere, the Spanish Muslims were fully aware of who Charles Martel was and what he had done to their aspirations. Indeed, Muslims in Spain had learned from their defeat that the Franks were not a sedentary people served by mercenary garrison troops, nor were they a barbarian horde. They, too, were empire builders, and the Frankish host was made up of very well trained citizen volunteers who possessed arms, armor, and tactics superior to those of the Muslims.[30] Indeed, when the Muslims tried to invade Gaul again in 735, Charles Martel and his Franks gave them another beating, so severe that Muslim forces never ventured very far north again. Forty years later, Martel's grandson joined the long process of driving them from Spain.

THE RECONQUEST OF SPAIN

Despite their attacks into France, the Muslims never conquered all of Spain. As the Spanish nobility retreated from the initial Muslim onslaught, they eventually reached the Bay of Biscay on the northern coast, and having nowhere left to go, they made their stand in an area known as Asturias, protected on three sides by mountains and by the sea to the north. This area became the Christian kingdom of Asturias, and from the start the Asturians were committed to reconquering Spain. So, in 741, while Muslim Spain was ravaged by a Berber uprising, Asturia annexed Galicia—the coastal region to the west. However, the next step in the Christian *Reconquista* was initiated by a Muslim faction.

In 777, more than sixty years after the initial Muslim invasion of Spain, the Muslim governor of Barcelona sought the aid of the great Frankish emperor Charlemagne against his rival the emir of Cordova, offering "Saragossa and other [northern] cities to Charlemagne in return for his help."[31] In the spring of 778 Charlemagne assembled two armies and directed them into Spain. One army marched through the East Pyrenees and approached Barcelona. Charlemagne led the other through the West Pyrenees toward Pamplona. Oddly enough, although Pamplona was a city of Christian Basques, and despite Charlemagne's intense Christianity, when he reached Pamplona, Charlemagne ordered that the city be taken. Then, joined by his other army, Charlemagne led his forces on to the promised city of Saragossa, accepting surrenders from several cities along the way, only to discover that the Muslim governor had switched sides and refused to surrender the city.[32]

At this point Charlemagne received news that Saxony had revolted against his rule, so he gathered his forces and quickly marched north to settle this threat. As his rear guard passed through the narrow Roncevaux Pass in the Pyrenees, they were ambushed by a coalition of Muslims and Basques, the latter having been angered by the sack of Pamplona. Trapped and greatly outnumbered, this Frankish contingent was massacred, and among the dead was Charlemagne's nephew Duke Roland of Brittany—fated to be celebrated in the great medieval epic poem *La Chanson de Roland* (*The Song of Roland*).

This was not the end of Charlemagne's Spanish adventures. Several years later he sent a new army and forced the Muslims south of Barcelona. This new area of Christian Spain became known as the Marca Hispanica (Spanish March). After Charlemagne's death in 814, Frankish control weakened and the Christian areas broke up "to become tiny states enjoying practical autonomy."[33] Acting singly and sometimes together, these Christian states continued to push the Muslims slowly south. Their efforts were assisted in 835 when it was believed that the bones of Saint James had been discovered in Galicia. These holy relics served as "a great inspiration to the Christian cause," and in addition, almost at once Christian pilgrims began to flock to the Shrine of Saint James in the Cathedral of Santiago de Compostela, bringing "a substantial flow of wealth into Galicia."[34] Then, in 1063 the local forces received reinforcements and renewed spirit from the north.

Alexander II became pope in 1062—one of a series of reforming popes who brought renewed respect and power to the office. A year after his election, Alexander proposed that knights who went to help drive the Muslims out of Spain would receive remission for their sins, thus launching "a crusade before the crusade" as Menéndez Pidal put it so well.[35] The response was very modest. A small number of Frankish knights seem to have ventured into Spain, and their participation may have helped recover more Muslim territory, but no significant battles were fought.

It is worth noting that the pope was very concerned that the knights setting out to fight the Muslims not attack Jews along the way. Having directed that the Jews be protected, he subsequently wrote that he was glad to learn "that you protect the Jews who live among you, so that they may not be killed by those setting out for Spain against the Saracens . . . for the situation of the Jews is greatly different from that of the Saracens. One may justly fight against those [Saracens because they] persecute Christians."[36]

In 1073 Pope Alexander II died and was replaced by another dedicated reformer who also favored the reconquest of Spain. In fact, immediately following his election, Pope Gregory VII wrote to those knights wishing to go to Spain, promising to "dispose of Spanish lands to any Frenchman who conquered them."[37] Again the turnout was very small, but it seems to have been sufficient to encourage local Christian forces, which resulted in the taking of Toledo on May 25, 1085. The fall of Toledo was a strategic and psychological "disaster for the Muslims."[38] Located at the very center of Spain, Toledo was home to one of the wealthiest Muslim dynasties, which had maintained a splendid court there for generations. Indeed, Toledo had been the capital of Visigothic Spain. Now it was back in Christian hands.

Then, in 1092 Alfonso VI, king of León-Castile, recalled Spain's most famous knight from exile. With the king's permission, Rodrigo Díaz de Vivar, widely known as El Cid, raised an army and, after a two-year siege, conquered Valencia on June 16, 1094. The Muslims reacted quickly, sending a very large field army to Valencia in December. To their surprise, El Cid did not accept a siege but sallied forth and met the Muslim army at Cuarte, a town near Valencia. El Cid was a brilliant tactician who never lost a battle against Muslims, and in this instance he conducted a daring night attack, inflicting a crushing and bloody defeat. Shortly thereafter he squelched a revolt of Muslims in Valencia, expelling those involved and taking revenge by turning Valencia's nine mosques into Christian churches. In January 1097 El Cid defeated a new Muslim army sent against Valencia, meeting and beating them at the town of Bairén, and he then rode on to capture a number of other towns in the area.

El Cid's resounding victories over major forces "showed other Christian Spaniards what could be done."[39] Although Islamic armies won some subsequent battles, the tide had turned. Islamic Spain was receding toward the southern coast.

RETAKING ITALY AND SICILY

Perhaps the single most remarkable feature of the Islamic territories was almost ceaseless internal conflict; the intricate plots, assassinations, and betrayals form a lethal soap opera. North Africa was frequently torn by rebellions and by intra-Islamic wars and conquests. Spain was a patchwork of constantly feuding Muslim regimes that often allied themselves with Christians against one another. Recall that it was the Muslim governor of Barcelona who invited Charlemagne to enter Spain, and El Cid spent part of his career as a brilliant mercenary leader on behalf of the Muslim "king" of Saragossa, warring against other Muslims. And just as Muslim disunity made Spain vulnerable to Christian efforts to drive them out, so, too, in Italy and Sicily.

In 873 the Byzantine emperor Basil I, having murdered his co-emperor and driven the Muslims from the entire Dalmatian coast (facing Italy), decided to reclaim southern Italy from Muslim rule.[40] He landed his troops on the heel of Italy and soon accepted the surrender of Otranto. Three years later Bari came under his control, and during the next decade "virtually the whole of south Italy was restored to Byzantine authority."[41]

It did not, however, become a peaceful province. Time and again there were rebellions, coups, and new regimes, in addition to the constant intrigues back in Constantinople. But Byzantine rule prevailed, and then in 1038, determined to put an end to Muslim pirates and raiders operating from the ports of Sicily, the Italian Byzantines launched an invasion across the narrow Strait of Messina. They had chosen a most opportune time, as the Arab emirs in Sicily had fallen into one of their typical civil wars. In fact, al-Akhal, the Muslim ruler of Palermo, had sent an envoy to Constantinople in 1035 to ask for Byzantine help against his mounting enemies. The emperor agreed to send forces, but al-Akhal was assassinated, and that "removed this useful pretext for an unopposed landing."[42] However, the civil war continued to spread among the Sicilian Arabs, making it seem unlikely that they could offer serious resistance to a Greek invasion force.

So, in 1038, George Maniakes, the most famous of the living Byzantine generals, led an oddly assorted army across the strait. Although he had a Greek name, Maniakes probably was of Mongol origin, "a great bear of a man: strong, ugly, thoroughly intimidating . . . his military prowess was much respected in the capital, but he was a blunt man who had to survive under a regime increasingly given to palace intrigue and treachery."[43] His troops consisted of Lombards forced into service, a few Byzantine regulars, and various contingents of mercenaries, including one made up of Norman knights who were remarkable for their political awareness and their ambition, as well as for their unusual stature, they being of Scandinavian origins. (The word *Norman* derives from the Old Norse *Northmathr* ["Norseman"].)

The invasion began in late summer and was an immediate success. Messina fell almost at once. The invaders then won major battles at Rometta and Troina, "and within two years over a dozen major fortresses in the east of the island, plus the city of Syracuse, had been subdued."[44] Then everything fell apart. First, Maniakes so alienated the Normans by withholding their share of the booty that they returned to Italy, "angry, bitter, and dangerous,"[45] leaving the Byzantine force without its most effective contingent. In addition, antagonism had been building between Maniakes and the commander of the navy, the emperor's brother-in-law Stephen, who lacked military virtues but not ambition. When Stephen foolishly allowed the Muslim fleet to escape through the Byzantine blockade, Maniakes made the mistake of abusing him physically and calling him an effeminate pimp.[46] In revenge, Stephen sent a message to the emperor accusing Maniakes of treason. Summoned to Constantinople, Maniakes was immediately thrown into prison, and command in Sicily was given to Stephen, who made a complete mess of things and then died. He was replaced by a court eunuch named Basil, "who proved very little better."[47] The Byzantine army began a slow retreat. At this point, Lombard rebels rose up in Apulia, the southernmost province in the heel of Italy. The army was urgently recalled to quell the rebellion, leaving Sicily once again under uncontested Muslim rule.

The Norman mercenaries found the entire experience most edifying. First, they now knew that Sicily was rich, that the large Christian population would support an invasion, and that the Muslims were hopelessly divided. They also recognized that Constantinople was too far away and too corrupted by intrigues to sustain its rule in the West. So rather than hire out to suppress the Lombard uprising, the Normans decided to lead it. In 1041 the Norman knights sneaked across the mountains and descended into Apulia.

The Normans were led by William of Hauteville, whose heroic exploits in Sicily had earned him the nickname "Iron Arm," and they quickly seized the town of Melfi as their base—a well-situated and fortified hill town. From there, within several weeks they accepted the submission of all the surrounding towns, having successfully presented themselves as supporters of the rebellion. The Byzantine governor was much too experienced to just sit back and allow the Norman and rebel forces to expand. Assembling an army considerably larger than his opponents', he met them at the Olivento River. He then sent a herald to the Norman camp offering either a safe return of the Normans to Lombard territory or battle. Historians agree that the following actually happened in response: the enormous Norman knight holding the herald's horse struck a huge blow with his mailed fist, smashing in the horse's head, and it fell dead on the spot.[48] Provided with a new horse, the herald was sent back to the Byzantine camp, whereupon the battle ensued the next day.

Although vastly outnumbered, the Normans routed the Byzantine forces, most of whom were killed in battle or drowned while trying to flee across the river. The Byzantine governor quickly responded by importing many regular troops from Constantinople and marching them off to confront the Normans and their Lombard allies at Montemaggiore. Again led by William Iron Arm, the Normans slaughtered this new Byzantine army. Even then the Byzantines did not accept defeat, but gathered another army and fought one more battle near Montepeloso. And again Iron Arm and his Normans prevailed, even taking the Byzantine governor prisoner and holding him for ransom. Never again were the Byzantines willing to fight an open battle with Normans in Italy; they instead contented themselves with defending strongly fortified towns and cities. In this manner they avoided any further military catastrophes, but they also failed to hold southern Italy as it was slowly transformed into a Norman kingdom.

Meanwhile, the Normans had not lost interest in Muslim Sicily. In 1059, after Robert Guiscard, duke of southern Italy, had designated himself in a letter to Pope Nicholas II as "future [lord] of Sicily,"[49] the Norman plans for an invasion began to take shape. Guiscard was a remarkable man. The Byzantine princess Anna Comnena described him as "overbearing," "brave," and "cunning," and as having a "thoroughly villainous mind." She continued: "He was a man of immense stature, surpassing even the biggest men; he had a ruddy complexion, fair hair, [and] broad shoulders," but was remarkably "graceful."[50]

In 1061 Guiscard, his brother Roger, and a select company of Normans made a night landing at Messina and in the morning found the city abandoned. Guiscard immediately had the city fortified and then formed an alliance with Ibn at-Tinnah, one of the feuding Sicilian emirs, and took most of Sicily before having to return to Italy to see after affairs there. He made several minor gestures toward expanding his control of part of Sicily but concentrated on overwhelming the remaining Byzantine strongholds in southern Italy, finally driving the Greeks out of southern Italy in 1071. The next year he returned to Sicily, captured Palermo, and soon took command of the entire island. In 1098 Robert Guiscard's eldest son, Bohemond, led the crusader forces that took the city of Antioch and became the ruler of the princedom of Antioch. Then, in 1130, Guiscard's nephew Robert II established the Norman kingdom of Sicily (which included southern Italy).[51] It lasted for only about a century, but Muslim rule never resumed.

CONTROL OF THE SEA

During the 1920s, the Belgian historian Henri Pirenne (1862–1935) gained international fame by claiming that the "Dark Ages" descended on Europe not because of the fall of Rome or the invasion of northern "barbarians," but because Muslim control of the Mediterranean isolated Europe. He wrote: "The Mediterranean had been a Roman lake; it now became, for the most part, a Moslem lake,"[52] and, cut off from trade with the East, Europe declined into a backward collection of rural economies.

To support this claim Pirenne cited fragmentary evidence that overseas trade had declined sharply late in the seventh century and remained low until early in the tenth. Although Pirenne's thesis was very influential for many years, eventually it lost plausibility as scholars discovered convincing evidence that the alleged decline in trade on which it rested had been greatly overstated. Perhaps there had been some interruptions of seaborne trade with the East during the first fifty years of Muslim expansion, but there is evidence that extremely active Mediterranean trade quickly resumed, even between western Europe and Islamic countries.[53]

Oddly enough, historians have failed to pay much attention to the most fundamental and easily assessed of Pirenne's assumptions: that Muslim sea power ruled the Mediterranean.[54] It is difficult to know how Pirenne came to this view. Perhaps he simply believed Ibn Khaldūn (1332–1406), who wrote that "the Muslims gained control over the whole Mediterranean. Their power and domination over it was vast. The Christian nations could do nothing against the Muslim fleets, anywhere in the Mediterranean. All the time the Muslims rode its waves for conquest."[55] Nevertheless, even with the advantages provided by possession of some strategically placed island bases, the Muslim fleet never ruled the waves.

Granted, soon after the conquest of Egypt the Muslims acquired a powerful fleet, and in 655 they defeated a Byzantine fleet off the Anatolian coast. But only twenty years later the Byzantines used Greek fire to destroy a huge Muslim fleet, and in 717 they did so again. Then, in 747 "a tremendous Arab armada consisting of 1,000 donens [galleys] representing the flower of the Syrian and Egyptian naval strength" encountered a far smaller Byzantine fleet off Cyprus, and only three Arab ships survived this engagement.[56] Muslim naval forces never fully recovered, in part because they suffered from chronic shortages "of ship timber, naval stores, and iron," all of which the Byzantines had in abundance.[57] Hence, rather than the Mediterranean becoming a Muslim lake, the truth is that the eastern Mediterranean was a Byzantine lake, the Byzantine navy having become "the most efficient and highly trained that the world had ever seen, patrolling the coasts, policing the high seas and attacking the Saracen raiding parties whenever and wherever they might be found."[58] It is true that the Muslims were able to sustain some invasions by sea in the western Mediterranean in the eighth and ninth centuries, far from the Byzantine naval bases, but by the tenth century they were driven to shelter by Western fleets as well as those of a renewed Byzantium.

Muslim naval weakness should always have been obvious. For one thing, the Muslims quickly realized that they must withdraw their fleets from open harbors, where they risked destruction from surprise attacks. Thus, for example, Carthage was abandoned, and the fleet stationed there was moved inland to Tunis and a canal dug to provide access to the sea. Being so narrow as to accommodate only one galley at a time, the canal was easily defended against any opposing fleet.[59] In similar fashion, the Egyptian fleet was removed from Alexandria and rebased up the Nile. While these were sensible moves, they also revealed weakness.

That the Muslims lacked control of the seas also was obvious in the ability of Byzantium to transport armies by sea with impunity—for example, their landing and supplying of the troops that drove Islam from southern Italy. Nor could the Muslim navies impede the very extensive overseas trade of the Italian city-states such as Genoa, Pisa, and Venice.[60] Indeed, in the eleventh century, well before the First Crusade, Italian fleets not only preyed on Muslim shipping but successfully and repeatedly raided Muslim naval bases along the North African coast.[61] Hence, during the Crusades, Italian, English, Frankish, and even Norse fleets sailed to and from the Holy Land at will, transporting thousands of crusaders and their supplies. Finally, as will be demonstrated in the next chapter, contrary to Pirenne's thesis, Muslim sea barriers to trade could not have caused Europe to enter the "Dark Ages," because the "Dark Ages" never took place.

CONCLUSION

All of these Christian victories preceded the First Crusade. Consequently, when the knights of western Europe marched or sailed to the Holy Land, they knew a lot about their Muslim opponents. Most of all, they knew they could beat them.

Chapter Three

WESTERN "IGNORANCE" VERSUS EASTERN "CULTURE"

Contrary to frequent claims, Muslim technology lagged far behind
that of the West. The knights shown here are armed with crossbows that
were far more accurate and deadly than Muslim bows—Muslim arrows
could seldom penetrate the chain-mail armor worn by these and most other
crusaders, but very few Muslims had such armor.

© British Library / HIP / Art Resource, NY

I T HAS LONG BEEN the received wisdom that while Europe slumbered through the Dark Ages, science and learning flourished in Islam. As the well-known Bernard Lewis put it in his recent study, Islam "had achieved the highest level so far in human history in the arts and sciences of civilization . . . [intellectually] medieval Europe was a pupil and in a sense dependent on the Islamic world."[1] But then, Lewis pointed out, Europeans suddenly began to advance "by leaps and bounds, leaving the scientific and technological and eventually the cultural heritage of the Islamic world far behind them."[2] Hence, the question Lewis posed in the title of his book: *What Went Wrong?*

This chapter documents my answer to Lewis's question: *nothing* went wrong. The belief that once upon a time Muslim culture was superior to that of Europe is at best an illusion.

DHIMMI CULTURE

To the extent that Arab elites acquired a sophisticated culture, they learned it from their subject peoples. As Bernard Lewis put it, without seeming to fully appreciate the implications, Arabs inherited "the knowledge and skills of the ancient Middle east, of Greece, of Persia and of India."[3] That is, the sophisticated culture so often attributed to Muslims (more often referred to as "Arabic" culture) was actually the culture of the conquered people—the Judeo-Christian-Greek culture of Byzantium, the remarkable learning of heretical Christian groups such as the Copts and the

Nestorians, extensive knowledge from Zoroastrian (Mazdean) Persia, and the great mathematical achievements of the Hindus (keep in mind the early and extensive Muslim conquests in India). This legacy of learning, including much that had originated with the ancient Greeks, was translated into Arabic, and portions of it were somewhat assimilated into Arab culture, but even after having been translated, this "learning" continued to be sustained primarily by the *dhimmi* populations living under Arab regimes. For example, the "earliest scientific book in the language of Islam" was a "treatise on medicine by a Syrian Christian priest in Alexandria, translated into Arabic by a Persian Jewish physician."[4] As in this example, not only did most "Arab" science and learning originate with the *dhimmis;* they even did most of the translating into Arabic.[5] But that did not transform this body of knowledge into Arab culture. Rather, as Marshall Hodgson noted, "those who pursued natural science tended to retain their older religious allegiances as *dhimmis*, even when doing their work in Arabic."[6] That being the case, as the *dhimmis* slowly assimilated, much of what was claimed to be the sophisticated Arab culture disappeared.

Although not a matter of intellectual culture, Muslim fleets provide an excellent example. The problems posed for their armies by the ability of Byzantium to attack them from the sea led the early Arab conquerors to acquire fleets of their own. Subsequently, these fleets sometimes gave good account of themselves in battles against Byzantine and Western navies, and this easily can be used as evidence of Islamic sophistication. But when we look more closely, we discover that these were not really "Muslim" fleets.

Being men of the desert, the Arabs knew nothing of shipbuilding, so they turned to their newly acquired and still-functioning shipyards of Egypt[7] and the port cities of coastal Syria (including Tyre, Acre, and Beirut) and commissioned the construction of a substantial fleet. The Arabs also knew nothing of sailing or navigation, so they manned their Egyptian fleet with Coptic sailors[8] and their Persian fleet with mercenaries having Byzantine naval backgrounds. A bit later, when in need of a fleet at Carthage, the Muslim "governor of Egypt sent 1,000 Coptic shipwrights . . . to construct a fleet of 100 warships."[9] While very little has been written about Muslim navies (itself suggestive that Muslim writers had little contact with them),[10] there is every reason to assume that Muslims never took over the construction or command of "their" fleets but that they continued to be designed, built, and sailed by *dhimmis*. Thus in 717, when the Arabs made their last effort against Constantinople by sea, a contributing factor in their defeat was "the defection to the Byzantine side of many of the Christian crews of Arab vessels."[11] Finally, when an enormous Muslim fleet was sunk by Europeans off the coast of Lepanto in 1571, "the leading captains of both fleets were European. The sultan himself preferred renegade Italian admirals."[12] Moreover, not only were the Arab ships copies of European designs; "[t]hey were built for the sultan by highly paid runaways,"[13] by "shipwrights from Naples and Venice."[14]

The highly acclaimed Arab architecture also turns out to have been mainly a *dhimmi* achievement, adapted from Persian and Byzantine origins. When Caliph Abd el-Malik had the great Dome of the Rock built in Jerusalem, and which became one of the great masterpieces attributed to Islamic art, he employed Byzantine architects and craftsmen,[15] which is why it so closely resembled the Church of the Holy Sepulchre.[16] Similarly, in 762, when the caliph al-Mansūr founded Baghdad, he entrusted the design of the city to a Zoroastrian and a Jew.[17] In fact, many famous Muslim mosques were originally built as Christian churches and converted by merely adding external minarets and redecorating the interiors. As an acknowledged authority on Islamic art and architecture put it, "the Dome of the Rock truly represents a work of what we understand today as Islamic art, that is, art not necessarily made by Muslims . . . but rather art made in societies where most people—or the most important people—were Muslims."[18]

Similar examples abound in the intellectual areas that have inspired so much admiration for Arab learning. Thus, in his much-admired book written to acknowledge the "enormous" contributions of the Arabs to science and engineering, Donald R. Hill noted that very little could be traced to Arab origins and admitted that most of these contributions originated with conquered populations. For example, Avicenna, whom the *Encyclopaedia Britannica* ranks as "the most influential of all Muslim philosopher-scientists," was a Persian. So were the famous scholars Omar Khayyám, al-Biruni, and Razi, all of whom are ranked with Avicenna. Another Persian, al-Khwarizmi, is credited as the father of algebra. Al-Uqlidisi, who introduced fractions, was a Syrian. Bakht-Ishū' and ibn Ishaq, leading figures in "Muslim" medical knowledge, were Nestorian Christians. Masha'allah ibn Atharī, the famous astronomer and astrologer, was a Jew. This list could be extended for several pages. What may have misled so many historians is that most contributors to "Arabic science" were given Arabic names and their works were published in Arabic—that being the "official" language of the land.

Consider mathematics. The so-called Arabic numerals were entirely of Hindu origin. Moreover, even after the splendid Hindu numbering system based on the concept of zero was published in Arabic, it was adopted only by mathematicians while other Muslims continued to use their cumbersome traditional system. Many other contributions to mathematics also have been erroneously attributed to "Arabs." For example, Thabit ibn Qurra, noted for his many contributions to geometry and to number theory, is usually identified as an "Arab mathematician," but he was a member of the pagan Sabian sect. Of course, there were some fine Muslim mathematicians, perhaps because it is a subject so abstract as to insulate its practitioners from any possible religious criticism. The same might be said for astronomy, although here, too, most of the credit should go not to Arabs, but to Hindus and Persians. The "discovery" that the earth turns on its axis is often attributed to the Persian al-Biruni, but he acknowledged having learned of it from Brahmagupta and other Indian astronomers.[19] Nor was al-Biruni certain about the matter, remarking in his *Canon Masudicus* that "it is the same whether you take it that the Earth is in motion or the sky. For, in both cases, it does not affect the Astronomical Science."[20] Another famous "Arab" astronomer was al-Battani, but like Thabit ibn Qurra, he, too, was a member of the pagan Sabian sect (who were star worshippers, which explains their particular interest in astronomy).

The many claims that the Arabs achieved far more sophisticated medicine than had previous cultures[21] are as mistaken as those regarding "Arabic" numerals. "Muslim" or "Arab" medicine was in fact Nestorian Christian medicine; even the leading Muslim and Arab physicians were trained at the enormous Nestorian medical center at Nisibus in Syria. Not only medicine but the full range of advanced education was offered at Nisibus and at the other institutions of learning established by the Nestorians, including the one at Jundishapur in Persia, which the distinguished historian of science George Sarton (1884–1956) called "the greatest intellectual center of the time."[22] Hence, the Nestorians "soon acquired a reputation with the Arabs for being excellent accountants, architects, astrologers, bankers, doctors, merchants, philosophers, scientists, scribes and teachers. In fact, prior to the ninth century, nearly all the learned scholars in the [Islamic area] were Nestorian Christians."[23] It was primarily the Nestorian Christian Hunayn ibn Ishaq al-'Ibadi (known in Latin as Johannitius) who "collected, translated, revised, and supervised the translation of Greek manuscripts, especially those of

Hippocrates, Galen, Plato, and Aristotle[,] into Syriac and Arabic."[24] Indeed, as late as the middle of the eleventh century, the Muslim writer Nasir-i Khrusau reported, "Truly, the scribes here in Syria, as is the case of Egypt, are all Christians . . . [and] it is most usual for the physicians . . . to be Christians."[25] In Palestine under Muslim rule, according to the monumental history by Moshe Gil, "the Christians had immense influence and positions of power, chiefly because of the gifted administrators among them who occupied government posts despite the ban in Muslim law against employing Christians [in such positions] or who were part of the intelligentsia of the period owing to the fact that they were outstanding scientists, mathematicians, physicians and so on."[26] The prominence of Christian officials was also acknowledged by Abd al-Jabbār, who wrote in about 995 that "kings in Egypt, al-Shām, Iraq, Jazīra, Fāris, and in all their surroundings, rely on Christians in matters of officialdom, the central administration and the handling of funds."[27]

Even many of the most partisan Muslim historians, including the famous English convert to Islam and translator of the Qur'an Marmaduke Pickthall (1875–1936),[28] agree that the sophisticated Muslim culture originated with the conquered populations. But what has largely been ignored is that the decline of that culture and the inability of Muslims to keep up with the West occurred because Muslim or Arab culture was largely an illusion resting on a complex mix of *dhimmi* cultures, and as such, it was easily lost and always vulnerable to being repressed as heretical. Hence, when in the fourteenth century Muslims in the East stamped out nearly all religious nonconformity, Muslim backwardness came to the fore.

ISLAM AND ARISTOTLE

Underlying the belief that the Muslims were more learned and sophisticated than the Christian West is the presumption that a society not steeped in Greek philosophy and literature was a society in the dark! Thus for the past several centuries many European writers have stressed the Arab possession of the classical writers, assuming that by having access to the advanced "wisdom" of the ancients, Islam was the much superior culture. Although medieval European scholars were far more familiar with the "classics" than was claimed, the fact is that because of the persistence of Byzantine/Greek culture in most of the conquered Arab societies, the most-educated Arabs did have greater knowledge of the work of classical Greek authors such as Plato and Aristotle. What is less known is the rather negative impact that access to Greek scholarship had on Arab scholarship.

The works of Plato and Aristotle reached the Arabs via translations into Syrian late in the seventh century and then into Arabic by Syrians in, perhaps, the ninth century. However, rather than treat these works as *attempts* by Greek scholars to answer various questions, Muslim intellectuals quickly read them in the same way as they read the Qur'an—as settled truths to be understood without question or contradiction—and thus to the degree that Muslim thinkers analyzed these works, it was to reconcile apparent internal disagreements. Eventually the focus was on Aristotle. As the respected Muslim historian Caesar Farah explained, "[I]n Aristotle Muslim thinkers found the great guide; to them he became the 'first teacher.' Having accepted this a priori, Muslim philosophy as it evolved in subsequent centuries merely chose to *continue* in this vein and to enlarge on Aristotle rather than to innovate."[29] This eventually led the philosopher Averroës and his followers to impose the position that Aristotle's physics was complete and infallible, and if actual observations were inconsistent with one of Aristotle's teachings, those observations were either in error or an illusion.[30]

Attitudes such as these prevented Islam from taking up where the Greeks had left off in their pursuit of knowledge. In contrast, knowledge of Aristotle's work prompted experimentation and discovery among the early Christian scholastics. Indeed, then as now, one's reputation was enhanced by disagreeing with received knowledge, by innovation and correction, which motivated scholastics to find fault with the Greeks.[31] And there were many faults to be found.

BOOKS AND LIBRARIES

As noted, central to all claims concerning the superiority of Muslim culture has been their possession of translations of many books by classical authors. But books must be kept somewhere, and large collections of books can be identified as libraries—whether these are the collection of books belonging to individuals or are institutions devoted to acquiring and preserving books. There is sufficient evidence of the existence of both kinds of libraries in Islam, dating back to early days. Indeed, libraries confronted the conquering Muslim armies all across the Middle East and North Africa. Some of these libraries had survived from pagan times; others were created by Christians and Jews. Among the Copts in Egypt, "every monastery and probably every church once had its own library of manuscripts."[32] All across Byzantium, the Orthodox clergy sustained libraries. At their great centers of learning, the Nestorian Christians maintained huge collections of books. There seems to have been nothing very unusual about the story of a Nestorian monk who checked out a book from the monastery library every week and devoted most of his waking hours to pondering and memorizing it.[33] Thus it was demonstrated to the early Muslims that if they "were to make use of the diversified knowledge to which they fell heir, they must have books, preferably in the Arabic language, and these books must be preserved in safety and rendered accessible to readers."[34]

However, the notion that Muslims valued libraries is contrary to the controversial claim that they burned the huge library at Alexandria.[35] The story is told that after the conquest of Alexandria, the Muslim commander inquired of the caliph 'Umar back in Damascus as to what should be done with this immense library, said to contain hundreds of thousands of scrolls. 'Umar is said to have replied, "[I]f what is written in them agrees with the Book of God [the Qur'an], they are not required: if it disagrees, they are not desired. Therefore destroy them."[36] Thus the general distributed the scrolls to the four thousand baths of the city to be used as fuel, and the burning took six months.

This story has provoked very angry responses from many admirers of Islam despite the fact that the leading Western historians (including Edward Gibbon) have rejected it, most being satisfied with the tradition that the library was burned by accident when Julius Caesar conquered Egypt. Nevertheless, Asma Afsaruddin angrily charged that the story reflects nothing more than Christian hatred of Muslims,[37] ignoring the fact that the story first appeared in the thirteenth century in an account written by a Muslim Egyptian historian! It was then repeated by other Muslim writers, including the famous Ibn Khaldūn.[38] That the charge that the caliph caused the great library to be burned was leveled by Muslims does not increase the likelihood that it is true; the first account was written about six hundred years after the alleged event. But that the story was believed by so many Muslim intellectuals suggests something far more interesting: that many Muslims, including heads of state, were hostile to books and learning!

This anti-intellectual attitude seems obvious if one reads Muslim political history rather than accounts of the glories of Muslim science. The former notes that when Mutawakkil became caliph in 847 he immediately "began to stifle independent research and scientific inquiry and increase the suppression of religious dissent by force."[39] So did his successors. Then with the collapse of the caliphate, it no longer was possible to apply any policies—whether "enlightened" or "repressive"—to a Muslim empire now shattered into a mosaic of emirates, subject to a series of internal invasions. From then on, some Muslim rulers were more tolerant than others of scholars, their books, and their learning, but most were not very tolerant. Indeed, Saladin, the famous twelfth-century Muslim hero so greatly admired by Western writers, closed the official library in Cairo and discarded the books.[40] All of this would seem to indicate a prevailing tension between the sophisticated, so-called Muslim culture sustained by the *dhimmis* and the actual culture of the Muslim elites.

THE MYTHICAL DARK AGES

The claim that Muslims possessed a more advanced culture also rests on illusions about the cultural backwardness of Christendom—on the widespread but unfounded belief that subsequent to the fall of Rome, Europe regressed into the Dark Ages and thus lost the cultural heritage that still was thriving in Islam. Voltaire (1694–1778) claimed that after Rome fell, "barbarism, superstition, [and] ignorance covered the face of the world."[41] According to Rousseau (1712–1778), "Europe had relapsed into the barbarism of the earliest ages. The people of this part of the world . . . lived some centuries ago in a condition worse than ignorance."[42] Edward Gibbon (1737–1794) also pronounced this era as the "triumph of barbarism and religion."[43]

Not surprisingly, this became the received wisdom on the matter. Thus, in his bestselling book *The Discoverers* (1983), Pulitzer Prize–winning historian and Librarian of Congress Daniel J. Boorstin (1914–2004) included a chapter titled "The Prison of Christian Dogma," in which he claimed that the "Dark Ages" began even before the fall of Rome. "Christianity conquered the Roman Empire and most of Europe. Then we observe a Europe-wide phenomenon of scholarly amnesia, which afflicted the continent from A.D. 300 to at least 1300." This occurred because "the leaders of orthodox Christendom built a grand barrier against the progress of knowledge."[44] And in the words of the distinguished historian William Manchester (1922–2004), this was an era "of incessant warfare, corruption, lawlessness, obsession with strange myths, and an almost impenetrable mindlessness . . . The Dark Ages were stark in every dimension."[45]

Some of these claims are malicious, and all are astonishingly ignorant. Granted, like the Muslim conquerors, the Germanic tribes that conquered Roman Europe had to acquire considerable culture before they measured up to their predecessors. But, in addition to having many Romans to instruct and guide them, they had the Church, which carefully sustained and *advanced* the culture inherited from Rome.[46] What is even more significant is that the centuries labeled as the "Dark Ages" were "one of the great innovative eras of mankind," as technology was developed and put into use "on a scale no civilization had previously known."[47] In fact, as will be seen, it was during the "Dark Ages" that Europe began the great technological leap forward that put it far ahead of the rest of the world.[48] This has become so well known that rejection of the "Dark Ages" as an unfounded myth is now reported in the respected dictionaries and encyclopedias that only a few years previously had accepted and promulgated that same myth. Thus, while earlier editions of the *Encyclopaedia Britannica* had identified the five or six centuries after the fall of Rome as the "Dark Ages," the fifteenth edition, published in 1981, dismissed that as an "unacceptable" term because it *incorrectly* claims this to have been "a period of intellectual darkness and barbarity."

As has been evident, the claims concerning a more advanced and sophisticated Muslim culture are often based on "intellectualism." But there is far more to culture than books or "book learning." No one can learn how to farm, sail, or win battles by reading Plato or Aristotle. Technology, in the broadest sense of the word, is the stuff of real life that determines how well people live and whether they can protect themselves. And whatever Muslim intellectuals did or didn't know about Aristotle's science or Plato's political philosophy in comparison with the knowledge of the learned Christian scholastics, Islamic technology lagged well behind that of Byzantium and Europe.

CONTRASTS IN TECHNOLOGY

It is far more difficult than it ought to be to contrast Christendom and Islam in terms of important technology, because the subject is dominated by Muslim authors who are too much given to absurd claims. Thus one can "discover" that "Ibn Firnas of Islamic Spain invented, constructed, and tested a flying machine in the 800s."[49] European shipbuilders did not invent the rudder; Muslim shipbuilders did. (Which Muslim shipbuilders were these?) The Chinese did not invent the compass; Muslims did. And on and on.[50]

Transport

What we do know with absolute certainty is that following the Muslim conquest of Egypt, the rest of North Africa, and Spain, the *wheel* disappeared from this whole area![51] For centuries there were no carts or wagons. All goods were hand-carried or packed on camels, donkeys, or horses. This did not happen because the Arabs lacked knowledge of the wheel, but because they thought it of little use. In their judgment, wheels required streets and roads. Camels and pedestrians required neither. Moreover, given their disdain for the wheel, it is doubtful that Muslims knew how to construct a proper harness to hook draft animals to carts and wagons.

In contrast, sometime early in the "Dark Ages," Europeans were the first to develop a collar and harness that would allow horses rather than oxen to pull heavy wagons—with a very substantial gain in speed. Properly harnessed, one horse could pull a wagon loaded with about two thousand pounds,[52] a burden that would require at least four pack camels and probably five.[53] The pulling capacity of European horses was increased again when, in the eighth century, iron horseshoes were invented and came into widespread use by the next century. Horseshoes not only protected the horse's hooves from wear and tear, especially on hard surfaces; they also allowed the horse to dig in on softer surfaces and gain better traction.[54] In addition, tenth-century Europeans were the first to discover a harness that would allow large teams of horses or oxen to be lined up in a column of pairs, as opposed to hooking them up abreast. This permitted the use of large numbers of draft animals to pull a single load,[55] such as giant catapults or assault towers during a siege.

An objection that Arabs may have had to wagons is that those in use at the time of the Muslim conquests and before had a fixed front axel that made them difficult to turn. They also had no brakes and could be very dangerous on downward slopes.[56] By no later than the ninth century Europeans had solved these problems, and their wagons had front axels that swiveled, as well as adequate brakes. This was a significant advantage when they undertook a major military campaign more than twenty-five hundred miles from home. Indeed, one contingent in the First Crusade is thought to have started out with at least two thousand wagons.[57]

Finally, despite having the swiftest riding horses in the world, the Muslims lacked the large draft horses used by Europeans.

Hence, for them the advantage of using wagons as opposed to pack camels would have been somewhat less. Of course, both Muslims and Europeans were expert at breeding horses, so these differences were a matter of preference.

Agriculture

Big draft horses also played a substantial role in the agricultural revolution that transformed Europe during the "Dark Ages." Food production per capita rose dramatically. Part of the reason was that horses could pull a plow twice as fast as could oxen; hence by switching to horses one farmer could plow twice as much land in the same amount of time. Of equal importance, the "Dark Ages" farmers' big horses were pulling a far superior plow.

Until some time in the sixth century, the most advanced farmers all over the world used some variant of the scratch plow, which is nothing more than a set of digging sticks arranged in rows on a flat surface. The scratch plow does not turn over the soil but is simply dragged over the surface, leaving undisturbed soil between shallow furrows, a process that often requires cross-plowing.[58] This was barely adequate for the thin, dry soils along the Mediterranean and was insufficient for the heavy, often damp, but extremely fertile soil of most of northern Europe. What was needed was a very heavy plow, with a large, sharp, heavy share (blade) that would turn over the soil and dig a deep furrow. To this was added a second share at an angle to cut off the slice of turf that was being turned over by the first share. Then was added a moldboard to completely turn over the sliced-off turf. Finally, wheels were added to the plow to facilitate moving it from one field to another and to make it possible to set the share to plow at different depths. Presto! Land that could not previously be farmed, or not farmed effectively, suddenly became very productive, and even on thinner soil the use of the heavy moldboard plow nearly doubled crop yields.[59]

During the eighth century came the next step in the agricultural revolution: the adoption of the three-field system, wherein farmland belonging to each village was divided into three plots[60] and each farmer had his own strip in each of the three fields. One plot was planted in a winter crop such as wheat; the second, in a spring crop such as oats (an especially important crop once the horse became the primary draft animal), legumes (such as peas and beans), or vegetables; and the third plot was allowed to lie fallow (unplanted). The next year the plot that had been fallow was planted in the winter crop, the second in a spring crop, and the plot that had grown a spring crop the previous year was left fallow. Not only did using the fallow plot for grazing keep down the weeds, but the manure spread by the cattle had dramatic effects on the land's fertility.

As a result, starting during the "Dark Ages" most Europeans began to eat far better than had the common people anywhere, ever. Indeed, medieval Europeans may have been the first human group whose genetic potential was not badly stunted by a poor diet, with the result that they were, on average, bigger, healthier, and more energetic than ordinary people elsewhere.

A far longer list of technological breakthroughs made by Europeans during the "Dark Ages" could be assembled, and I have done so elsewhere.[61] Here it seems adequate and more appropriate to conclude the matter by a close comparison of military technology.

Military Might

Consider that in 732, supposedly during the depths of the "Dark Ages," Charles Martel's heavy cavalry possessed high-backed saddles equipped with stirrups that allowed them to put the full weight of a charging horse and heavily armored rider behind a long lance without the rider's being thrown off by the impact.

In contrast, the opposing Muslim cavalry rode bareback or on thin pads, and lacked stirrups, thereby being limited to swinging swords and axes, just as had all previous cavalries including those of the Romans and Persians.[62] Muslim cavalry could avoid and flee the thundering charges by Western knights, but they could not stand up to them.

In addition, just as the Muslims lacked the big horses needed to pull plows and heavily loaded wagons, they lacked the big chargers needed by well-armored knights—a problem that also first became apparent at the Battle of Tours/Poitiers and never was overcome. In the era of the Crusades, the European knights rode horses weighing about twelve to thirteen hundred pounds, while the Muslim cavalry was mounted on horses weighing about seven to eight hundred pounds.[63] This gave the crusaders a considerable advantage when it came to man-to-man fighting, for the man on the larger, taller horse was striking down at his opponent, and his horse could push the other horse around. It also was important because the average crusader cavalryman weighed far more than did his Muslim counterpart. For one thing, he was a larger man. But the major weight factor was the difference in armor.

Unlike modern times, in those days there was no "standard equipment" issued to the troops. Although some of the nobility provided some arms and armor for their troops, this was not typical: most combatants supplied their own equipment. Consequently, comparisons of the equipment of Christian and Muslim armies are far less exact than, for example, comparisons between the equipment of American and Japanese soldiers in World War II. That said, crusaders wore considerably more and better armor than did their Muslim opponents. However, do not suppose that the Europeans were decked out in the complete, jointed suits of plate armor that stand around in museums. These suits came later, and only some knights of the heavy cavalry ever wore them, as they were dangerously impractical. Knights in plate-armor suits had to be lifted onto their saddles by booms; if they fell off they could not rise to their feet to fight on. Rather than armor suits, even the heavy crusader cavalry wore chain-mail coats sufficiently thick to turn aside all but the most powerful sword and axe strokes, and helmets that covered their head, neck, and sometimes part of their face. So did the infantry, who made up by far the greater proportion of any medieval Western army.

Chain mail was constructed of tiny iron rings, each threaded with four others, and it was fashioned into a long "shirt split at the groin, with flaps hanging down from the thighs to about the knees. These could be tied around the leg like a cowboy's chaps, or, more commonly, left to hang as a kind of split skirt."[64] Some crusaders also wore leggings made of chain mail, some of which also covered the foot.

Chain-mail armor was well known in the East but not widely employed. Metal scales attached to cloth or leather jackets were used instead—a variety of armor regarded as "outmoded in the West."[65] Having lighter and less armor contributed to the greater mobility of Muslim fighters, but it also made them far more vulnerable when forced to fight head-on. The chain-mail armor worn by the Franks was remarkably stout. For example, Muslim arrows could only partly penetrate it, "often without wounding the body. The image of the porcupine was sometimes used to describe the appearance of men . . . who had been under Turkish attack."[66] In his memoir of the First Crusade, Ralph of Caen summed it up correctly, noting that the Saracens "trusted in their numbers, we in our armour."[67]

But no armor, not even a plate-armor suit, was very effective against the invention that made the crusaders so lethal in battle— the crossbow. Although it was widely used by the crusaders, remarkably little has been written about the crossbow because it was thought to be quite shameful, even sinful, to use it. In 1139 the Second Lateran Council prohibited its use (except against infidels) "under penalty of anathema, as a weapon hateful to God and to Christians," and this ban was subsequently confirmed by Pope Innocent III.[68] However, European armies ignored the Church and made widespread use of the crossbow until it was made obsolete by firearms. Thus, for example, the Knights Templar garrison at the castle of Saphet in northern Galilee in about 1260 consisted of fifty knights and three hundred crossbowmen.[69]

The "moral" objections to the crossbow had to do with social class, as this revolutionary weapon allowed untrained peasants to be lethal enemies of the trained soldiery. It took many years of training to become a knight, and the same was true for archers. Indeed, it took years for archers to build the arm strength needed to draw a longbow, let alone to perfect their accuracy. But just about anyone could become proficient with a crossbow in less than a week. Worse yet, even a beginner could be considerably more accurate than a highly skilled longbow archer at ranges up to sixty-five to seventy yards.[70] This was because the crossbow was aimed like a rifle and fired by pulling a trigger that released the string and propelled a bolt (heavy arrow) that went in a straight line to wherever the weapon was pointed. Although longbows could be fired more rapidly and farther (by using a very high trajectory), they could not match the accuracy of the crossbow. The projectiles fired by crossbows were called bolts because they were much shorter and heavier than the arrows fired by regular bows. While this reduced the range of crossbows, it greatly increased their impact at shorter ranges. The fact that so little training was required meant that huge numbers of crossbowmen could be assembled quickly; the Genoese several times fielded as many as twenty thousand for a single battle.[71]

Against the crusader crossbows, the Muslims employed a short, composite bow of far less range and striking power than the crossbow. Muslim arrows were effective against lightly armored opponents such as other Muslims, but unless fired point-blank, they needed to hit a crusader in an unarmored spot. In contrast, a bolt from a crossbow, fired at a range of 150 yards or less, achieved remarkable penetration even of armor plate. As the Byzantine princess Anna Comnena (c. 1083–1153) reported in *The Alexiad*, her superb account of her father's reign, the crossbow fires with "tremendous violence and force, so that the missiles wherever they strike do not rebound; in fact they transfix a shield, cut through heavy iron breastplate and resume their flight on the far side."[72]

In the crusader armies, such as the one organized by Richard Lionheart, crossbows were served by three-man teams: one carried and braced up a huge shield, which they crouched behind in battle as protection from enemy arrows and missiles; one reloaded crossbows and passed them to the archer, who did the shooting. These teams could regularly fire eight times a minute, about the same as the rate of fire achieved by a single long bowman, but with far greater effect.[73]

Crossbow teams backing up well-armored, reliable infantry formations made a lethal combination: the enemy suffered severe losses inflicted by the crossbows while advancing for an attack and then had to confront intact infantry lines.[74] This was especially a problem for Muslim armies, since they had the additional disadvantage of being primarily a light cavalry force, ill suited to attack determined infantry unless they very greatly outnumbered them. The severe beatings administered in the eighth century by the Franks, even without crossbows, might have prompted Muslim leaders to reconsider the composition of their forces. But in such affairs tradition is very difficult to overcome; the Arabs had always been light cavalry, and they had achieved a brilliant series of early conquests with their traditional methods. Any tendency for the Muslims to rethink their overwhelming dependence on cavalry, perhaps in response to having been driven from Europe, was thwarted in the eleventh century when the Seljuk Turks, newly converted to Islam, overran the Arab Middle East. The Turks were mounted nomads who held infantry in contempt. Hence, the Muslim reliance on light cavalry remained a serious tactical and technological deficit that played a major role during the Crusades. Again and again in the Holy Land, despite having overwhelming numerical superiority, Muslim cavalry failed against Christian infantry. Even Christian knights often dismounted to fight as infantry, and their formations always included large numbers of crossbow teams.[75]

Crossbows not only were lethal on the battlefield, but were very effective at picking defenders off the walls of fortresses and at repelling attacks against a fortress. They also played a very important role in naval warfare.

The most significant fact to consider when attempting to compare Christian and Muslim fleets is that the ships of the latter were copies of those of the former and were built and crewed by Christian renegades and mercenaries. From this it follows that the crews of Muslim ships were not imbued with the same level of commitment as were the Christian fleets. Thus, after Saladin had rebuilt a Muslim fleet in the 1180s, it was completely destroyed in 1187 while anchored off Tyre to prevent the city, which was under siege by Saladin's forces, from being resupplied from the sea. Surprised by a crusader fleet, according to an Egyptian account, Saladin's crews abandoned their ships without a fight.[76]

In addition, having been built by Christians and copied from Christian boats, the Muslim fleets were always somewhat out-of-date. Therefore, in addition to superior seamanship and commitment, the Christian fleets enjoyed a "lead both in size and in the technological capabilities of their ships."[77] One of these advantages was to pack the "castles" of each galley with crossbowmen, which permitted Christian fleets to inflict considerable casualties on an opposing galley from a distance—just as the English fleet later used its canons against the Spanish Armada and refused to close for hand-to-hand fighting. In addition, Christians developed very heavy crossbows mounted on the decks of their galleys and used them to launch large projectiles—sometimes canisters of Greek fire—against their opponents. Another technological advantage involved special galleys that made it possible for Christian fleets to transport a company of knights together with their big war horses and land them on a hostile beach, mounted and ready to fight.[78]

CONCLUSION

Even if we grant the claims that educated Arabs possessed superior knowledge of classical authors and produced some outstanding mathematicians and astronomers, the fact remains that they lagged far behind in terms of such vital technology as saddles, stirrups, horseshoes, wagons and carts, draft horses and harnesses, effective plows, crossbows, Greek fire, shipwrights, sailors, productive agriculture, effective armor, and well-trained infantry. Little wonder that crusaders could march more than twenty-five hundred miles, defeat an enemy that vastly outnumbered them, and continue to do so as long as Europe was prepared to support them.

Chapter Four

PILGRIMAGE AND PERSECUTION

Entrance to the Church of the Holy Sepulchre built over what is believed to be the tomb in which Jesus was buried. The original church was built by Constantine between 326 and 335, but was destroyed by order of the caliph of Egypt in 1009. The present church was built on the ruins of the first, the work beginning in 1037.

© The Francis Frith Collection / Art Resource, NY

W HEN POPE URBAN II called upon the knights of Europe to join God's battalions, he justified it on the grounds that after many centuries of toleration, Muslims were desecrating the sacred Christian sites in the Holy Land and were inflicting savage mistreatment on Christian pilgrims. Was it true? Or did the pope make it all up? To fully assess these claims it is useful to trace the rise of Christian pilgrimage and to see how Muslims responded to it over time.

EARLY PILGRIMS

Christian pilgrims did not exist in the first century, and had they existed it is not clear where they would have gone. After all, Jesus spent nearly all of his ministry in Galilee and made only several[1] brief visits to Jerusalem. Even so, potential sacred sites in Galilee were not of compelling significance. Eventually Nazareth, Cana, and several other places in Galilee began to attract some pilgrims, and monasteries and churches were built there to commemorate the events involved. But that was later. Meanwhile, although there were extremely sacred sites in Jerusalem, the city had been destroyed by the Romans under Titus in the year 70 and razed again by Hadrian in 135 in the wake of the Bar Kokhba Revolt. So, although early Christians no doubt shared with Jews a special reverence for Jerusalem, we have little knowledge of when Christians began to visit its sacred sites.

What we do know is that pilgrims from the West were never more than a "tiny stream" compared with the "flow of pilgrims to Jerusalem from the East."[2] Unfortunately, nearly all specific knowledge of Byzantine pilgrims has been lost, so it is the "tiny stream" that we know more about, while we know relatively little about the throngs that came from the Eastern Christian areas.

One early Eastern pilgrim was Melito (died c. 180), bishop of Sardis, who provided the earliest known Christian canon of the Old Testament. Melito visited Jerusalem, and in *Peri Pasha* ("Concerning Passover," a work that was not discovered until the 1930s) he located major sacred sites in the city. Another visitor was the celebrated Alexandrian theologian Origen (c. 185–254), who traveled in the Holy Land and wrote of "the desire of Christians to search after the footsteps of Christ."[3] But even though Palestine was relatively close to the major Byzantine cities, there is no evidence that many pilgrims came in early times.[4]

That changed with the conversion of Constantine. His mother, the empress Helena, was elevated to sainthood after having visited Jerusalem, where she found many sacred relics and learned that strong local traditions had survived concerning the locations of the important sacred sites. Foremost among these was the belief that Christ's tomb lay buried beneath a temple of Venus built by Hadrian to spite the Christians.

What followed was one of the very earliest archeological undertakings, well told by the church historian Eusebius (c. 263–339) in his *Life of Constantine*.[5] Eusebius began by noting that apparently Hadrian's engineers had been "determined to hide" the tomb "from the eyes of men . . . After expending much labor in bringing in earth from outside, they covered up the whole place; then having raised the level of the terrain, and after paving it with stone, they entirely concealed the sacred grotto beneath a great mound."

On top of this the Romans had constructed "a dark shrine of life-less idols."

As Eusebius continued: "Constantine gave orders that the place should be purified . . . And as soon as he issued the orders, these deceitful constructions were torn down . . . images and demons and all . . . were overthrown and utterly destroyed . . . one layer after another was laid bare . . . then suddenly, contrary to all expecta-tion, the venerable and sacred monument to our Savior's resurrec-tion became visible, and the most holy cave." What the excavators seem to have uncovered was a tomb carved into the rock that fit the biblical description.

Constantine's response was to have the great Church of the Holy Sepulchre constructed over the site, and Eusebius, by then bishop of Caesarea, was present at its consecration. Constantine also had great churches built in Bethlehem and on the Mount of Olives. The discovery of what was believed to be the Holy Sepulchre and Constantine's other construction projects spurred a rapidly grow-ing stream of pilgrims.

The first of the known pilgrims from the West was a man from Bordeaux (France) who journeyed to the Holy Land in 333, when Constantine's churches were being finished. We don't know his name, but he wrote an extended itinerary, which has survived. Much of it is devoted to providing a route and listing good stop-ping places along the way. He crossed the Alps into Italy and then into Thrace, through Byzantium, across the Bosporus, and on down the coast to Palestine. According to his estimate, it was a trip of about 3,250 miles, and he changed horses 360 times.[6]

Once in the Holy Land, the author wrote descriptions of Constantine's churches and the locations of sacred sites: "On your left [as one heads north toward the city and the Damascus Gate] is the hillock Golgotha where the Lord was crucified, and about a stone's throw from it, the vault where they laid his body, and he arose again on the third day. By order of the emperor Constantine there now has been built there a basilica . . . which has beside it cisterns of remarkable beauty, and beside them a baptistery where children are baptized."[7]

In 1884 an Italian scholar discovered a manuscript in a monastery library that was part of a letter written by a woman named Egeria (also Aetheria) who made a pilgrimage to the Holy Land from about 381 to 384. Although some historians have supposed that Egeria was a nun, it seems far more likely that she was a wealthy laywoman who reported her tour of the sights in a letter written to her circle of women friends back home (probably on the Atlantic coast of Gaul). The portion of her letter that survives was copied from the original in the eleventh century by monks at Monte Cassino. No doubt this portion was valued because it describes monks in the Holy Land and their liturgical practices. But the surviving part of Egeria's letter also reports her visits to many holy sites and side trips to Egypt and Mount Sinai.

In 385 Saint Jerome (340–420) led a group of pilgrims from Rome to the Holy Land. Among them were Bishop Paulinus of Antioch; the wealthy widow Paula and her unmarried daughter Eustochium; and Paula's good friend, the widow Marcella. Paula was an upper-class Roman matron of immense wealth who had long been part of Jerome's entourage (which inspired rumors of immorality). After visiting the sacred sites, Jerome and his female circle went to Egypt. But in 388 they returned and took up residence near Bethlehem in a monastery built and funded by Paula. During the last thirty-two years of his life, Jerome lived there and translated the Bible from Greek and Hebrew into Latin.

Oddly enough, Jerome did not think it at all important for anyone to undertake a pilgrimage to the Holy Land, and many early church fathers condemned or ridiculed the practice. Saint Augustine (354–430) denounced pilgrimages, Saint John Chrysostom (c. 344–407) mocked them,[8] and Saint Gregory of Nyssa (c. 335–394) pointed out that pilgrimages were nowhere suggested in the Bible and that Jerusalem was a rather unattractive and sinful city. Jerome agreed, noting that it was full of "prostitutes . . . [and] the dregs of the whole world gathered there."[9]

But the public paid no attention. When the empress Eudocia (c. 401–460) settled in Jerusalem in 440, it was becoming a very fashionable residence, and women of the nobility dominated the ranks of the pilgrims.[10] Moreover, most pilgrims continued to come from the Byzantine East, it being a very long and expensive trip from the West. Even from Constantinople, it was more than a thousand miles along the Roman roads to Jerusalem.[11] But the numbers kept climbing, and by the end of the fifth century there were more than three hundred hostels and monasteries offering lodging to pilgrims in the city of Jerusalem alone.[12] If we assume that on average each of these could accommodate twenty guests, that would have been a daily capacity of six thousand, which is suggestive of very heavy travel, given that the resident population of the city at that time was only about ten thousand.[13]

The upward trend in pilgrim traffic continued through the sixth century, with an increasing number coming from the West by sea. Among them was Antoninus Martyr, who sailed from Italy to Cyprus and then to the coast of Palestine in about 570. In his narrative, he remarks at length on the beauty of Jewish women, and he is the first to report that there were three churches on Mount Tabor in lower Galilee—a claim now supported by surviving ruins.[14] His visit to the Church of the Holy Sepulchre occurred more than two centuries after its original construction, and, according to his descriptions, it had been constantly decorated by pious visitors: "[T]he stone by which the tomb was closed . . . is adorned with gold and precious stones . . . its ornaments are innumerable. From iron rods hang armlets, bracelets, chains, necklaces, coronets, waistbands, sword belts, and crowns of emperors made of gold and precious stones, and a great number of ornaments given by empresses. The whole tomb . . . is covered with silver."[15]

Byzantine embellishments of Jerusalem continued under the celebrated emperor Justinian (483–565), who also greatly expanded Byzantium by "recovering" North Africa, Italy, Sicily, and a portion of southern Spain from various "barbarian" invaders. Justinian built and restored so many buildings in every part of his empire that the ancient historian Procopius (c. 500–565), who was a member of Justinian's court, wrote an entire book about his constructions.[16] The most monumental of all his buildings was the New Church of Saint Mary, usually referred to as the Nea (new) Church, built in Jerusalem, probably to rival memories of Solomon's Temple. It was built of enormous blocks of stone, and according to Procopius no other church "can be compared."[17] Several modern Holy Land archaeologists suspect that the Nea Church served primarily to house the Temple treasures stolen by the Romans in 70 and said to have been recovered by Byzantium at this time.[18] In any event, the enormous complex included a hospice for pilgrims and was a major attraction.

But then it ended.

MUSLIM JERUSALEM

In 636 a Muslim army entered Palestine, and in 638 Jerusalem surrendered. Soon after his triumphant entry into Jerusalem, the caliph 'Umar wrote a letter of assurance to the city's population:

> *This is the covenant given by God's slave 'Umar, commander of the believers, to the people of Jerusalem: He grants them security, to each person and his property: to their churches, their crosses, their sick and the healthy, to all people of their creed. We shall not station*

Muslim soldiers in their churches. We shall not destroy the churches nor impair any of their property or their crosses or anything which belongs to them. We shall not compel the people of Jerusalem to renounce their beliefs and we shall do them no harm.[19]

Sounds humane and reasonable. However, the next sentence in this letter reads: "No Jew shall live among them in Jerusalem."

This seems a very odd prohibition, since Arab sources claim that local Jews had welcomed and often aided the Muslim forces in Palestine.[20] Some suppose that the prohibition was merely an extension of the Byzantine policy precluding Jews from Jerusalem; Saint Jerome revealed that the Jews "are forbidden to come to Jerusalem."[21] Remarkably, the Byzantines had merely extended the prohibition that Hadrian had first imposed against Jews occupying Jerusalem after he crushed their revolt in 135.[22] As for the Muslims continuing the ban, this was consistent with the prohibition against Jews living anywhere in Arabia and with Muhammad's persecutions of the Jews in Medina.[23] In any event, a few years later the Muslim rulers dropped this prohibition and allowed Jews to move back into the city. This was at best a mixed blessing, since neither Christians nor Jews could live in Jerusalem—or anywhere else under Muslim rule—unless they accepted the subordinate role of *dhimmi* and were willing to live with the contempt and occasional persecution that that status entailed. "Almost generation after generation, Christian writers recorded acts of persecution and harassment, to the point of slaughter and destruction, suffered at the hands of the Muslim rulers."[24] In a number of instances, the reports—not only from Christian but also from Muslim sources—implicate the Jewish community as participating in the attacks on Christians.[25]

In any event, mass murders of Christian monks and pilgrims were common. An unsystematic list based only on Moshe Gil's immense *History of Palestine, 634–1099* includes the following events:

- Early in the eighth century, seventy Christian pilgrims from Asia Minor were executed by the governor of Caesura, except for seven who converted to Islam.

- Shortly thereafter sixty pilgrims, also from Asia Minor, were crucified in Jerusalem.

- Late in the eighth century, Muslims attacked the Monastery of Saint Theodosius near Bethlehem, slaughtered the monks, and destroyed two nearby churches.

- In 796 Muslims burned to death twenty monks from the Monastery of Mar Saba.

- In 809 there were multiple attacks on many churches, convents, and monasteries in and around Jerusalem, involving mass rapes and murders.

- These attacks were renewed in 813.

- In 923, on Palm Sunday, a new wave of atrocities broke out; churches were destroyed, and many died.

These events challenge the claims about Muslim religious tolerance.

Eventually, Jerusalem became a city of great religious significance to Muslims, but it did not start out that way. There is no mention of Jerusalem in the Qur'an, although initially Muhammad taught that Muslims should face Jerusalem when they prayed; he later shifted this to Mecca when the Jews disappointed him by failing to embrace him as the Prophet. But what eventually caused Muslims to regard Jerusalem as a holy city is its centrality to Muhammad's famous "Night Journey."

Muslims believe that in 620, about ten years before his death, Muhammad was sleeping in the home of his cousin in Mecca when he was awakened by the Angel Gabriel, who led him by the hand to a winged horse, whereupon the two were quickly transported to Jerusalem. There he was introduced to Adam, Abraham, Moses, and Jesus, after which he and Gabriel flew up to heaven, where Muhammad was taken through each of the seven heavens and then beyond, where he was allowed to see Allāh, who appeared as a divine light. On his way back down through the seven heavens, Muhammad had a series of interactions with Moses concerning the number of times Muslims would be required to pray each day, the number gradually being reduced from fifty to five. By morning, Muhammad awoke safely in his bed in Mecca.[26]

The Dome of the Rock was built from 685 to 691 on the site of the long-destroyed Jewish Temple to symbolize that Islam had succeeded Judaism and Christianity.[27] Subsequently, those concerned with promoting Muslim pilgrimages to Jerusalem identified the Dome of the Rock as having been built on the very spot where Muslims believe Muhammad and Gabriel rose into the heavens. The combination of a splendid structure and its embodiment of this sacred tradition soon made Jerusalem holy to Muslims, although not nearly as significant to Islam as it is to Judaism and Christianity. Jerusalem's being holy to all three faiths has led to conflicts ever since, nicely illustrated by the fact that on the side of the Dome of the Rock, facing the Church of the Holy Sepulchre, it is written in Arabic: "God has no son." But there also have been bitter conflicts among Christians in Jerusalem ever since the split took place between the Roman and Greek Churches.

Before the Muslim invasion, Jerusalem had been controlled by the Byzantine Orthodox Church, and Roman (Latin) Catholics were merely tolerated. Orthodox dominance continued under the Muslims until about 800, when Caliph Haroun al-Rashid agreed to allow Charlemagne to endow and maintain facilities, including hostels, for pilgrims from the West, and these were placed under the control of Roman Catholics. Of course, this was deeply resented by the Orthodox,[28] and after the death of Charlemagne they soon reasserted their authority, leaving only one church in Latin hands, "and the Latin nuns serving in the Holy Sepulchre."[29] (Even today fistfights break out between Roman Catholic and Orthodox monks involved with the Sepulchre.)[30] In 1056 Pope Victor II complained that not only did Byzantine officials impose a head tax on Western pilgrims passing through their territory, but Orthodox monks also charged westerners a fee at the Holy Sepulchre.[31]

As noted, local Muslim authorities had hoped that by stressing the religious significance of Jerusalem they could attract a flow of Muslim pilgrims, their motive being the same as that of every promoter of tourism: attracting spenders from out of town. But few Muslim pilgrims ever arrived. For a time after Jerusalem came under Muslim rule, there also seem to have been few Christian pilgrims. But their numbers soon began to increase, and by the eighth century they were coming in substantial numbers, some of them from as far away as England and Scandinavia. There was a short interruption in the ninth century due to conflicts over control of Sicily and southern Italy, but this soon passed with the defeat of Muslim naval forces in the western Mediterranean, and soon many pilgrims journeyed by boat from Venice or Bari.[32]

The pilgrims were welcomed in the Holy Land because they "brought money into the country and could be taxed."[33] So by the tenth century the stream of Christian pilgrims had turned into a flood.

WAVES OF PENITENT PILGRIMS

Pilgrimage can be defined as "a journey undertaken from religious motives to a sacred place."[34] Among Christians, especially in the West, the "religious motives" increasingly had to do with atonement—with obtaining forgiveness for one's sins. Some who made the long journey were seeking forgiveness for the accumulated sins of a lifetime, none of them particularly terrible. But by the ninth and tenth centuries, the ranks of pilgrims had become swollen with those who had been told by their confessors that their only hope of atonement lay in one pilgrimage, or even several, to Jerusalem. For example, when Count Thierry of Trier murdered his archbishop in 1059, his confessor demanded that he undertake a pilgrimage, and he went.[35]

Perhaps the most notorious pilgrim was Fulk III, Count of Anjou (972–1040), who was required to make four pilgrimages to the Holy Land, the first as penance for having his wife burned to death in her wedding dress, allegedly for having had sex with a goatherd. All things considered, four pilgrimages may have been far too few, given that Fulk was a "plunderer, murderer, robber, and swearer of false oaths, a truly terrifying character of fiendish cruelty . . . Whenever he had the slightest difference with a neighbor he rushed upon his lands, ravaging, pillaging, raping and killing; nothing could stop him."[36] Nevertheless, when confronted by his confessor Fulk "responded with extravagant expressions of devotion."[37]

Fulk's case reveals the most fundamental aspect of medieval Christian pilgrimage. The knights and nobility of Christendom were very violent, very sinful, and very religious! As Sidney Painter (1902–1960) put it: "[T]he ordinary knight was savage, brutal, and lustful. At the same time he was, in his own way, devout."[38] Consequently, the knights and nobles were chronically in need of atonement and quite willing to accept the burdens involved to gain it; there was widespread agreement that for terrible crimes, only a pilgrimage could possibly suffice. Consider these excerpts from the "Laws of Canute," written about 1020 and attributed to the Viking king of England and Denmark:

39. If anyone slays a minister of the altar, he is to be an outlaw before God and before men, unless he atone for it very deeply by pilgrimage.

. . .

41. If a minister of the altar becomes a homicide or otherwise commits too grave a crime, he is then to forfeit both his ecclesiastical orders and his native land, and to go on a pilgrimage." [39]

And so they came. Toward the end of the tenth century, the huge and energetic monastic movement based at Cluny (in France) built hostels and hotels all along the route east to accommodate the pilgrim traffic. Parties of a thousand were common, and one group from Germany is known to have begun with at least seven thousand male pilgrims (including a number of bishops) and probably grew substantially by picking up small groups along the way.[40] This party was attacked both going and coming home by Bedouin robbers, and ultimately only about two thousand of them survived the trip.[41]

By the tenth century, many Norse pilgrims were coming even though most of their countrymen were still pagans.[42] "Most Scandinavian pilgrims liked to make a round tour, coming by sea through the Straits of Gibraltar and returning overland through Russia."[43] Like the Franks, the Norse converts were "very devoted to Christ if not to his commandments."[44] Among them was Thorvald the Far-Traveled, who came all the way from Iceland. Thorvald was a renowned Viking who had converted to Christianity and then "tried to preach the new faith to his countrymen in 981."[45] He undertook a pilgrimage in 990 seeking to atone for having killed two poets who had mocked his faith and another man who had criticized his preaching. Following his pilgrimage he devoted his missionary activities to Russia and died there, presumably without murdering any Russian pagans. Another Norse pilgrim was Lagman Gudrödsson, the king of the Isle of Man, who sought atonement for having murdered his brother. Swein Godwinsson was also a royal Norse pilgrim. He died in the mountains, having been required to make the trip barefoot in order to atone for murders.

And so it went.

THE DESTRUCTION OF THE HOLY SEPULCHRE

In 878 a new dynasty was established in Egypt and seized control of the Holy Land from the caliph in Baghdad. Initially, nothing much changed. But in 996 Tāriqu al-Hākim became the sixth Fatimid caliph in Egypt, at the age of eleven, and ruled until he disappeared at age thirty-six.

Whether or not Hākim was mad has been debated. The illustrious Marshall Hodgson admitted he was "eccentric" but claimed he was "an effective ruler."[46] It is true that Hākim lived simply. It also is true that sometimes he traveled around the streets and had conversations with ordinary people. On the other hand, he ordered that all the dogs in Cairo be killed, that no grapes be grown or eaten (to prevent the making of wine), that women never leave their homes, and that shoemakers cease making women's shoes. Hākim also outlawed chess and the eating of watercress or of any fish without scales. He suddenly required that everyone work at night and sleep during the day since these were his preferred hours. He murdered his tutor and nearly all of his viziers, large numbers of other high officials, poets, and physicians, and many of his relatives—often doing the killing himself. He cut off the hands of the female slaves in his palace. To express his opposition to public baths for women, he had the entrance to the most popular one suddenly walled up, entombing alive all who were inside.

Hākim also forced all Christians to wear a four-pound cross around their necks and Jews to wear an equally heavy carving of a calf (as shame for having worshipped the Golden Calf). Finally, Hākim had his name substituted for that of Allāh in mosque services.[47]

None of this changed history. But then Hākim ordered the burning or confiscation of all Christian churches (eventually about "thirty thousand were burned or pillaged")[48] and the stripping and complete destruction of the Church of the Holy Sepulchre in Jerusalem, including all traces of the carved-out tomb beneath it. According to the eleventh-century Arab chronicler Yahya ibn Said of Antioch, Hākim ordered Yaruk, the governor of Palestine, "to demolish the church [of the Holy Sepulchre] and to remove its symbols, and to get rid of all traces and remembrance of it." Yaruk's son and two associates "seized all the furnishings that were there, and knocked the church down to its foundations, except for what was impossible to destroy . . . [and they] worked hard to destroy the tomb and to remove every trace of it, and did in fact hew and root up the greater part of it."[49]

Word of this outrage caused an enormous wave of anger all across Europe—a bitter grievance that was later rekindled by those who recruited volunteers for the First Crusade. As for Hākim, he disappeared during a ride in the hills where he usually practiced astrology; his donkey came home with blood on its back. The Druze believe that Hākim is "hidden" and will return as the Mahdi on judgment day. Most others think he was murdered by order of his sister, who feared he meant to kill her as he had so many others.

In return for the release of five thousand Muslim prisoners held by Byzantium, Hākim's successor permitted reconstruction of the Church of the Holy Sepulchre,[50] although most of the destruction done to the cavern could not be undone. Work began in 1037, by which time the flow of pilgrims from the West had resumed:

"[A]n unending stream of travellers poured eastward, sometimes travelling in parties numbering thousands, men and women of every age and class, ready . . . to spend a year or more on the voyage."[51] Just as they could no longer visit the original Church of the Holy Sepulchre, neither could they visit Justinian's enormous Nea Church, which also lay in ruins; it is uncertain who destroyed it, and when.[52] Still the pilgrims came, despite the fact that in addition to the usual hardships and dangers involved in such a long trip, Muslim attacks on Christian pilgrims had become more frequent and bloody:[53]

- In 1022 Gerald of Thouars, abbot of Saint-Florent-lès-Saumur, had reached the Holy Land when he was imprisoned and then executed by Muslims.

- In 1026 Richard of Saint-Vanne was stoned to death for having been detected reciting the Mass in Islamic territory.

- In 1040 Ulrich of Breisgau was stoned by a mob near the river Jordan.

- In 1064 Bishop Gunther of Bamberg and his large party of pilgrims were ambushed by Muslims near Caesarea, and two-thirds did not survive.

Despite the dangers along the way, once again pilgrims were welcomed in Jerusalem for their substantial contributions to the local economy.

But in 1071, things changed dramatically.

THE TURKISH INVASION

Late in the tenth century a large tribe of nomadic raiders in the area southeast of the Aral Sea that today is divided between Uzbekistan and Turkmenistan encountered Islam and soon converted, first by treaty and later by conviction. (Pagans usually converted far more rapidly to Islam than did Jews, Christians, or Zoroastrians.)[54] However, the Islam to which they converted differed considerably from the prevailing Muslim orthodoxy. Claude Cahen (1909–1991) described it as "a folk-Islam," not only for its lack of sophistication, but for its militant intolerance of "heretical" Islamic groups, especially the Shiites. Cahen continued: "[N]aturally the Turks, on adopting the new faith[,] did not entirely forget all the customs, beliefs, and practices of their non-Moslem ancestors."[55] Hence, even as Muslims, the Seljuk Turks continued as brigands, "pillaging and plundering wherever the opportunity arose."[56] And although they sometimes hired on as mercenaries to various Muslim rulers, their conversion to Islam did not shield other Muslims or Muslim-ruled societies from their attacks. Eventually, however, instead of hit-and-run raids, the Turks began to impose permanent control on territories—substituting the systematic, organized plundering committed by states for mere brigandage.

In the eleventh century the Seljuk Turks began to move west, and, under an effective leader named Tughrul Bey, by 1045 they had seized Persia and set themselves up in Baghdad as the heirs of the Abbasid Caliphate, whereupon Tughrul Bey proclaimed himself "Sultan and King of East and West." Still in an expansionist mode, Tughrul Bey turned his forces north and attacked Armenia, a Monophysite Christian kingdom that recently had fallen captive to Byzantium and was subjected to fierce religious persecution led by Orthodox Byzantine bishops. Given the prevailing bitterness against Byzantium, the Armenian princes offered little resistance, although they surely would have done so had they known what was in store. Thus in 1048, while the Byzantines were distracted by a revolt at home, the Turks overran the city of Ardzen and massacred the men, raped the women, and took the children into slavery.[57]

However, the Turks did not occupy Armenia, but were content to continue raiding it. More massacres followed. In 1063 Tughrul Bey died and was succeeded by his thirty-three-year-old nephew Alp Arslan. The next year Arslan led a large army into Armenia and laid siege to its capital of Ani. Although enjoying a superb defensive position, the city surrendered after only twenty-five days, obviously thinking that would avoid needless suffering. But according to the Arab historian Sibt ibn al-Gawzi (d. 1256), who claimed to be quoting an eyewitness: "The army entered the city, massacred its inhabitants, pillaged and burned it . . . The dead bodies were so many that they blocked all the streets."[58] In 1067 Arslan's forces pushed through Byzantine defenses to Cappadocian Caesarea, in the center of modern Turkey, and committed another massacre. Finally, these depredations drew a serious Byzantine response.

To make this possible, however, it was necessary for the Byzantines to overcome the convoluted and cowardly political intrigues of the Greek court, made acute by the death of the emperor Constantine X, notorious for his neglect of the army and the interests of the empire. With the crowning of Romanus Diogenese in Constantinople as the Byzantine emperor on January 1, 1068, it appeared as if responsible and competent leadership had been restored. Romanus was a successful and very experienced general— young, vigorous, brave, and fully aware of the Seljuk menace.

Emperor Romanus's first act was to begin rebuilding the Byzantine army, which had become a demoralized collection of mercenaries—ill equipped, poorly trained, and owed enormous sums in back salaries. He spent two years on the task, devoting much time and effort to recruiting new forces. In 1071 he was prepared to move against the Turks with about sixty to seventy thousand fighting men. (Some Muslim sources claim the Byzantine army numbered six hundred thousand, and the Armenian historian

Matthew of Edessa placed the total at one million!) Although Romanus had devoted two years to upgrading the army, he had been able to do little more than assemble a larger force that was not much better equipped, trained, or loyal than before. To make matters worse, it "was a motley force" composed of mercenaries from many different nations, some of them bitter enemies of one another.[59] Indeed, a major contingent was made up of Uzes, Turks with ties to the Seljuks, and who promptly deserted to the enemy during the crucial battle.

Although upset by various omens and fully aware of the defects of his battalions, Romanus marched east to engage the Turks. Having camped near Erzurum, Romanus inexplicably split his army, giving command of the larger portion to Joseph Tarchaniotes and sending it to attack Khelat (now Ahlat), on the shores of Lake Van, while he led the smaller contingent toward the town of Manzikert. No one knows what happened next, except that the larger force fled and never returned to the campaign. Some Muslim historians claim that Alp Arslan and a much smaller Muslim force won a pitched battle against Tarchaniotes and his Greeks. Others claim that when word of the pending arrival of a Turkish force circulated among Tarchaniotes' Byzantines, they simply ran away. However, that no word of the debacle was sent to Romanus, who was only thirty miles away, is consistent with the conclusion reached by Viscount Norwich that Tarchaniotes was a traitor in league with plotters back in Constantinople and that he simply abandoned Romanus and marched to the rear.

Now with only about a third of his army, Romanus still attempted to deal with the Turks. A series of hit-and-run engagements followed, and finally came the major battle at Manzikert, whereupon the Uzes changed sides and the Byzantines were routed. Romanus fought on until wounds made it impossible for him to grip his sword, and then he was captured. He was taken to

Alp Arslan, and the two seem to have hit it off quite well: a peace treaty was signed. It ceded an area to the Turks and settled on an annual tribute payment; further, Romanus agreed to give one of his daughters in marriage to one of Alp Arslan's sons. All things considered, it was not a bad deal for the Byzantines.

Meanwhile, back in Constantinople, not only did word of the defeat and the loss of territory reach the congenital conspirators of the court, but at this time they also learned that their forces in Italy had been overwhelmed by Iron Arm and his Normans. So the conspirators gathered troops from the nearby garrisons and rode out to meet the returning emperor Romanus. Perhaps there was some fighting. In any event Romanus was seized. As the contemporary Byzantine historian John Scylitzes told it: "[H]arsh men took him and pitilessly, mercilessly, put out his eyes. Carried forth on a cheap beast of burden like a decaying corpse, his eyes gouged out and his face and head alive with worms, he lived a few days in pain with a foul stench all about him until he gave up the ghost."[60]

The new emperor, Michael V, was incompetent, and his reign was nothing but one insurrection and riot after another all across the empire. In 1078 things got so out of control that Michael abdicated and fled, and was replaced by an aged general. Three years later he, too, abdicated, in favor of a brilliant young commander: Alexius Comnenus. Although he was unable to recapture the lost territories, Comnenus restored order, established a reliable army, and eventually wrote the letter that prompted Pope Urban II to launch the First Crusade.

At that point the Turks might have settled down to life as a ruling elite over a substantial and wealthy territory, but for religious antagonism. The Turks were orthodox Sunni Muslims, but the Fatimid Caliphate in Cairo was ruled by Shiites—heretics "guilty" of splitting Islam. So the Turks moved west and south, invading Fatimid territory, including the Holy Land.

The Turkish commander was Atsiz bin Uwaq, who had served in Alp Arslan's court until he deserted to serve the Fatimids in Palestine, whereupon he deserted the Fatimids and in 1071 became commander of the Turkish invasion forces. Historians debate[61] whether Atsiz took Jerusalem in 1071 during the first year of his campaign, or in 1073, but it is agreed that Acre was taken in 1074 and Damascus in 1075. At that point Atsiz turned south, intent on driving the Fatimids from Egypt, but he was badly defeated in 1077. In the wake of the Fatimid victory over the Turks, there were risings by Fatimid Muslims in Palestine, and Atsiz was forced to flee all the way to Damascus. But he soon returned and laid siege to Jerusalem. Given Atsiz's promise of safety, the city opened its gates, whereupon the Turkish troops were released to slaughter and pillage, and thousands died. Next, Atsiz's troops murdered the populations of Ramla and Gaza, then Tyre and Jaffa.[62]

In the midst of all this turmoil and bloodshed, it cannot have been a good time to be a Christian pilgrim. And it soon got worse. Not only because the Turkish rulers persecuted pilgrims, but because they did not (possibly they could not) interfere with the hordes of bandits and local village officials who preyed upon them. A few large, well-armed groups got through, such as the one led by Robert I of Flanders in 1089. But most either were victimized or decided to turn back.[63] Even the twelfth-century Syrian historian al-'Azimi acknowledged that in 1093 Muslims in Palestine prevented Christian pilgrims from going to Jerusalem. He also suggested that the survivors' going home and spreading the word caused the Crusades to be organized. Moshe Gil pointed out that by speaking of survivors, al-'Azimi clearly suggested "that there had been a massacre,"[64] and perhaps many of them.

Finally, the nobility of Europe were not dependent on the pope or on Alexius Comnenus for information on the brutalization of Christian pilgrims. They had trustworthy, independent information from their own relatives and friends who had managed to survive and who had returned "to the West weary and impoverished, with a dreadful tale to tell"[65]—the very people mentioned by al-'Azimi.

CONCLUSION

The Crusades were not unprovoked. Muslim efforts at conquest and colonization still continued in the eleventh century (and for centuries to come). Pilgrims did risk their lives to go to the Holy Land. The sacred sites of Christianity were not secure. And the knights of Christendom were confident that they could put things right.

Chapter Five

ENLISTING CRUSADERS

A knight kneels in prayer as he prepares to set off on the First Crusade.
At the top right, his servant leans over the turret with his master's helmet.
© *British Library / HIP / Art Resource, NY*

IT WAS ONE THING for Pope Urban II to conclude that Europe should rally in support of Eastern Christianity and the liberation of the Holy Land. But how was he able to bring it about? How were tens of thousands of people convinced to commit their lives and fortunes to such a challenge? Many of them, especially those recruited by Peter the Hermit, may have been unaware of what really lay ahead. But the great nobles and knights were neither foolish nor naive. They knew much about the journey itself: some had already been to the Holy Land on a pilgrimage, and all of them had close relatives and associates who had been there. So they knew they faced a very long and perilous journey at the end of which there would be many bloody battles against a dangerous and determined foe. They also were fully aware that there was no pot of gold awaiting them in the sands of Palestine. So, how were they recruited?

PREACHING THE CRUSADES

No matter how eloquent Pope Urban II was when addressing the crowd at Clermont, one speech could not have launched thousands of knights to the Holy Land. Indeed, by the time he reached Clermont the pope had been on the road for four months visiting important Frankish (French) nobles, abbots, and bishops. Since most of them subsequently played leading roles in mounting the First Crusade, we can be sure that the pope used his visits to enlist their support. If we credit the story that during his famous speech at Clermont some in the audience began to cut out crosses and sew them onto their chests, we can assume they had prepared to do this in advance: knights did not usually carry sewing kits. Moreover, according to one account, when the pope had finished speaking "envoys from Raymond, count of Toulouse, appeared and announced that their lord had taken the cross."[1]

But whatever the pope had done ahead of time to line up support, Clermont was still only the beginning; the plan had yet to be widely "sold" before it could happen. Consequently, according to the account by Baldric, archbishop of Dol, at the end of his speech at Clermont, Urban turned to the bishops and said, "You, brothers and fellow bishops; you fellow priests and sharers with us in Christ, make this same announcement through the churches committed to you, and with your whole soul vigorously preach the journey to Jerusalem."[2] But even had they all done so, their efforts probably would have been insufficient. The First Crusade became a reality only because the pope was able to recruit hundreds to preach it who had not been at Clermont. To understand how he achieved this, it will be helpful to see just what kind of a pope he was and the churchly resources available to him.

Two Churches

In many ways, the conversion of Constantine was a catastrophe for Christianity. It would have been enough had he merely given Christianity the legal right to exist without persecution. But when he made Christianity "the most favoured recipient of the near-limitless resources of imperial favour,"[3] he undercut the authentic commitment of the clergy. Suddenly, a faith that had been meeting in homes and humble structures was housed in magnificent public buildings; the new church of Saint Peter built by Constantine in Rome was modeled on the basilican form used for imperial throne halls. A clergy recruited from the people and modestly sustained by member contributions suddenly gained immense power, status, and wealth as part of the imperial civil service. Bishops "now became grandees on a par with the wealthiest senators."[4] Consequently, in the words of Richard Fletcher, the "privileges and exemptions granted the Christian clergy precipitated a stampede into the priesthood."[5]

As Christian offices became another form of imperial preferment, they were soon filled by the sons of the aristocracy. There no longer was an obligation that one be morally qualified, let alone that one be "called." Gaining a church position was mainly a matter of influence, of commerce, and eventually of heredity. Simony became rife: an extensive and very expensive traffic in religious offices developed, involving the sale not only of high offices such as bishoprics, but even of lowly parish placements. There soon arose great clerical families, whose sons followed their fathers, uncles, and grandfathers into holy office, including the papacy.[6] As a result, many dissolute, corrupt, lax, and insincere people gained high positions: Pope Benedict IX (1012–1055), the nephew of two previous popes, took office without even having been ordained as a priest and caused so many scandals by "whoring his way around Rome" that he was bribed to leave office.[7]

Of course, many who entered the religious life were not careerists or libertines; even some sons and daughters of the clerical families were deeply sincere. Consequently, there arose what became, in effect, two parallel churches. These can usefully be identified as the *Church of Power* and the *Church of Piety*. The Church of Power was the main body of the Church as it evolved in response to the immense power and wealth bestowed on the clergy by Constantine. It included the great majority of priests, bishops, cardinals, and popes who ruled the Church most of the time until the Counter-Reformation set in during the sixteenth century. In many ways the Church of Piety was sustained as a reaction against the

Church of Power. It might have been silenced or at least shunted aside but for the fact that it had an unyielding base in monasticism, which, in turn, had very strong support among the ruling elites: 75 percent of ascetic medieval saints were sons and daughters of the nobility, including many sons and daughters of kings.[8]

Remarkably, at the same time that there had begun a "stampede" into the priesthood by the sons of privilege, there was a rapid expansion of monasticism: by the middle of the fourth century there were many thousands of monks and nuns, nearly all of them living in organized communities. Naturally, those living an ascetic life felt themselves spiritually superior to the others, as was in fact acknowledged by Catholic theology. However, their antagonism toward the regular clergy and, especially, the Church hierarchy had a different basis; it was not merely that these men were not leading ascetic lives, but that so many were leading dissolute lives. This was an issue that would not subside. Again and again leaders of the Church of Piety attempted to reform the Church of Power, and during several notable periods they managed to gain control of the papacy and impose major changes. It was during one of these interludes of control by the Church of Piety that Urban II rose to the Chair of Peter.

Otho (or Odo) of Lagery was born into the northern French nobility in 1042. During his early teens he entered the Church and quickly rose to be archdeacon of the cathedral at Rheims. In 1067 he entered the monastery of Cluny, which had rapidly become the largest and most aggressive of Europe's monastic organizations. Here Otho soon gained the office of grand prior, second only to the abbot, and in 1078 Pope Gregory VII (himself a former monk and an ardent member of the Church of Piety) appointed him cardinal-bishop of Ostia. He was elected pope by acclamation in 1088 and took the name Urban II. He died on July 29, 1099, two weeks after the crusaders had taken Jerusalem but before word of their victory had reached the West.

That Urban II was an esteemed member of the Church of Piety was important because it gave him credibility with the friars and monks who did most of what little preaching was done in medieval Europe; "preaching to the laity was, at best, sporadic"[9] in this era. Local parish priests did very little preaching. It was not required that they do so during Mass, and in any event, Mass attendance was extremely low.[10] What effective preaching took place was done by monks and wandering friars, usually in the marketplace rather than in a church, and it was they who accepted the pope's request to preach support for the First Crusade. Hence, hundreds (perhaps thousands) of friars and monks spread the pope's message in every hamlet, village, and town. Among them were three very distinguished men who had turned away from very successful church careers to live as ascetics in the forest of Craon: Robert of Arbissel, Vitalis of Mortain, and Bernard of Tiron. At the invitation of the pope, each emerged from seclusion to preach the First Crusade, and subsequently each successfully founded a new monastic order.

And just as these three men, like the pope himself, were from upper-class backgrounds, the same was true of most monks, which enabled them to witness for the Crusade directly to their noble relatives. In this era, monks usually entered their orders through the process of *oblation* (or offering), wherein a young boy (far less often a girl) was enrolled in a religious order by parents who paid a substantial entry fee. Too often this practice has incorrectly been interpreted as a method for disposing of "excess" sons who did not stand to inherit.[11] In fact, the entry fee usually was equal to a quite substantial inheritance.[12] In any event, oblation was such a common practice that most of the nobility had uncles, sons, brothers, and nephews living nearby in religious cloisters with whom they usually remained in close touch. This arrangement sustained strong ties between the Church of Piety and the nobility and had very significant effects on the religiousness of the privileged families.

However, the pope did not simply delegate the task of preaching the Crusade. From Clermont he took to the road once more, spending the next nine months traveling more than two thousand miles through France, "entering country towns, the citizens of which had never seen a king or anyone of such international importance . . . accompanied by a flock of cardinals, archbishops, and bishops . . . whose train must have stretched across miles of countryside."[13] Everywhere he went, the pope consecrated local chapels, churches, cathedrals, monasteries, convents, and cemeteries and blessed local altars and relics. Most of these occasions were public ceremonies, and huge crowds turned out—or at least "huge" in terms of the size of the local population (the population of Paris was about twenty-five thousand).[14] The pope used all these opportunities to preach the Crusade. Perhaps even more important, the pope's visit and his preaching stimulated many locals, including bishops, to continue preaching the Crusade long after the pope and his party had departed.[15] Moreover, while the pope "toured France, papal letters and legates travelled swiftly to England, Normandy, and Flanders, to Genoa and Bologna, exhorting, commanding and persuading . . . Later in the same year the pope sent the bishops of Orange and Grenoble to preach the crusade in Genoa, and bring the formidable Genoese sea-power into the war."[16]

In many ways, those preaching the Crusade were too successful. They convinced not only thousands of fighting men to volunteer, but also even larger numbers of men and women with no military potential. Soon thousands of these people, many of them peasants, traveled east under the leadership of Peter the Hermit, doing a great deal of harm along the way, and then suffered pointless deaths—as will be seen.

Penitential Warfare

Many skeptics have noted that the pilgrimages often failed to improve the subsequent behavior of pilgrims. The main issue here is not that some pilgrims were like Fulk III, who returned from each of his four pilgrimages ready and eager to sin again. The issue seems to be the expectation that an authentic pilgrimage ought to have fundamentally transformed a pilgrim's character and personality—or at least to have changed an individual into a far more peaceful and forgiving sort of person. But that was not a typical outcome. Instead, most of the fighting men who went on a pilgrimage returned as fierce and ready to do battle as before. For example, according to the *Chronicle of Monte Cassino* (c. 1050s), "[F]orty Normans dressed as pilgrims, on their return from Jerusalem, disembarked at Salerno. These were men of considerable bearing, impressive-looking, men of the greatest experience in warfare. They found the city besieged by Saracens. Their souls were inflamed with a call to God. They demanded arms and horses from Gaimare the prince of Salerno, got them, and threw themselves ferociously upon the enemy. They killed and captured many and put the rest to flight, achieving a miraculous victory with the help of God. They swore they had done all this only for the love of God and of the Christian faith; they refused reward and refused to remain in Salerno."[17]

That even very pious knights found pacifism incomprehensible may puzzle some having modern sensibilities, but that assumption was fundamental to Pope Urban's call for a Crusade. Having come from a family of noble knights, the pope took their propensity for violence for granted. He fully understood that from early childhood a knight was raised to regard fighting as his chief function and that throughout "his life the knight spent most of his time in practicing with his arms or actually fighting. Dull periods of peace were largely devoted to hunting on horseback such savage animals as the wild boar."[18] Since the pope could not get the knights of Europe to observe a peace of God, at least he could enlist them to serve in God's battalions and to direct their fierce bravery toward a sacred cause. And to bring this about, Urban proposed something entirely new—that participation in the Crusade was the moral equivalent of serving in a monastic order, in that special holiness and certainty of salvation would be gained by those who took part.

As Guibert of Nogent recalled Urban's words at Clermont: "God has instituted in our time holy wars, so that the order of knights . . . [who] have been slaughtering one another . . . might find a new way of gaining salvation. And so they are not forced to abandon secular affairs completely by choosing the monastic life or any religious profession, as used to be the custom, but can attain some measure of God's grace while pursuing their own careers, with the liberty and dress to which they are accustomed."[19] In this way Urban took a realistic view not only of the knighthood, but also of the military situation. Tens of thousands of dedicated pacifists could do nothing to liberate the Holy Land. It was going to take an army of belligerent knights who were motivated but not transformed by the promise of salvation. Thus, the invention of penitential warfare.

Many recent historians have followed Carl Erdmann (1898–1945) in arguing that Pope Urban's call to the Crusade was nothing new, that it was a potpourri of well-known ideas and practices—holy war, pilgrimage, and indulgences.[20] And besides, religious motives were of minor importance to the knights, since they went primarily in pursuit of gain. These historians also have followed Erdmann's remarkable claim that Pope Urban had far less interest in liberating the Holy Land than he had in sending reinforcements to the Byzantines and perhaps thereby gaining authority over the Eastern church.

None of these claims is sustained by the evidence, not even that cited by Erdmann, who "rummaged through the versions of the [pope's] sermon [at Clermont] isolating and taking out of context [phrases] . . . to support his thesis that it was not the liberation of Jerusalem which Urban had in mind but the fulfillment of Gregory VII's plan for the unification of the Christian church."[21]

Since all surviving versions of Urban's speech at Clermont were recalled and written down well after the fact, there is perhaps some license as to what the pope may have actually preached. But there is nothing ambiguous about the statement issued by the Council of Clermont, convened by the pope just prior to his speech: "Whoever goes on the journey to free the church of God in Jerusalem out of devotion alone, and not for the gaining of glory or money, can substitute the journey for all penance for sin."[22] Nothing here about saving Byzantium.

In addition, in his campaign for volunteers the pope wrote several letters that survive, each of which specifically gives Jerusalem as the destination of the Crusade then being organized. For example, in his letter to Bologna: "We have heard that some of you have conceived the desire to go to Jerusalem, and you know that it is pleasing to us, and you should also know that if any among you travel. . . . only for the good of their souls and the liberty of the churches, they will be relieved of the penance for all of their sins."[23]

As for the claim that the pope's idea of penitential warfare was nothing new, he did not propose it in a theological vacuum. Penance and pilgrimage had been linked for many centuries. Nor was the idea of a "just war" anything new; it had been assessed at length by Saint Augustine (354–430), among many other theologians. But putting these notions together was creative. And as we have seen, again and again Urban explained in the most direct ways, unadorned by theological quibbles or qualifiers, that anyone who went on the Crusade in the proper spirit would have their sins forgiven. That idea was so new that many theologians opposed it at the time as inconsistent with previous Christian doctrines on violence, which held that fighting always was sinful. Indeed, the "idea of penitential warfare was revolutionary . . . because it put the act of fighting on the same meritorious plane as prayer, works of mercy and fasting."[24]

Finally, even if Erdmann had been right and the pope had not placed the primary emphasis on liberating Jerusalem, the far more important fact is that liberating Jerusalem is what the crusaders believed their mission to be, as they explained in many documents that survive. Godfrey of Boullion and his brother Baldwin of Boulogne issued a document to their mother to go into effect should they not return from their "fight for God in Jerusalem."[25] Raymond of Saint-Gilles claimed he was going "on pilgrimage to wage war on foreign peoples and defeat barbaric nations, lest the Holy City of Jerusalem be held captive and the Holy Sepulchre of the Lord Jesus be contaminated any longer."[26]

In addition to such words came the deeds. The knights were not content with having won some decisive victories over Muslim forces and pushing them far back from Constantinople. No! Starving, riddled with disease, having eaten most of their horses, and with greatly reduced numbers, they pushed on to Jerusalem and against all odds stormed over the walls to victory.

NETWORKS OF ENLISTMENT

The primary sources on the Crusades—on the routes marched, the suffering endured, and the battles fought—have been well known for centuries. But only recently have historians recognized the immense amount of data available on the crusaders themselves—on who went and how they financed their participation. As first noted by Giles Constable,[27] these data are contained in "legal documents describing transfers of property by endowment, sale, or pledge, many of [which] . . . record benefactions and other financial arrangements made by the members of the property-owning classes who crusaded, wills drawn up on their behalf, and disputes in which their heirs and families were involved."[28] These treasures took on added significance when Jonathan Riley-Smith entered them in a computer database.[29] He did so because he wished to shift the focus from events to individuals, to shed light on why some people decided to become crusaders—given that most of their peers did not.

Riley-Smith's most important insight was thrust upon him by the data: crusading was dominated by a few closely related families! It appears that it was not so much that individuals decided to accept the pope's summons, but that families did so. Unbeknownst to Riley-Smith, this is entirely consistent with a very large social scientific literature on recruitment to social movements, be they political campaigns or new religions. People become active in social movements in response to the fact that many of their friends, relatives, or other close associates already have done so. Put another way, collective social activities are not the summation of a number of independent choices made by individuals; rather, they are the product of social networks. So, for example, reconstruction of the initial set of converts to new religions, from Buddhism to Mormonism, shows those religions to have begun as family affairs.[30] And so it was with crusading.

Consider the family headed by Count William Tête-Hardi of Burgundy. He had five sons. Of these, three went on the First Crusade and the fourth became a priest who, as Pope Calixtus II (1119–1124), inaugurated an extension of the Crusade to attack Damascus in 1122. Count William also had four daughters. Three were married to men who joined their brothers-in-law and went on the First Crusade, and the fourth was the mother of a First Crusader. As for the Second Crusade, this family sent ten crusaders in 1147. There were many similar examples. Baldwin of Ghent went on the First Crusade, accompanied by his brother, his uncle, and his two brothers-in-law. As for the four Montlhéry sisters, they had so many spouses, children, and other close relatives involved in the Crusades, and in sustaining the crusader kingdoms, that it took Riley-Smith a whole chapter to cover them all.[31] Riley-Smith also discovered that, in addition to crusaders' being highly clustered into immediate families, these crusader families also were extensively tied to one another by marriage and kinship, ties that even crossed the two major nationality groups involved in the First Crusade: the Franks and the Normans. For example, Count William Tête-Hardi's granddaughter Florina was married to Sven of Denmark and accompanied him on the First Crusade.

In addition to the fact that networks form the basis for joining social movements, there was a second reason that families were so prominent in generating crusaders: families were inevitably deeply involved in the ability of a knight to go crusading. Substantial sums had to be raised to fund the venture, and arrangements had to be made about estates and heirs in case of death. Indeed, that's why Riley-Smith was able to assemble such an elaborate body of data on the crusaders: these arrangements were recorded in formal, written documents. In many instances, these took the form of very large mortgages, promissory notes, or loan agreements.

FINANCES

Crusading was a very expensive undertaking. A knight needed armor, arms, at least one warhorse (preferably two or three), a palfrey (a riding horse), and packhorses or mules, all of them being very costly items. For example, Guy of Thiers paid ten pounds for a warhorse, which was equal to more than two years of salary for a ship's captain.[32] A knight also needed servants (one or two to take care of the horses), clothing, tenting, an array of supplies such as horseshoes, and a substantial amount of cash to buy supplies along the way, in addition to those supplies that could be looted or were contributed, and he needed to pay various members of his entourage. In those days, money consisted entirely of coins, and because coins are so heavy, a group of knights often shared a treasury wagon.[33]

Most crusaders also needed funds to sustain their families and estates while they were away in the East. The best estimate is that a typical crusader needed to raise at least four or five times his annual income before he could set forth.[34] This reveals the absurdity of all claims that the crusaders were mostly landless younger sons, since it would have been cheaper for families to have kept such sons at home and provided them an adequate inheritance.

Pope Urban asked the richer crusaders to subsidize those lacking sufficient funds, and in response some great nobles put a substantial number of knights on their payrolls. But that still left large numbers, especially among the lesser nobility, in need of very large sums. A few financed their participation by selling property, and some huge sales were involved. In order to raise needed crusading funds, Godfrey of Bouillon sold the entire county of Verdun to King Philip of France. The Viscount of Bourges sold both the city and the county of that name; the buyer also was King Philip.[35] In similar fashion, "part of the county of Chalon and the castle Couvin"[36] changed owners. And on a smaller scale, there are many records involving the sale of vineyards, mills, and forests, and even of peasants being sold new rights to their land.

However, medieval families placed so much emphasis on *never* surrendering any property that most aspiring crusaders preferred to borrow rather than sell. Some approached their relatives and friends for loans. Of course, since crusading was so concentrated in families, that often was a dead end, as all who might otherwise have lent the money were themselves seeking funds. Consequently, only about

10 percent of the crusaders obtained their funding from relatives.[37] One of these was Robert, Duke of Normandy, who "pawned the entire duchy of Normandy" to his brother King William II of England for ten thousand marks in 1096,[38] a sum that would have paid the wages of twenty-five hundred ship's captains for a year.[39] To obtain such a sum, the king had to impose a new tax on the nation despite many angry protests.[40] And even having sold the county of Verdun, Godfrey of Bouillon mortgaged his county of Bouillon to the bishop of Liège for fifteen hundred marks.[41]

Since banks had yet to be invented, in this era monastic orders served as the primary financiers in Europe,[42] and it was to them that most aspiring crusaders turned. Because the Church still clung to its opposition to interest payments (on grounds of usury), the transactions were quite creative. Today one pledges property such as a farm or a factory to a lender and repays the principal, plus interest—the latter being payment for use of the principal. Meanwhile, the borrower retains possession of the mortgaged property and receives any income the property produces. In the eleventh century, however, a lord would borrow a sum of money in the form of a *vifage,* an arrangement whereby control of the property and all or part of the income it generated passed to the lender until such time as the principal was repaid. The income gained from the property by the lender was, of course, a substitute for interest, but it was not defined as such by the Church, and hence no sin of usury was involved. Thus, for example, in order to go on the First Crusade, William of Le Vast pledged his land for three silver marks to the abbey of Fécamp. In return, the abbey would collect all the rents until William repaid them. (Repayment was not taken from the rents.) Bernard Morel was able to get better terms when he borrowed against his farm from the nuns of Marcigny. His *vifage* agreement awarded only half of all the income from the farm to the nuns until he, or his heirs, repaid the loan.[43]

Of course, as with modern mortgages, failure to pay resulted in foreclosure, and because such a high percentage of those knights and nobles who went on the First Crusade died from disease or starvation or were killed in battle, foreclosures were widespread. Thus, the mortgage agreement signed by Achard of Montmerle with the monks of Cluny pledged his property in return for two thousand solidi with the provision that "[n]o person can redeem [this mortgage] except myself. Thus if I die . . . that which is the subject of this mortgage . . . shall become the rightful and hereditary possession of the monastery of Cluny in perpetuity." Achard was killed in fighting near Jerusalem.[44]

But it wasn't only raising the funds needed for crusading that caused knights who had taken the cross to enter into negotiations with religious orders. They wanted to insure, as best they could, their fate and that of their families. Thus, Stephen of Blois gave a forest to the abbey of Marmoutier "so that God, at the intercession of St. Martin and his monks, might pardon me for whatever I have done wrong and lead me on the journey out of my homeland and bring me back healthy and safe, and watch over my wife Adela and our children."[45] Robert of Burgundio of Sablé gave a vineyard and a farm to the same abbey "so that God may keep me healthy and safe in going and returning."[46] Many others gave substantial property to monastic groups in return for regular prayers for their souls and their success.

Finally, it must be kept in mind that about 85 to 90 percent of the Frankish knights *did not* respond to the pope's call to the Crusade.[47] This gives further support to the claim that those who went were motivated primarily by pious idealism. It must be supposed that if it had been widely believed that great returns were to be had from looting a land of "milk and honey," there would have been a much greater turnout.

INITIATING A DEBACLE

The pope made frequent efforts to limit crusading to warriors and their needed support personnel. At Clermont he said: "We do not ... advise that the old or feeble, or those unfit for bearing arms, undertake this journey; nor ought women set out at all, without their husbands or brothers or legal guardians. For such are more of a hindrance than aid, more of a burden than advantage."[48] He also forbade clerics from taking part unless given permission to do so by their superiors.

In the groups organized by the nobility, the pope's advice prevailed to at least a modest extent, although even these contingents contained substantial numbers of noncombatants: monks and clergy, those too elderly to fight, some wives, and the unarmed poor, as well as the usual large contingents of camp followers and whores.[49] Unfortunately, the largest groups to head east for the First Crusade paid little heed to the pope's sensible limitations. Instead, they consisted mainly of peasants and villagers, including many women and children. There were a few knights among them, and although many of the other men had secured some arms, they had no training in using them—a fatal deficiency, as matters turned out. These groups have come to be known as the "People's Crusade." They were aroused and led by Peter the Hermit.

Peter the Hermit was so small that his friends called him "Little Peter." He was "swarthy and with a long lean face, horribly like the donkey that he always rode and which was revered almost as much as himself. He went barefoot; and his clothes were filthy. He ate neither bread nor meat, but fish, and he drank wine."[50] Peter was born near Amiens and apparently had attempted a pilgrimage to Jerusalem sometime before 1096 but was turned back and tortured by the Turks, according to Anna Comnena.[51] It is uncertain whether he was at Clermont to hear the pope speak, but he quickly embraced the call to crusade and began a remarkably effective evangelistic campaign in support. According to William of Tyre, "[H]e was sharp witted, his glance was bright and captivating, and he spoke with ease and eloquence."[52] At a time when most people had rarely if ever heard any impassioned preaching, at each stop Peter's charismatic harangues caused outbreaks of public excitement. Guibert of Nogent, who actually met him, wrote that Peter "was surrounded by so great throngs of people, he received such enormous gifts, his holiness was lauded so highly, that no one within my memory has been held in such high honor."[53] Indeed, as he moved from town to town, he inspired so many to leave their homes and follow along that by the time Peter reached Cologne, his train of followers is thought to have numbered fifteen thousand men, women, and children,[54] or equal to the population of London and not far below that of Paris.[55]

Peter called a brief halt in Cologne in order to preach to the Germans and gather a larger force. But many of his French followers, especially the knights, were in no mood to wait. In early April 1096 (nearly five months ahead of the August 15 departure date fixed by Pope Urban), several thousand marched off toward Hungary under the leadership of Walter the Penniless. Very little is known about Walter, aside from the fact that he was a Frankish knight from Burgundy and was "a well-known soldier" according to Albert of Aachen.[56] His true name was Walter Sans-Avoir, but he wasn't poor. His contingent included some of the knights who had joined Peter and "a great company of Frankish foot-soldiers,"[57] and they had adequate funds to pay their way across Europe. However, by jumping the gun Walter put irresistible pressure on Peter for a prompt departure, and so he and his great mass of followers, perhaps numbering twenty thousand, began their march east about ten days later. Their unexpectedly early arrival in Constantinople upset the Emperor Comnena's timetable and damaged the relationship between the crusaders and the Byzantines.

CONCLUSION

The knights of Europe sewed crosses on their breasts and marched east for two primary reasons, one of them generic, the other specific to crusading. The generic reason was their perceived need for penance. The specific reason was to liberate the Holy Land.

Just as it has today, the Church in medieval times had many profound reservations about violence, and especially about killing. This created serious concerns among the knights and their confessors, because war was chronic among the medieval nobility and any knight who survived for very long was apt to have killed someone. Even when victims were evil men without any redeeming worth, their deaths were held to constitute sins,[58] and in most instances the killer enjoyed no obvious moral superiority over the victim—sometimes quite the reverse. In addition to violence, the lifestyle of medieval knights celebrated the Seven Deadly Sins and was in chronic violation of the commandments against adultery, theft, and coveting wives.[59] Consequently, knights were chronically in need of penance, and their confessors imposed all manner of acts of atonement, sometimes even demanding a journey all the way to the Holy Land.

Thus the call to crusade was not a call to do something novel; no doubt many knights had long been considering a pilgrimage (and a few had already gone and returned). Now the pope himself was assuring them that crusading would wash away all their sins and that at the same time they could rescue the Holy Land, including Christ's tomb, from further damage and sacrilege at the hands of the enemies of God. It was an altogether noble and holy mission, and the knights treated it as such. The Burgundian Stephen I of

Neublans put it this way: "Considering how many are my sins and the love, clemency and mercy of Our Lord Jesus Christ, because when he was rich he became poor for our sake, I have determined to repay him in some measure for everything he has given me freely, although I am unworthy. And so I have decided to go to Jerusalem, where God was seen as man and spoke with men and to adore the place where his feet trod."[60]

Had the crusaders been motivated not by religion but by land and loot, the knights of Europe would have responded earlier, in 1063, when Pope Alexander II proposed a Crusade to drive the infidel Muslims out of Spain. Unlike the Holy Land, Moorish Spain was extremely wealthy, possessed an abundance of fertile lands, and was close at hand. But hardly anyone responded to the pope's summons. Yet only thirty-three years later, tens of thousands of crusaders set out for the dry, impoverished wastes of faraway Palestine. What was different? Spain was not the Holy Land! Christ had not walked the streets of Toledo, nor had he been crucified in Seville.

Chapter Six

GOING EAST

Knights wearing their chain-mail armor head for the Holy Land,
with bishops leading the way. Perhaps more than 60,000 crusaders set
out, but only about 15,000 of them reached Jerusalem, most of the
rest having died or been killed along the way.
© *Erich Lessing / Art Resource, NY*

N O ONE REALLY KNOWS how many people set out for the East during the First Crusade. Fulcher of Chartres claimed that 6 million fighting men began the journey east and that six hundred thousand reached Nicaea.[1] This is impossible, since the total population of France, from which most crusaders came, was less than 5 million in 1086.[2] Anna Comnena reported that Peter the Hermit's force alone consisted of "80,000 infantry and 100,000 horsemen."[3] In fact, Peter's entire following, including all the women and children, numbered only about twenty thousand.[4] The other original sources are equally absurd.[5]

The best modern estimate is that around 130,000 set out for the Holy Land, of which about 13,000 were nobles and knights[6] accompanied by perhaps 50,000 trained infantrymen and 15,000 to 20,000 noncombatants, including clergy, servants, and the usual camp followers.[7] The rest were peasants and villagers who had been swept up in the excitement. These numbers are at least compatible with the estimates that, having suffered huge losses along the way, about 40,000 Western Christians lay siege to Nicaea in June 1097 and that 15,000 reached Jerusalem in 1099.[8]

Whatever their numbers, the First Crusade was composed of three primary elements. First came the *People's Crusade*—the main body led by Peter the Hermit, with an advance party led by Walter the Penniless. Several later-leaving groups also were associated with the People's Crusade but are more appropriately treated separately as the *German Crusade*. One of these groups was led by a priest named Volkmar; another was led by Peter's disciple, a monk named Gottschalk. The third was recruited by a minor Rhineland nobleman, Emicho of Leisingen (or Leiningen) and probably was not associated with Peter's expedition. Aside from the fact that those involved in these groups were mostly Germans rather than Franks, a major reason to examine these three groups separately from the People's Crusade is that they committed a series of Jewish massacres along the Rhine River in preparation to going east. All three were, in turn, annihilated when they tried to force their way through Hungary. Not long afterward, those participants in the main body of the People's Crusade who had managed to reach Constantinople were killed after they crossed into Turkish territory.

The success of the First Crusade was achieved by the companies of well-armed, well-trained knights who left several months to a year later than the groups involved in either the People's Crusade or the German Crusade. These battalions often are identified as the *Princes' Crusade,* because that's who organized and led them; the leaders of three of the five major contingents were the sons of kings.

The pope had set August 15, 1096, as the departure date so that the crops would have been gathered along the routes east. This was crucial since medieval armies of necessity lived off the land, it being impossible to transport sufficient supplies of food and fodder very far overland. All of the groups setting out, including the People's Crusaders, were prepared to pay for supplies, but if the locals were uncooperative, armies had no choice but to take what they needed, which easily and often turned into looting and worse.[9] Availability of supplies also was the reason that the crusader contingents followed several different routes in an effort not to overload local capacities.

All the crusader groups planned to meet at Constantinople, where they expected that they would join forces with a Byzantine army and that this combined force would be under the command of Emperor Alexius Comnenus. As it turned out, Comnenus neither took command nor provided significant Byzantine forces, and the westerners had to go it alone.

THE PEOPLE'S CRUSADE

Many myths surround the People's Crusade. Based on Ekkehard of Aurach's account, many modern historians have claimed that Peter could so easily arouse ordinary people to go on a Crusade because economic conditions in Europe were dreadful at this time,[10] an argument frequently extended to explain why younger sons of the nobility were eager to go as well.[11] Not so. The Crusades were possible only because this was not a period of economic hardship but rather a boom time of rapid economic growth,[12] which explains why even the People's Crusade was relatively well funded, not only by participants, but by sympathetic donors. Despite being known as Walter the Penniless, he and his followers were able to pay for their supplies all the way to Constantinople. It was lack of discipline, not poverty, that produced episodes of pillaging by Peter's contingent. He set out with an adequate treasure wagon, and many, perhaps most, of his followers had funds of their own.[13]

That brings us to the second myth: that Peter's followers were overwhelmingly made up of the dregs of society—an utterly impoverished and hopelessly ignorant, "ramshackle horde,"[14] mostly "drawn from the lower classes."[15] That charge also goes back to early chroniclers: Ekkehard dismissed Peter's followers as chaff, and Guibert of Nogent did as well.[16] According to Albert of Aachen, Peter's contingent included "all the common people, the chaste as well as the sinful, adulterers, homicides, thieves, perjurers, and robbers."[17] In reality, these views merely reflected the snobbery of the times. The worst that can be said of these people is that they were commoners and that they probably sold everything they had in order to finance their participation.

Walter the Penniless

Walter's group led the way along what was known as the northern route. Leaving Cologne, they marched through Swabia, Bavaria, and Austria and on through Hungary, entering the Byzantine Empire at Bulgaria. From there they went through Nish to Sophia and on to Constantinople. The march was not entirely uneventful. When they entered Bulgaria, sixteen of Walter's contingent lingered in the town of Semlin, just west of Belgrade, hoping to purchase arms. According to Albert of Aix, "[S]eeing the absence of Walter and his army, [locals] laid hands upon those sixteen and robbed them of arms, [armor], garments, gold and silver and so let them depart naked and empty-handed."[18] Walter refused to be provoked and marched on to Belgrade, where a new crisis arose. Having had no knowledge that crusaders were headed his way, the local Byzantine magistrate sent urgent word to the governor at Nish asking for instructions. Meanwhile, he stupidly refused to allow Walter's troops to buy food. Rather than starve, the crusaders went out foraging and rounded up some local herds, which upset some Bulgarians to the point that they drove one foraging party into a church and burned the building, killing about sixty crusaders. Knowing that retaliation would cost him time and casualties, as well as lead to greater hunger, Walter marched his troops through the forests to Nish, the provincial capital, where they were well received and able to resupply. Then, moving right along, they arrived at Constantinople on July 20, having been 102 days on the road. Once at their destination, Walter and his contingent were welcomed by the emperor and set up camp outside the walls to wait for Peter.

Peter's Progress

Peter the Hermit led his people east from Cologne on April 19 and followed the route taken by Walter's contingent. The march to the Hungarian border was peaceful and uneventful. King Colo-man granted them passage across Hungary provided "there should be no plundering, and that whatever the army required should be purchased without contention and at a fair price."[19] Peter's company observed these rules all across Hungary. But Bulgaria was another matter. Just as Walter had trouble at Semlin, so did Peter.

As he approached Semlin, Peter got word that the Bulgarians planned to ambush his contingent and seize its treasury. Peter dismissed this as mere rumor, but as his company approached the city, they saw the armor that had been robbed from Walter's sixteen stragglers hanging from the walls. This enraged many in the advance guard, and Peter lacked sufficient control to prevent them from assaulting the city and killing a large number of its inhabitants. Albert of Aix reported that Peter and his forces remained there for five days and systematically looted both the city and surrounding area, taking "an abundance of grain, flocks of sheep, herds of cattle, a plentiful supply of wine, and an infinite number of horses."[20] Moving on, the crusaders suffered serious losses while attempting to cross a river. Eight days later they reached Nish, and Peter sought permission to purchase food. This was granted, but the next day some German stragglers got into a dispute and set fire to some mills near the city. Peter hurried to the rear to try to put things right, but he was too late to prevent thousands of his men from getting into a battle with the Bulgarians. As many as a third of Peter's contingent were killed,[21] and many of their wagons were lost to the Bulgarians, including Peter's treasure wagon.

When word of all this reached Constantinople, Emperor Alexius sent officials with large gifts to meet Peter and supervise the remainder of the journey. After traveling for more than three months, Peter's forces reached Constantinople on August 1 (fourteen days before the departure date set by the pope). Shortly thereafter Peter met with the emperor, who gave him a substantial amount of gold coins, and the two agreed that Peter should lead his contingent across the Sea of Marmara and establish camp at Hellenopolis. He was joined there by Walter the Penniless and his knights.

The plan was that this combined force would wait for the arrival of the other crusader groups just then leaving for the Holy Land. Peter's people had ample supplies, and Hellenopolis was a safe haven so long as they did not venture into Turkish territory; Nicaea, the Seljuk capital of Asia Minor, was only twenty-five miles away. It probably was too much to expect this poorly disciplined company to mind their own business for the period it was going to take for groups in the Princes' Crusade to reach them. After two months, monotony led to pillaging raids in the direction of Nicaea. Initial success led to "war fever," and while Peter was absent, all of his fighting men marched out to attack the Turks, whereupon they were slaughtered; Albert of Aachen claimed that Walter the Penniless was killed by seven arrows. A Byzantine relief force managed to rescue a few survivors who had taken refuge in a deserted castle on the shore. These seem to have been knights. Apparently all of the noncombatants, including women and children, had perished or been enslaved.

Many historians have blamed the debacle on the emperor for stationing the People's Crusaders at Hellenopolis. But Hellenopolis served as a secure haven so long as the Europeans remained there. The proximate cause of this disaster was simply that Peter's people arrived far too early and then failed to understand the strength and abilities of their enemy. But the fundamental cause was lack of authority.

THE GERMAN CRUSADE AND THE JEWISH MASSACRES

Historians often claim that the main body of Peter's followers attacked Jews along the way to Constantinople.[22] This is careless.

As Frederic Duncalf (1882–1963) pointed out, Peter's followers "do not seem to have been guilty of the persecution of the Jews which became so prevalent in the Rhine valley after their departure."[23] Several of these massacres were committed by two groups that were following in the wake of Peter's expedition, but most of them were the work of German knights who seem not to have been involved with Peter.

Emicho of Leisingen was a minor Rhineland count who responded to the pope's call to crusade by assembling a small army of German knights. Then, on May 3, 1096, two weeks after Peter's group had set out for the Holy Land, Emicho led his troops in an attack on the Jewish population of Speyer (Spier).[24] Some historians believe that Emicho's attacks on the Jews were cynical, prompted primarily by greed, while others accept that he sincerely believed that all "enemies of Christ" should be converted or killed. In any event, warned of Emicho's approach and intentions, the bishop of Speyer took the local Jews under his protection, and Emicho's forces could lay their hands on only a dozen Jews who had somehow failed to heed the bishop's alarm. All twelve were killed. Then Emicho led his forces to Worms. Here, too, the bishop took the local Jews into his palace for protection. But this time Emicho would have none of that: his forces broke down the bishop's gates and killed about five hundred Jews. The pattern was repeated the next week in Mainz. Here, too, the bishop attempted to shield the Jews but was attacked and forced to flee for his life. The same again in Cologne, and again in Metz. As the distinguished historian of anti-Semitism Léon Poliakov (1910–1997) summed up: "It is important to note that almost everywhere . . . bishops attempted, sometimes even at the peril of their own lives, to protect the Jews."[25] At this point a portion of Emicho's forces broke away and set out to purge the Moselle Valley of Jews. Being careful only to attack towns *without a resident bishop,* they managed to kill several thousand Jews.

Meanwhile, two of Peter the Hermit's followers, who had remained behind to organize stragglers, also attacked Jews. Volkmar overwhelmed the opposition of the local bishop and massacred Jews in Prague. Gottschalk led a murderous attack on the Jews of Ratisbon (Regensberg). The pope "harshly condemned" all these attacks, "but there was little more he could do."[26] However, it turned out that there was a lot that the knights of Hungary could do. When Volkmar and his forces reached Hungary and began to pillage, they were wiped out by Hungarian knights. The same fate befell Gottshalk. And when Emicho and his forces reached Hungary they were denied passage, and when they tried to force their way through, they also were dispatched by Hungarian knights.

According to the revered historian of the Crusades Sir Steven Runciman (1903–2000), these defeats struck "most good Christians" as "punishments meted out from on high to the murderers of Jews."[27] This is consistent with the efforts of local bishops to preserve the Jews, and with the fact that other armies gathered for the First Crusade did not molest Jews—with the possible exception of several hundred Jews who may have died in Jerusalem during the massacre subsequent to its fall to crusaders.

THE PRINCES' CRUSADE

Five major groups made up the Princes' Crusade—appropriately named, since not only were these groups led by princes, but many others of equally high rank were enrolled. The groups left at different times and followed different routes, but all of them reached Constantinople (see table 6.1).

Hugh of Vermandois

King Philip I of France was ineligible to go on the Crusade, having been excommunicated for marrying another man's wife

TABLE 6.1   *Elements of the First Crusade*

CRUSADE	LEADERS	DATE OF DEPARTURE	DATE OF ARRIVAL IN CONSTANTINOPLE
People's	Walter the Penniless	April 3, 1096	July 20, 1096
	Peter the Hermit	April 19, 1096	August 1, 1096
German	Volkmar	April 1096	Did not arrive. Probably killed by Hungarian knights.
	Gottschalk	May 1096	Did not arrive. Killed by Hungarian knights.
	Emicho of Leisingen	June 3, 1096	Did not arrive. Returned home after defeat in Hungary.
Princes'	Hugh of Vermandois	August 1096	December 1096
	Godfrey of Bouillon	August 1096	December 23, 1096
	Bohemond of Taranto	October 1096	April 9, 1097
	Raymond IV of Toulouse	October 1096	April 21, 1097
	Robert, Duke of Normandy	October 1096	May 1097

without either of them getting divorced and for refusing to give her up when the Church demanded that he do so. However, he supported the crusading enterprise by buying several large counties from nobles raising money to enable them to go, and he encouraged his brother Hugh to take part.

Hugh, Count of Vermandois (1053–1101), was the son of King Henry I of France and a Scandinavian princess, Anne of Kiev. When he left to go east he was about forty and, as will be seen, remarkably arrogant even for these times. He was long remembered as Hugh the Great ("Hugh Magnus") because he was so designated by William of Tyre. This turns out to have been a copyist's error, mistaking *Minus,* meaning "the younger," for *Magnus.*[28] This correction is consistent with reality, because despite all his boasting and posturing, Hugh was an ineffectual commander. But given his royal connection he was able to assemble a very select group of noble knights from the area near Paris, and just before he left he was joined by knights who had survived Emicho's defeat in Hungary. Hugh's contingent left in August, in accord with the pope's plan.

Hugh chose to make part of the journey by sea from the port of Bari in the Norman kingdom of southern Italy. His march down the Italian Peninsula was uneventful, and he arrived at Bari in October, where he found the Norman prince Bohemond organizing a company of crusaders. But Hugh did not want to wait for the Normans despite warnings that it was a bad time of the year for voyaging. Before setting sail, according to Anna Comnena, Hugh sent this message ahead to Emperor Alexius: "Know, Emperor, that I am the King of Kings, the greatest of all beneath the heavens. It is my will that you should meet me on my arrival and receive me with the pomp and ceremony due to my noble birth."[29]

The emperor was not favorably impressed by this message. Nor, it would appear, was Neptune. The predicted winter storms took place, and most of Hugh's ships were sunk off the Byzantine port of Dyrrhachium. Many of his men drowned, but Hugh managed to reach shore, where Byzantine officials found him "bewildered and bedraggled."[30] The Greeks reequipped his surviving knights and flattered Hugh, but they kept him under house arrest. Escorted to Constantinople, he was greeted by Alexius Comnenus, but not given his freedom until he swore an oath of loyalty to the emperor.

After the crusader conquest of Antioch in 1098, Hugh went back to France. There he was shamed for having failed to keep his vow to go to Jerusalem—the new pope, Paschal II, even threatened to excommunicate him for it—so he went back to Palestine in 1101, where he was wounded in a battle and died of his wounds.

Godfrey of Bouillon

Godfrey of Bouillon (c. 1060–1100) was also Duke of Lower Lorraine, which was part of the German Holy Roman Empire, and (through his mother) he was a direct descendent of Charlemagne. He was tall, sturdy, very blond, and admired for his pleasant manners. Godfrey was greatly influenced by the Cluniac monks and so committed to the Crusade that he made very substantial financial sacrifices to go: he sold two major estates and borrowed against his castle from the bishop of Liège. This allowed him to equip and supply a large army. He was joined in this venture by his two brothers, Eustace III and Baldwin of Boulogne.

Eustace was not eager to go crusading but performed very well once he arrived in the Holy Land. Baldwin had been destined to the Church but lacked a taste for contemplation and chastity. He was even taller than Godfrey and as dark as Godfrey was fair. When he set out on the Crusade, Baldwin took along his Norman wife, Godehilde of Toeni, and their small children. He seems not to have intended to come back to Europe. In any event, he had a glorious career in the crusader states, eventually becoming king of Jerusalem, succeeding his brother Godfrey (although the latter had never permitted himself to be crowned).

Godfrey decided to journey to the Holy Land via the northern route. He left Lorraine at the end of August and marched up the Rhine Valley and then down the Danube Valley until he reached Hungary. King Coloman of Hungary was still angry about his experiences with the People's Crusaders. So when Godfrey sent a delegation ahead to arrange for passage, Colomon arranged to meet directly with Godfrey. This meeting convinced the king to allow the crusaders to pass (for a very substantial price), but only if Baldwin and his wife and children would serve as hostages to guarantee the behavior of the army. Although reluctant to place this burden on his family, Baldwin eventually agreed, whereupon Godfrey sent heralds to announce to everyone in his army that any infractions against Hungarians or their property would be punished by death. No violations were reported, and when Godfrey's forces reached Bulgaria, Baldwin and his family were released.

Having entered Bulgaria, Godfrey's army passed by Belgrade, still a deserted ruin since its pillage five months earlier by Peter's forces, and, heading for Nish, they were met halfway there by representatives of Emperor Alexius, who made arrangements to resupply the crusaders. Gregory then led his forces uneventfully to Sleymbria, on the coast of the Sea of Marmora. There, for entirely unknown reasons, Godfrey lost control of his troops, and they pillaged the countryside for eight days. Some have said that they were angered from having heard that Hugh of Vermandois was being held as a prisoner—at least that's what Godfrey used as an excuse when he met with Byzantine representatives sent by the emperor.[31] In any event, order was restored, and Godfrey's army reached Constantinople on December 23, 1096.

The arrival of this large, well-armed, and unruly force of trained soldiers at his gates caused Emperor Alexius a great deal of worry.

Therefore, he attempted to assure himself of Godfrey's allegiance and to get him and his troops some distance from the capital as soon as possible. As to the first, he invited Godfrey to come to see him and to swear an oath of homage to him, using Hugh of Vermandois to carry the invitation. Godfrey refused. Eventually Alexius resorted to threats, marching to Godfrey's camp with a large army of Byzantine veterans. Faced with overwhelming force, Godfrey consented to swearing the oath and to having his troops transported across the Bosporus to an encampment at Pelecanum.

Just behind Godfrey's army came an assortment of small groups of knights, "probably composed of various vassals of Godfrey who had preferred to travel through Italy"[32] and come from there by sea. They were a truculent lot and also resisted swearing an oath to the emperor. Eventually they did so, but only after an intervention by Godfrey. Then they, too, were quickly transported across the Bosporus; the emperor was convinced that the crusaders really meant to seize his empire and not go to Jerusalem. The party that came next was the one most likely to have imperial designs—Normans who already had repeatedly beaten Greek armies led by Alexius and who ruled over the former Byzantine colonies in southern Italy.

Bohemond of Taranto

On April 9, 1097, Bohemond, Prince of Taranto (c. 1058–1111), arrived in Constantinople, followed by his large army of veteran Norman knights. This was a quite remarkable event, since Bohemond was the son of Robert Guiscard, who had led the Norman conquest of Sicily and southern Italy by repeatedly defeating the best armies that Byzantium could send to defend them. Worse yet, father and son had fought, and usually won, a number of battles against Byzantine armies led by the Emperor Alexius Comnenus himself.

No wonder that when Alexius discovered that a major contingent of crusaders were Normans recruited in Italy and led by
Bohemond, he was very apprehensive. His daughter Anna, who
was fourteen at the time she met Bohemond, wrote a remarkable
sketch of the man many years later in her *Alexiad:* "The sight of
him inspired admiration, the mention of his name terror . . . His
stature was such that he towered almost a full cubit [about twelve
inches] over the tallest men." In fact, his real name was Mark; his
father had nicknamed him Bohemond (after the mythical giant)
because of his great size as an infant. Anna continued, "He was
slender of waist . . . perfectly proportioned . . . His skin was . . . very
white . . . His hair was lightish-brown and not so long as that of
other barbarians (that is, it did not hang to his shoulders) . . . There
was a certain charm about him, but it was somewhat dimmed by
the alarm his whole person inspired; there was a hard, savage
quality in his whole aspect, due, I suppose to his great stature and
his eyes; even his laugh sounded like a threat to others . . . His arrogance was everywhere manifest; he was cunning, too."[33]

The emperor was fully aware that Bohemond was undoubtedly
the most experienced, talented, and politically astute commander
among the crusaders, having learned it the hard way. Back in 1081,
having placed his new Norman kingdom of Italy and Sicily firmly
under his control, Robert Guiscard and his son Bohemond had
sailed their Norman troops across the Adriatic Sea, taking Corfu
and Durazzo, coastal cities within the primary Byzantine area.
Emperor Alexius Comnenus marched north to expel the Normans,
only to be badly defeated at the Battle of Dyrrhachium. Next, the
Normans conquered nearly all of northern Greece. Desperate to
prevent the Normans from taking his entire empire, Alexius paid
an enormous sum (said to be 360,000 gold pieces) to Henry IV, the
Holy Roman Emperor, to attack the pope, who was the Normans'
ally in Italy. Robert Guiscard rushed back to Italy to meet this

threat, leaving Bohemond in command in Greece. Although still in his early twenties, Bohemond proved a brilliant leader, especially gifted at recognizing and countering enemy tactics, and he defeated Alexius in two battles, thus putting the Normans in control of Macedonia and nearly all of Thessaly. At this point Alexius managed to convince the Seljuk Turks that the Normans were a threat to them, too, and so, with a new army including thousands of Turks, Alexius was barely able to defeat the Normans at Larissa. At this point, in large part because Bohemond lacked the funds to pay his troops their back salaries, the bulk of the Norman army sailed back to Italy, although Corfu and a substantial area along the Adriatic were still in Norman hands. To regain these, Alexius hired Venetians, who successfully attacked from the sea and restored the area to the empire.

Now, about fifteen years older and nearing forty, Bohemond had raised sufficient funds to fully support a large force to go crusading. Accompanied by the anonymous author of the *Gesta Francorum,* the most influential eyewitness account of the First Crusade, he boarded his forces on ships at Bari and sailed to the Bulgarian coast and from there marched on to Constantinople. His meetings with the Emperor Alexius were tense. Bohemond was as leery of the situation as was Alexius. Aware of the Greek penchant for palace poisonings, he refused to eat any food offered at court. However, he fully retained his political acumen and readily agreed to swear an oath of allegiance to Alexius. Then he led his troops across the Bosporus to join Godfrey's contingent at Pelecanum.

Raymond IV of Toulouse

The fourth group of crusaders was led by Raymond IV of Toulouse (c. 1041–1105), also known as Count Raymond of Saint-Gilles. Although extremely devout, he was excommunicated twice for marrying women to whom, according to Church rules, he was too closely related. In keeping with the network aspect of crusading, the second of Raymond's three wives was Bohemond's niece.

Raymond had decided that he wished to be buried in the Holy Land, and so when the pope first began to circulate his proposal for a Crusade, Raymond was one of the first to respond; his representatives followed Urban's speech at Clermont with the announcement that Raymond had already taken the cross. At fifty-five, Raymond was certainly the oldest of the leading crusaders, and he probably was the richest as well. He departed in October 1096 at the head of a large company of knights, accompanied by his third wife (the daughter of King Alfonso VI of Castile) and their infant son (who died on the journey).

Raymond's party crossed the Alps, and because of the season Raymond decided he did not want to sail across the Adriatic Sea, so he marched on until he was able to descend the eastern shore—an unwise choice, as it turned out. The roads were very bad; it was winter, and the weather was foul; and the locals were mostly wild Slavs who refused to sell them any supplies, harassed and stole from their rear guard, and murdered stragglers. Hungry and miserable, the contingent reached Dyrrhachium early in February. There they were met by Byzantine officials and were escorted by local troops. This seems to have caused antagonism among Raymond's knights, who already were angry. A series of minor skirmishes began with their escorts, but nothing too serious took place until they reached Roussa in Thrace. With Raymond having gone ahead to Constantinople and not there to exert control, his followers, finding there were no provisions for sale at Roussa (Bohemond's man having bought everything two weeks earlier), scaled the walls of the city and pillaged all the homes. Then, as they continued on, they were intercepted by a major Byzantine army and suffered a serious defeat.

Meanwhile, Raymond was negotiating with Emperor Alexius. The emperor tried to play on Raymond's fear that Bohemond would become leader of the Crusade, reassuring Raymond that he would never give Bohemond an imperial command. However, instead of swearing the oath of allegiance to Alexius, Raymond pledged himself to support the emperor only if Alexius led the Crusade in person. Then he and his forces, reassembled after their battle with the Byzantines, were ferried across the Bosporus.

Robert, Duke of Normandy

Robert, Duke of Normandy (c. 1051–1134), the eldest son of William the Conqueror, was denied the throne of England for having allied himself with the king of France and plotting against his father. Although he held the duchy of Normandy, he was very lacking in wealth and had to mortgage Normandy to his brother, King William of England, in order to support an army to go crusading. His party included Norman knights from England and Scotland as well as Normandy; the many notables among them included his cousin Robert II, Count of Flanders; his brother-in-law Stephen, Count of Blois; and the cleric Fulcher of Chartres, who wrote a lengthy history of the whole undertaking.

Having crossed the Alps, Robert's forces marched south through Italy until they reached the Norman Kingdom. Because it was so late in the year, Robert wintered his forces in Calabria. Seeming to be in no hurry, Robert finally went to Brindisi in April and set sail. The first ship to leave was hardly under way when it suddenly broke in half and about four hundred were drowned. Some of the more weak hearted deserted at this point, but the bulk of the army was safely transported to Dyrrhachium. From there they marched, reaching Constantinople in early May. They were cordially received by the emperor, Robert swore the required oath to Alexius, and then he and his troops were ferried across the Bosporus.

Finally, the entire cast of crusaders had been assembled.

ABANDONED BY BYZANTIUM

It turns out Alexius had never anticipated that thousands of high-ranking European nobles and knights would answer his call for help against the Turks. He had assumed that companies of mercenaries would be sent; few upper-class Byzantines engaged in any military activities, and for centuries the armies of the empire had consisted of mercenaries, and even slaves—often under the command of a eunuch.[34] Now Alexius was confronted with thousands of men who had come of their own free will, were dedicated to a cause, and already had fully demonstrated that they were difficult to manage. Alexius and his court thought them to be dangerous barbarians. In turn, the crusaders thought Alexius and his court were a bunch of decadent, devious plotters; the *Gesta Francorum* often attaches a nasty adjective when referring to Alexius, using phrases such as "the wretched emperor."[35]

Both sides were correct. The dangerous barbarians won battle after battle against staggering odds, even though they had been abandoned by the devious plotters. For when the time came to attack the Turks, Alexius did not take command. Nor did he merge his army with the crusaders. Instead, he sent a small contingent to accompany the crusaders into Asia Minor only as far as needed to recover recently lost Byzantine territory; he interpreted the oath sworn to him by leading crusaders as giving him full and exclusive rights to all these recovered cities and areas. Once the Western knights had accomplished that goal, Alexius seems not to have intended that even a token Byzantine army go any further. His position was that if the crusaders wanted to push on to the Holy Land, that was their own concern, but that "Jerusalem was strategically irrelevant to the empire."[36] Henceforth, the "barbarians" would have to go it alone, even though the most difficult battles still lay ahead. Consequently, feeling that they had been tricked by the emperor, many leading crusaders rejected Alexius's territorial claims and their oaths to him, on grounds that he had not kept his word. Thus began an antagonism between East and West that ultimately resulted in the sack of Constantinople in 1204 during the Fourth Crusade.

CONCLUSION

A very frustrating feature of the literature on the Crusades is the lack of reliable numbers. Not only is it extremely difficult to know how many people actually set out on the First Crusade, but few plausible attempts have been made to estimate how many were lost along the way. We know that a substantial proportion of the People's Crusaders were killed in their several battles in Bulgaria. Surely many more died of the natural causes that always beset such groups in those days; even during the American Civil War, the Union Army lost three men from disease for every one lost in battle.[37] So it is very difficult to guess how many of Peter's people survived to be slaughtered by the Turks. Similarly, although many, perhaps most, of Hugh of Vermandois's contingent who set sail from Bari drowned, we can't estimate how many they were, let alone how many fell out along the way.

All that having been said, I estimate that of the perhaps 130,000 who set out on the First Crusade in 1096, 90,000 did not take part in the siege of Nicaea in June 1097. That is a loss rate of roughly 35 per mile who died or turned back. And by the time Jerusalem was taken, perhaps as many as 115,000 (or 88 percent) of the original crusaders had been lost. If this seems excessive, consider that of Bohemond's Normans who were sufficiently prominent to be named in the *Gesta Francorum,* a third were dead before 1099 and another fourth were unaccounted for.[38] In addition, these estimates of losses do not include the several thousand additional knights who arrived by sea during the course of the campaign. So the total number who died or deserted probably totaled about 120,000—most of whom perished.

It was not until the upper-class sons of Europe were slaughtered in the trenches during World War I that Europe suffered the loss of a generation of leaders equal to that which took place during the First Crusade. Those who marched east were among the best and the brightest of their time. When they died, the responsibilities for managing many major estates and dealing with many important concerns fell upon widows and minor sons, and on those who failed to serve, just as it did in England, France, and Germany in the 1920s. Even so, commitment to crusading remained high for many more years as the families involved in the First Crusade continued to send their subsequent generations to defend the Holy Land. Indeed, when Europe began to sour on crusading, it appears that it was not the families who had given the most who lost heart; rather, it was families who had never sent a crusader who opposed continuing to pay the taxes required to sustain the crusader kingdoms.

Chapter Seven

BLOODY VICTORIES

Against all odds, following their capture of Jerusalem, the crusaders quickly marched
south and defeated a huge Egyptian army at Ascalon. Here Godfrey of Bouillon is
shown directing his victorious troops as they sack the Egyptian camp.
© *Réunion des Musées Nationaux / Art Resource, NY*

THE ACTUAL MILITARY PHASE of the First Crusade began when the combined forces of the Princes' Crusade, accompanied by "a small detachment of Byzantine engineers, with siege machines,"[1] left their encampment on the banks of the Bosporus and marched twenty-five miles south to Nicaea, the first Muslim stronghold between them and the Holy Land. Little did they know that more than a year later, after fierce fighting and very heavy losses, they would still only be in Antioch. And it was another year before they reached the gates of Jerusalem, on June 7, 1099 (see map 7.1).

NICAEA

Nicaea was the capital of the Seljuk sultanate of Rûm, ruled by Kilij Arslan. *Rûm* was the Turkish word for "Rome," and this sultanate consisted of the large portion of Anatolia that the Turks had conquered from the Byzantines, who still referred to theirs as the Roman Empire. It was an opportune time to attack Nicaea, because the sultan was so contemptuous of the crusaders after his easy slaughter of Peter the Hermit's followers that he had ignored the nearby gathering of "Franj" (Frank) forces and led his army eastward to confront a challenger to his rule. In fact, he was so unconcerned that he left his wife, his children, and his treasure store within Nicaea.

The siege of Nicaea began on May 14, 1097. When word reached Sultan Arslan that the crusaders had surrounded Nicaea and then

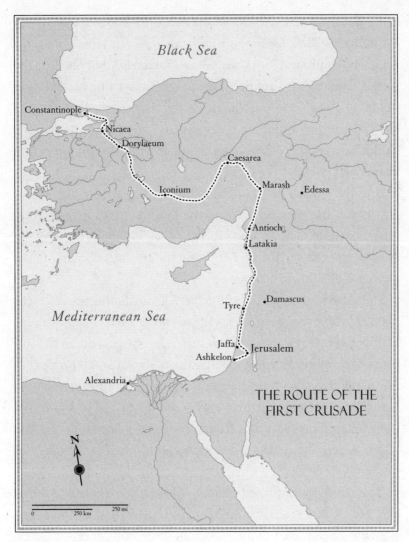

MAP 7.1

had easily repelled a sortie by troops from the city, he hurriedly led his army back. Upon arrival he immediately attacked the forces of Raymond of Toulouse, whose troops blocked the way to the southern entrance to the city. Robert of Flanders brought some of his troops to Raymond's aid, and the battle with Sultan Arslan's army lasted all day. Arslan was stunned to discover that, "man for man, his Turks were no match for the well-armed westerners on open ground."[2] As the *Gesta Francorum* described it, the Turks "came along gleefully . . . but as many as came . . . had their heads cut off by our men, who threw the heads of the slain into the city by means of a sling, in order to cause more terror among the Turkish garrison."[3] After dark the sultan withdrew his forces and abandoned Nicaea to its fate.

But the victors had suffered badly, too. Again the *Gesta:* "[M]any of our men suffered martyrdom there and gave up their blessed souls to God with joy and gladness."[4] Despite these losses, Nicaea was still in Turkish hands. So the crusaders began to plan a general assault.

Unbeknownst to them, Emperor Alexius had quite different plans. He sent several of his agents to conduct secret negotiations, and they convinced the Turks to surrender the city. So, as the sun rose on the morning when the assault on Nicaea was scheduled to begin, the crusaders were greeted with the sight of Byzantine banners flying over the defensive towers of Nicaea and of Byzantine troops patrolling the walls, having been smuggled in during the night. Western crusaders were permitted to enter the city only in groups of six or less at a time.

This further confirmed for the Western leaders that Alexius and his court were not to be trusted, thus adding to the growing antagonism toward the emperor—especially since no Greek troops had helped with the fighting. Suspicions of Alexius grew even more intense when the Turkish commanders and the sultan's family, instead of being held for ransom, were taken to meet the emperor in Alexandria. "The emperor, who was a fool as well as a knave," treated them as distinguished guests and then sent them home safely and in style, leaving them, as the *Gesta* put it, "ready to injure the Franks and obstruct their crusade."[5] Bohemond, of course, reminded his colleagues that Alexius had once used Turkish forces against him.

Perhaps seeking to appease the knights, Alexius decided to reinforce the tiny Byzantine contingent accompanying the crusaders. This impressed no one in the crusader camp because, although the Byzantine army stationed in and around Constantinople greatly outnumbered the crusaders, Alexius sent only a surprisingly small detachment of about two thousand soldiers,[6] commanded by a general named Taticius, the son of an enslaved Turk.

DORYLAEUM

A week after the surrender of Nicaea, the crusaders began to move again. Historians long believed that they headed toward the ruined city of Dorylaeum—for which their next major battle is named. It now is accepted that they followed a more western route and that the battle occurred about forty miles west of Dorylaeum.[7] Meanwhile, the Turks had regrouped under Kilij Arslan and been heavily reinforced by other Turkish princes as well as by Persian and Albanian mercenaries. After the crusaders had traveled for three days, their scouts alerted them that major Turkish forces were approaching and that a battle could be expected soon. At dawn on July 1, this large Turkish force attacked the crusader vanguard made up of Bohemond's forces, and inflicted substantial casualties while the Normans were getting organized. Bohemond gathered the noncombatants at the center of the encampment, where there were springs, and assigned them the task of carrying water to the troops; crusader women often performed this vital task bravely and effectively. Bohemond dismounted his knights and placed them with his infantry to form a solid defensive perimeter. The Turkish army consisted entirely of light cavalry armed with bows and swords,[8] and although they inflicted some casualties with their arrows, they could make no headway against the infantry line. It seems that the Turks mistook Bohemond's force for the entire crusader army and were caught entirely unprepared when the main body of knights launched a thundering heavy-cavalry charge against their flank and rear.

Both sides suffered serious losses, but the Turkish casualties were far greater. According to the *Gesta:* "As soon as our knights charged, the Turks, Arabs, Saracens, and Agulani and all the rest of the barbarians took to their heels and fled . . . God alone knows how many there were of them. They fled very fast to their camp, but they were not allowed to stay there for long, so they continued their flight and we pursued them, killing them, for a whole day, and we took much booty . . . If God had not been with us in this battle and sent us the other army quickly, none of us would have escaped."[9] The defeat was so swift and complete that once again Arslan lost his entire treasury, which he had managed to raise to replace the one he had lost at Nicaea.[10] Nevertheless, before he took his forces off to the mountains Arslan had his troops ravage the countryside to "make it impossible [for the crusaders] to feed themselves as they advanced."[11]

After resting for two days following the battle, the crusaders set out to cross Anatolia on their way to Antioch. It was a dreadful march. The summer heat was intense. There was no water: the wells and cisterns (built to store rainwater) had all been destroyed by the Turks. As the *Gesta* tells it, they were passing through "a land which was deserted, waterless and uninhabitable, from which we barely emerged or escaped alive, for we suffered greatly from hunger and thirst, and found nothing at all to eat except prickly plants . . . On such food we survived wretchedly enough, but we lost most of our horses."[12]

The crusaders slogged on until they reached Iconium, in a fertile valley filled with streams and orchards. In addition to claiming the city, the crusaders rested there for a few days and then marched on to Heraclea, also located in a fertile valley. There they found a substantial Turkish army, led by two emirs who seem to have thought their mere presence would be sufficient to cause the crusaders to change course. But the crusaders attacked at once, and soon the Turks withdrew at full speed—the crusaders' shortage of horses saving the Turks from being slaughtered.

At Heraclea the crusaders had their choice of two routes to Antioch. One was more direct but very mountainous. The other passed through Caesara Mazacha and was longer but less easily defended. Bohemond chose to cross the mountains. The rest went through Caesara, which they found to have been deserted by the Turks. The forces were reunited at Coxon. There they found plentiful supplies and a cordial welcome from the largely Christian population. After three days of rest, they moved on and discovered that the journey from Coxon to Antioch "was the most difficult that the crusaders had to face."[13] As the *Gesta* reported: "[W]e set out and began to cross a damnable mountain, which was so high and steep that none of our men dared to overtake another on the mountain path. Horses fell over the precipice, and one beast of burden dragged another down. As for the knights . . . [some] threw their arms away and went on."[14] The armor was discarded because of the loss of pack animals; it was very heavy to carry.

Once across the mountain, the crusaders reorganized their units at Marash. Here Baldwin of Boulogne and about a hundred mounted knights, accompanied by the historian Fulcher of Chartres, left the Crusade and traveled east, where Baldwin was adopted by Thoros, the childless Armenian ruler of Edessa. (Secret negotiations had gone on for some time.) Soon after, Thoros was murdered by a mob of citizens, Baldwin became the first count of Edessa, and the county of Edessa became the first of the crusader kingdoms.

Meanwhile, the crusaders marched to the city of Antioch, then the capital of Syria.

ANTIOCH

Antioch is situated on the Orontes River where it cuts through the mountains, about twelve miles from the Mediterranean. At the start of the Christian era it was the third-largest city in the Roman Empire; only Rome and Alexandria were larger.[15] Under Muslim rule it suffered a substantial decline of both population and commerce. Having been recovered briefly by Byzantium in the tenth century, it regained some importance, but declined again when lost to the Turks. Nevertheless, in 1098 it was a city of substantial size, with very impressive fortifications.

The city stood partly on a mountainside, and its massive walls climbed steep slopes, crossed a river, and included a citadel a thousand feet above the main part of the city. Four hundred towers punctuated the walls, "spaced so as to bring every yard of them within bow shot."[16] Because these defenses were so strong, the conquest of Antioch in the past usually had been achieved by treachery. That is precisely what Bohemond had in mind this time, too. But he kept this to himself as the other leaders considered the military situation. Meanwhile, things were not so good inside the city. For one thing, the garrison was too small to fully man the walls. For another, by recently mistreating the Christian residents (who were the majority) and converting their cathedral into a horse stable, the emir had created a substantial population of potential traitors.[17]

While the crusaders considered their options, the emir sent ambassadors far and wide in search of military support—with some success, although no relief forces could arrive for some time. Meanwhile, in October 1097 the crusaders undertook a siege of the city. Unfortunately, just as the Muslim commander did not have enough troops to fully man the walls, there were too few crusaders to fully surround the city. Hence, the flow of supplies to Antioch continued. In November, the crusaders received an important reinforcement: thirteen Genoese galleys and transports arrived on the coast, carrying more crusaders and supplies. Nevertheless, the crusader forces soon consumed all of the available supplies, including fodder.

As winter set in, the besiegers suffered far more from hunger and disease than did those besieged within Antioch—since they continued to be resupplied. Large numbers of the poor noncombatants with the crusaders actually starved to death. Obviously, Alexius could have sent ample supplies by sea. But he did not. Instead, in February he ordered Tatikios and his contingent of Byzantine troops to withdraw, and they sailed away on ships that had been sent for that purpose but had not used the opportunity to bring any supplies. Tatikios made matters even worse by pretending that he was not deserting but going back to get abundant supplies for the crusaders. The crusaders knew better. The *Gesta* put it this way: "[H]e is a liar, and always will be. We were thus left in direst need."[18] Things soon got so bad in the crusader encampments that Peter the Hermit and William the Carpenter (who had taken part in Emicho's massacre of Jews) deserted and headed for Constantinople. Bohemond's nephew Tancred pursued them and brought them back in disgrace. After humiliating them at length in public, Bohemond let them live. Shortly thereafter, William fled once more and probably found sanctuary with Alexius.[19]

It was then that a very substantial Muslim relief force advanced on Antioch. The battle was fought on Shrove Tuesday, February 9, 1098. Despite being greatly outnumbered, the crusaders won a smashing victory. Having very few horses, nearly all the knights joined the ranks of the heavy infantry, against which the Muslim cavalry suffered terrible losses during each attack. At the appropriate moment Bohemond suddenly appeared on the Muslim flank with the remaining heavy cavalry of perhaps three hundred knights. At the same time, the crusader infantry also charged. The Muslim force was massacred. Beyond their amazing victory, the crusaders also gained desperately needed supplies from the enemy camp. As the *Gesta* summed up: "Thus, by God's will, on that day our enemies were overcome. Our men captured plenty of horses and other things of which they were badly in need, and they brought back a hundred heads of dead Turks to the city gate."[20] A month later, a small Norman fleet from England arrived off the coast, bringing additional supplies and more crusaders.

Even so, the prospects for storming the city seemed grim. Consequently, a trickle of desertion began. It soon swelled to major proportions when Stephen of Blois and a large group of northern Franks defected without warning; they left a day too early, as will be seen. This defection had far more devastating effects than a simple reduction in the crusader ranks. For at this time Alexius, having decided that despite everything the crusaders were going to take Antioch, had quickly led a large Byzantine army south in order to be in on the victory and to claim Antioch. Stephen of Blois and other noble deserters met Alexius at Alexandretta, only about forty miles north of Antioch. There they told Alexius that the situation in Antioch was hopeless. Rather than quickly move on to redress the situation, Alexius decided to stay put while awaiting further information.

Meanwhile, Bohemond was attempting to suborn someone in Antioch who could open a gate so that a bloody and very risky assault on the walls of the city could be avoided. Bohemond's subversive efforts were made possible by the fact that the city was full of Christians who hated the Turkish commander and thus provided Bohemond with an extensive network for communicating within the city. Even so, the traitor he found was not a Christian;

rather, he was a Muslim convert in command of a tower, a postern gate, and a segment of wall on the southeastern side of the city. On the night of June 2–3, a day after Stephen of Blois had deserted, Bohemond led a small group of his Normans through the unlocked gate and took control of ten towers and a long stretch of the wall, whereupon elements of the Christian population of the city attacked Muslim troops from within while the crusaders poured into the city. The Muslim troops were quickly wiped out—even most of those who fled the city, including their commander.

Antioch was again a Christian city. But it appeared to be an empty victory. A very large and imposing Muslim army had been gathering for some time, made up of forces supplied by many sultans and emirs and led by the Turkish sultan Kerbogah. Fearing this development, more desertions took place, including Bohemond's brother-in-law William of Grant-Mesnil. The deserters reached the Byzantine encampment at Alexandretta just when Alexius, having heard that Antioch had been taken, was about to resume his march south to stake his claim; indeed, Stephen of Blois was getting ready to return to Antioch as well. But news of the impending arrival of Kerbogah's powerful forces decided the issue. All agreed that it was too late to save the Crusade, and all turned tail and headed north. It should be noted that when Stephen of Blois reached home he was universally defined as a coward, even by his wife, who was so unrelenting in her contempt that in 1101 Stephen recruited a new army, led it back to the Holy Land, and was killed in an ill-advised charge at the Egyptians in the Battle of Ramla. It also should be noted that by his retreat, Alexius had destroyed any remaining credibility he had with the crusaders. When they really needed his support, he had left them to their fate.

Kerbogah's large, well-trained force arrived at the gates of Antioch on June 9, 1098. The situation appeared hopeless: by this time the crusaders may have been down to fewer than two hundred warhorses.[21] Consequently, Kerbogah assumed that the crusaders would go on the defensive and man the walls, necessitating a siege. And that's what many of the Crusade commanders thought was the only possible strategy other than surrender.

So, for a few days fierce fighting took place between Kerbogah's attackers and the crusaders defending the walls, with heavy losses on both sides. Then, religion intervened. On June 11 a priest reported that Christ had appeared to him during the night and promised divine aid to the crusaders in five days. In response, the leaders all swore not to abandon their mission. Then, on June 14, Count Peter Bartholomew reported that Saint Andrew had appeared to him in a vision and revealed to him the location of the Holy Lance—this being the spear used by the Roman soldier to pierce the side of Jesus during the Crucifixion. Many of the clergy were skeptical, but several nobles accepted this story and helped Bartholomew dig in the promised spot. They dug up a piece of iron that they proclaimed to indeed be a spearhead, and the news caused excitement throughout the army. With the lance leading the way, they would certainly be invincible. Incredibly, they were!

On June 20, 1098, Bohemond was acknowledged as the overall commander of the crusader army in recognition of his greater experience and the severity of the situation. He immediately prepared the army to sally forth and attack the Turks—not only because of the divine reassurances, but because he realized that this was the best military option, albeit "a dangerous gamble."[22] So, on June 28, with the historian Raymond of Aguilers carrying the Holy Lance, the remaining crusader forces marched through the Bridge Gate of Antioch to face Kerbogah's far larger host. The Turks attacked immediately but recoiled after colliding with the unmovable, well-armored, disciplined heavy infantry formations, whose members were confident that they were God's battalions. It was, in many ways, the Battle of Tours all over again. The Muslim forces attacked and died. The crusader ranks seemed impregnable. Soon the Turks began to withdraw and then to flee. The crusaders tromped along in their close formations, overran Kerbogah's camp, and killed everyone within reach. The only reason some Turkish forces escaped was that the crusaders lacked the horses needed to catch them. To have triumphed so completely against such a powerful enemy seemed incomprehensible to many crusaders, even after the fact. The story spread that a contingent of mounted saints had descended from heaven and joined in the attack.[23]

So it was that another major Turkish force was destroyed, and now the road to Jerusalem lay open before them. But Bohemond did not plan to march down it. Instead, he began negotiations to become the ruler of a new kingdom based in Antioch. The initial agreement with Emperor Alexius, sworn to by the crusader leaders, acknowledged his claim to all territories that recently had been part of Byzantium. That included Antioch. But, Bohemond argued, when Alexius deserted them, that invalidated all oaths and obligations. Moreover, since Bohemond had arranged for the unlocked gate and had led the troops that took the city, and because he was very popular with the Christian residents of the city, he claimed the right to rule. Although most leaders agreed with Bohemond that Alexius had no claims, they were not prepared to cede him Antioch. The rest of the year was spent in disputes and maneuvers over Bohemond's claims. This delay did not reflect any loss of determination to take back Jerusalem, and it was agreed that they would wait until early spring before heading south. The crusaders used this interim to write letters to Pope Urban begging him to come and take command of the crusader forces. Some historians suppose that the crusaders knew the pope would not come east, but that writing to him "enabled them to postpone once more the need to decide upon the fate of Antioch."[24]

Meanwhile, the army suffered. An epidemic broke out (it may have been typhoid),[25] and many died. They ran short of food and began to eat their remaining horses. Soon many were eating "leaves, thistles, and leather."[26] Again, as at Nicaea, many of the poor starved to death. In December, under the leadership of some dispossessed knights, a group of poor men armed themselves with the abundant captured Muslim weapons and formed a fighting brigade. Known as the Tafurs, they were remarkable for their religious fanaticism and ferocity. Lacking the funds needed to buy what little food was available, the Tafurs overwhelmed the Muslim town of Ma'arrat al-Numan. A massacre followed, and, according to some reports, so did incidents of cannibalism.[27]

Finally, in February the crusaders began the march to Jerusalem. Bohemond accompanied them for about fifty miles, as far as Latakia, and then by mutual consent returned to assume full control of Antioch. Latakia was a port, and the crusaders continued along the coast and were several times supplied by fleets from Genoa, Pisa, and even England. The ships kept coming, not only because their owners favored the crusader cause, but perhaps primarily because the crusader leaders had money to pay well for supplies. In addition, each trip brought a few more late-coming crusaders willing to pay for passage. Of course, the ships were able to come because the Byzantine navy controlled the eastern Mediterranean and Alexius was willing to allow the European ships access to his ports on Cypress. Offsetting this gesture was the fact that Alexius had written to the Fatimid court in Cairo to "repudiate any connection with [the crusader] advance" on Jerusalem.[28] Later, when the crusaders captured copies of this correspondence, they were astounded at such treachery.

Finally, on June 7, 1099, the crusaders reached the walls of Jerusalem.

JERUSALEM

According to Steven Runciman, "The city of Jerusalem was one of the great fortresses of the medieval world ... The walls were in good condition and [it was manned by] a strong garrison of Arab and Sudanese troops."[29] Note that these were not Turkish troops. A year before the crusaders reached the city, it had been captured from the Turks by the Fatimids of Egypt under the command of their grand vizier, al-Afdal, who had taken advantage of the Turkish defeats at Antioch to move against them. With Jerusalem securely in Fatimid hands, the vizier returned to Cairo, leaving Ifitkhar al-Dawla as governor of the city.

When he became aware of the approaching crusaders, Ifitkhar had all wells around the city polluted or blocked, drove away all the livestock, and set workmen to constructing defensive machines such as catapults. He also expelled the city's Christian population. This was a wise move, as Christians had outnumbered the Muslims in the city, and, as demonstrated by Bohemond at Antioch, they were unlikely to have been loyal to the regime. Sending away the Christians also reduced by about half the demand on Jerusalem's stockpile of supplies. But Ifitkhar's hole card was that he did not believe he would need to defend the city for very long because an overwhelming relief force would soon arrive.

The crusader force that gathered to attack Jerusalem consisted of only about thirteen hundred knights and perhaps ten thousand infantry,[30] having been reduced by about two-thirds from the crusader army that had besieged Nicaea two years previously. As always, in addition to the fighting men, there were many noncombatants as well. All things considered, the crusaders were reasonably fit, the march down the coast having been both well supplied and leisurely; on average they had traveled only about eight miles a day and had taken many full days of rest.[31] Along the way, they were welcomed by some cities; the others they simply bypassed. But now time was of the essence. It was getting hot, and their food and water would soon run out.

So, on June 13, the crusaders launched an attack. Initially things went well as they smashed through the outer defenses. However, it turned out that they lacked the number of ladders needed to make it over the walls in sufficient numbers, and they were repelled. This was a very serious defeat, because there were no materials in the area that could be used to construct more ladders, let alone siege machines such as portable towers. At this critical moment six Christian ships—two from Genoa and four from England—arrived at Jaffa, about twenty-five miles away. All six carried food, but the Genoese ships also had cargoes of ropes, nails, and bolts needed for making siege machines.

Meanwhile, Tancred and Robert of Flanders led expeditions in search of wood and returned with logs and planks, many of them carried by Muslim prisoners captured along the way. As the crusaders set to work on scaling ladders and constructing two wooden towers on wheels and equipped with catapults, they suffered greatly from heat and thirst: they had to send detachments as far as the Jordan River to bring back water. There were desertions, since it appeared to many that even with ladders and siege equipment, the odds were not in their favor, especially since they knew that a huge army had set out from Egypt to attack them. Once again, a solution was sought in religion.

A priest received a vision that promised victory if the crusaders stopped bickering, fasted, and walked barefoot around the walls of Jerusalem. The vision was accepted as authentic, and a three-day fast was observed. Then, on July 8, 1099, the procession began: bishops, clergy, princes, knights, foot soldiers, and noncombatants—all of them barefoot as they marched around the city. Residents of Jerusalem crowded the walls to mock them, but "they gloried in such mockery."[32] The procession ended on the Mount of Olives, where Peter the Hermit (once again in good graces) preached an impassioned sermon.

The next two days were a blur of activity as the siege towers were completed and all the necessary preparations made. During the night of July 13–14 the ditches around the walls were filled in at several widely separated points so the towers could be rolled against the walls. By the evening of the 14th, Raymond of Aguilers's men succeeded in placing their tower against the south wall. Despite fierce fighting, the crusaders could not gain a foothold. But the next morning, Godfrey of Bouillon's force was able to place their tower against the north wall. Godfrey is reported to have stood atop the tower firing his crossbow.[33] We should assume that many others in his squadron had crossbows, too (see chap. 3), and that their lethal fire enabled Godfrey's men to be firmly in control of a stretch of wall by noon. This allowed scaling ladders to be set up without resistance, and a strong crusader force mounted the walls and soon was fighting in the city streets. The Muslim forces were overwhelmed, and a massacre began; by the morning of the 16th the city was littered with corpses.

This is the horror story that has been used again and again to vilify the crusaders. Consequently, let us pause here to consider the matter from several perspectives. First of all, it is not only absurd but often quite disingenuous to use this event to "prove" that the crusaders were bloodthirsty barbarians in contrast to the more civilized and tolerant Muslims. Dozens of Muslim massacres of whole cities have been reported in previous chapters, and the crusaders knew of such occurrences. Second, the commonly applied "rule of war" concerning siege warfare was that if a city did not surrender before forcing the attackers to take the city by storm (which inevitably caused a very high rate of casualties in the besieging force), the inhabitants could expect to be massacred as an example to others in the future. That is, had the Muslims surrendered Jerusalem on June 13 when the towers were ready to be rolled against the walls, they would no doubt have been given terms that would have prevented a massacre.

Another rule of medieval war was "To the victor go the spoils." Loot and booty were major motivating factors, especially for the common soldiers in all armies. Hence, surrender agreements with cities usually provided for very substantial settlements, which then were shared out. But when cities were taken by storm, the spoils were obtained by looting. As Guibert of Nogent described the looting of Jerusalem: "Palaces and other buildings lay open, and silver, gold, and silken garments were seized as booty . . . and in the houses they found a great abundance of every kind of food. This was right and proper for the army of God, that the finest things that offered themselves to each man, no matter how poor, became his by right, without doubt or challenge, no matter the social class of the man who first came upon them."[34] When troops began to loot, things often got out of hand. In this instance, as Guibert put it, "[t]he army ran amok," and a killing spree began. Soon Jerusalem "was filled with so many corpses that the Franks were unable to move without stepping on dead bodies." Captives were set to work collecting the bodies and carrying them from the city. Placed in front of the main gates in huge piles, they then were burned. Thus, "God repaid them . . . by exacting a retribution equal to their hideous crimes."[35]

Granted, it was a cruel and bloody age, but nothing is to be gained either in terms of moral insights or historical comprehension by anachronistically imposing the Geneva Convention on these times. Moreover, the sources may have greatly exaggerated the extent of the massacre: these same writers routinely reported armies of nearly a million men and hundreds of thousands of casualties on each side in various battles. Surely, no sensible person will believe Raymond of Aguilers's report that "men rode in blood up to their knees and bridle reins."[36] What most likely happened was, as the distinguished John France put it, "not far beyond what common practice of the day meted out to any place that had resisted."[37]

Caution should especially be applied to the claim that when the Jewish residents of Jerusalem fled to their major synagogue, they all died when angry crusaders burned the building down around them. This is the favorite example of those determined to condemn the Crusades and one I repeated in an earlier study of anti-Semitic outbursts.[38] On the face of it, the story is plausible. As reported in several previous chapters, Jews frequently sided with the Muslims against the Christians in the Holy Land. In this instance, there were Jews in Ifitkhar's regular forces as well as in the city militia.[39] Hence, there is no reason to assume that the Jews would have received special treatment; people inside synagogues were as endangered as those inside mosques. Nor can there be any doubt that there were substantial taints of anti-Semitism among the crusaders.

Even so, there is very credible evidence that most of the Jews were spared and that the story that all the Jews were burned alive may be false! Some of the Christian accounts report that the Jews were taken captive and later forced to clear the corpses out of the city, which is what the Israeli historian Moshe Gil believes happened.[40] Indeed, one of the famous Geniza letters discovered in Cairo in 1952 was written in Hebrew by Jewish community leaders seeking funds to ransom Jews taken captive at the fall of Jerusalem.[41] It is possible, too, that some Jews died when their synagogue was burned while most Jews in Jerusalem did not take shelter in a synagogue and were taken captive.

Despite taking several years and costing thousands of lives, the capture of Jerusalem was, in many ways, only the beginning of the story. In fact, it was only about three weeks before the next chapter took place: a battle against a newly arrived Fatimid army from Cairo.

ASCALON

When al-Afdal, grand vizier to the Fatimid caliph of Egypt, first heard that the crusaders were advancing on Antioch, he assumed that they were Byzantine mercenaries and would be excellent allies against the Seljuk Turks. Emperor Alexius strengthened that impression and even coaxed the crusader commanders into negotiating with the Fatimids. Eventually al-Afdal realized that the crusaders were on an independent mission, and he scrambled to assemble a mighty army. It was too late to save Jerusalem, which at this time had been a Fatimid possession, but it was not too late to take it back.

Part of al-Afdal's army marched across the Sinai Desert to Palestine. Another part sailed with al-Afdal and landed at Ascalon, about fifty miles southwest of Jerusalem. The rest of the army joined him there, as did a number of other contingents, including various Bedouin tribes. The crusaders were, of course, kept fully abreast of these developments by their agents and scouts, and even had they not been they would have learned of this threat when al-Afdal sent them a message suggesting negotiations. Instead, the crusaders marched off to Ascalon, leaving all their noncombatants behind under the protection of a tiny garrison. Peter the Hermit also was left behind with instructions to hold constant services of intercession for victory. At this point, the crusader force could not have numbered more than ten thousand, and al-Afdal's force probably totaled around twenty thousand.[42]

On the 11th of August the crusaders arrived just north of Ascalon, where they discovered immense herds that had been brought to feed the Muslim army. Taking control of these, they then rested for the night. In the early morning the crusaders formed up their ranks and advanced on al-Afdal's camp. Incredibly, they took the enemy completely by surprise; once again, an arrogant Muslim leader had not even posted sentries, let alone sent out scouts. The Muslims offered no sustained opposition and fled for their lives, but there were few survivors. The vizier managed to escape with a few of his officers by sailing away to Egypt.

The booty taken by the crusaders seems incredible, not only for the staggering amounts involved, but why it was there at all: "[b]ullion and precious stones were found in huge quantities."[43]

CONCLUSION

What Pope Urban had begun in that field in Clermont had now come to pass. God's battalions had been victorious, and the unbelievers had been driven from Jerusalem. Almost immediately, large numbers of crusaders began to head for home; after all, they had been gone much longer than anyone had expected. Within several months the crusader forces remaining in the Holy Land had fallen to perhaps no more than three hundred knights and an unknown, but not very large, number of foot soldiers. This was a very dangerous development, for surely Muslim forces would come again; the Holy Land remained encircled by a large Muslim world. Unfortunately, no plans had been made at the outset for maintaining a liberated Jerusalem, because it was thought that the Byzantines would take the lead. No one believed that now. Thus the question that had been bothering many leading crusaders for several years was, How can our miraculous achievement be sustained?

Chapter Eight

THE CRUSADER KINGDOMS

In order to defend the crusader kingdoms with the very small
number of knights available, the Templars and the Hospitallers built
superb fortresses such as the Krac des Chevaliers, shown here.
© *DeA Picture Library / Art Resource, NY*

W HEN THEY BEGAN their journeys east, the crusader princes were not concerned about what would happen once the Holy Land was back in Christian hands. They assumed that it would simply become part of Byzantium, just as they assumed that Alexius Comnenus would lead them into battle. But, of course, the Byzantine emperor had done no leading, and everyone from the West now regarded him as a treacherous fraud who had repeatedly betrayed them. It also was clear that Alexius was not interested in defending the Holy Land and would gladly restore it to Islam if offered an attractive treaty. So, if their victories were to have lasting significance, some crusaders would need to stay in the East, even though their ranks had become precariously slim as most of their comrades went home. The solution was to create a permanent state, ruled and defended by Christians. Thus, in 1099, they founded the kingdom of Jerusalem. It also came to be known at Outremer, the French word for "overseas" (*outre-mer*).

The kingdom of Jerusalem occupied essentially the same area as ancient Palestine (see map 8.1). It was created by and initially ruled by Godfrey of Bouillon, who had led the capture of Jerusalem and then the defeat of the Egyptian army that tried to re-capture the city. Godfrey refused to be crowned king on grounds that he could not wear "a crown of gold" where Christ had worn "a crown of thorns."[1] Instead, he settled for the title of Defender of the Holy Sepulchre.

In addition to the kingdom of Jerusalem, there were three other minor crusader kingdoms. These were the county of Edessa,

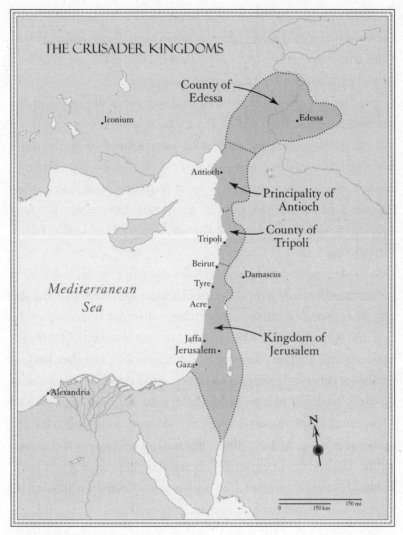

MAP 8.1

named for its major city (and the only one of the kingdoms that
was landlocked); the principality of Antioch, which surrounded
the city of Antioch in what is now southern Turkey; and the
county of Tripoli, located just south of Antioch and named for the
Lebanese coastal city of that name. To keep a proper perspective, it

is useful to note how small these "cities" were. Antioch was much the largest city of the area, having about forty thousand residents. Edessa had about twenty-four thousand; Tripoli, about eight thousand; Jerusalem had only about ten thousand.[2]

The foundings of Edessa and Antioch were discussed in the previous chapter. Baldwin of Boulogne rose to power in Edessa in 1098, having marched there with a small force while the main body of crusaders attacked Antioch. When his brother Godfrey died in 1100, Baldwin became king of Jerusalem, and Edessa soon became a fief of the kingdom of Jerusalem. Edessa was not only the first crusader kingdom but also the first to be retaken by Islam, in 1144.

The same year that Baldwin took power in Edessa, Bohemond of Taranto became prince of Antioch after he negotiated the betrayal of a gate that allowed the crusaders to enter and conquer the city, and subsequently he had led the successful defense of Antioch against what seemed like overwhelming odds. The other leading crusaders eventually supported Bohemond's decision to remain in Antioch because "somebody had to defend the lines back to Asia Minor and Christian territory,"[3] and no one wished to trust the emperor Alexius to do so. From the start, Antioch was threatened by the Byzantines as rightfully theirs, but they never got it back. Instead, Antioch remained an independent kingdom until 1119, when it was joined to the kingdom of Jerusalem.

The county of Tripoli was the last of the four crusader states to be established—in 1102. It came into being when Count Raymond IV of Toulouse laid siege to the port city of Tripoli. When Raymond died suddenly in 1105, he left his infant son as heir, and the county became a vassal state of the kingdom of Jerusalem.

The three minor kingdoms will receive only passing mentions; the story of the Christians in the Holy Land following the First Crusade is primarily the story of the kingdom of Jerusalem. That story stretches over nearly two centuries, but this chapter will be limited to sketching the history, economy, and social organization of the kingdom as it developed during the first few decades of the twelfth century. Then the chapter turns to the claim that the crusader kingdoms were the first manifestation of European colonialism and, as such, justifiably still provoke Muslim wrath. What cannot be contested is that, whatever else they may have been, the crusader kingdoms were embattled enclaves surrounded by a large, militant, and powerful Muslim world. In fact, the kingdom of Jerusalem was never entirely cleared of fortified Muslim cities that remained enemy outposts and from which raiding parties continued to attack small settlements and travelers—especially groups of Christian pilgrims. Consequently, defense was the primary preoccupation of rulers of the kingdom. The latter part of this chapter concerns the founding of two knightly religious orders that were dedicated to the defense of the Holy Land.

THE KINGDOM OF JERUSALEM

The kingdom of Jerusalem hugged the Mediterranean coast; the eastern border was, on average, only about fifty miles from the sea, and aside from Jerusalem, all the principal cities were ports. The coastal plain was mostly a sandy waste, with few farmable areas, but for many centuries it served as a thriving caravan route. Back from the coastal plain were mountain ranges, and most of the good agricultural land lay in a valley between them. Given how narrow the kingdom was, and that populous Muslim nations lay just beyond the eastern and southern borders, all four of the crusader kingdoms "had to be garrison states."[4]

The initial steps to create the kingdom of Jerusalem took place against the sense of urgency caused by the massive departures of crusaders and their entourages for home. According to Fulcher of Chartres, soon after the conquest of Jerusalem there were no "more than three hundred knights and as many footmen to defend [the kingdom] . . . We scarcely dared to assemble our knights when we wished to plan some feat against our enemies. We feared that in the meantime they would do some damage against our deserted fortifications."[5] These totals do not include the troops available in the other three kingdoms, but these would have been only minor forces, too. Perhaps the most amazing thing about this entire era was that the kingdoms were not retaken at once by Muslim armies.

Although the massive departures posed a serious problem for the defense of the Holy Land, they pose two serious questions for the historian: who stayed, and why did they do so?

Just as enlistment in the Crusades was a network phenomenon, so was staying. That is, those who stayed were not scattered individuals but overwhelmingly were members of a *domus,* or household—a group of noblemen, knights, and retainers associated with a leading figure such as Godfrey of Bouillon. When Godfrey decided to stay, his household stayed with him just as they had followed him when he went on the Crusade. Many who favor the notion that the kingdoms were colonies suggest that it was the landless with little awaiting them back in Europe who opted to stay. But according to a careful "census" of those who stayed by Jonathan Riley-Smith, the decisions to stay that mattered were those made by the heads of households, and these were "rich men who certainly had no financial need to stay in the East."[6] As to why they chose to stay, Riley-Smith concluded that most did so out "of idealism or [in the case of followers] of dependence on the close emotional ties binding lord and vassal, patron and client."[7]

This helps to explain why the governance of the kingdoms was based on the European feudal system. This is what they all knew and accepted. Hence, almost at once Godfrey began to assign fiefs to various members of his household, who were thereby committed to supplying a quota of knights and foot soldiers for the defense of the kingdom—which was the basis of feudalism. But there was a crucial difference. European feudalism was based on agricultural land. It was the productivity of this land that paid the bills. But in the kingdom there was very little agricultural land, and the nobility could not base themselves on their "estates" as in Europe; consequently, manor houses "did not exist in the kingdom."[8] Instead, the "overwhelming majority [of knights] were simply salaried warriors,"[9] and poorly paid ones at that. The average knight's salary was barely sufficient to meet the costs of keeping his horses and necessary retainers. Because they were not supported by rural estates, knights and nobles preferred to live in cities and towns as did most everyone else. For the times, the kingdom was remarkably urban: Jerusalem, Antioch, and Edessa were nearly as large as Paris and Venice, and were far larger than London or Rome.[10] Acre, Jaffa, Sidon, Gaza, and Tyre also were sizable.

Godfrey lived only long enough to establish feudalism, dying on July 18, 1100, a year and three days after his victory at Jerusalem. His brother Baldwin was called from Edessa to take his place and was crowned king of Jerusalem in Bethlehem on Christmas Day 1100; his cousin Baldwin of LeBourg replaced him as count of Edessa, which subsequently became a fief of the kingdom of Jerusalem. Baldwin was the real founder of the kingdom, and he greatly expanded its territory. Reinforced by a contingent of newly arrived Norwegian crusaders led by Magnus Barefoot, he conquered important port cities such as Acre, Beirut, and Sidon, which enabled the kingdom to establish trade relations with Genoa, Pisa, and Venice.

Pilgrims continued to be a major source of revenue, and they also often served as a temporary source of defenders.[11] Additional funds were raised by taxing the large Muslim caravans that had long followed the coastal route north from Arabia and Egypt to Damascus. Several major castles, including the famous Krak de Montréal, were built along the caravan route for this purpose. Given the constant warfare that marked the entire history of the kingdom, booty also played a significant role in the kingdom's economy,[12] and by the end of the twelfth century the spice trade became quite profitable—passing through the kingdom's ports to merchants from the Italian city-states. But in early days, the rulers of the kingdom and their retainers relied greatly on their own European wealth, and when Baldwin's funds ran low he recouped by marrying a rich widow from Sicily, who brought him "a huge treasure of money, weapons, and supplies."[13] The bottom line was that the kingdom could be sustained in Christian hands only, as it was supported by subsidies sent from Europe, many of them raised by special "crusader" taxes (see chap. 10).

After King Baldwin of Jerusalem died in 1118 during a campaign against Egypt, once again the barons turned to Edessa for a new king, and Baldwin of LeBourg was crowned as Baldwin II. He reigned for thirteen years and added the city of Tyre to the kingdom.

In 1144 Islam struck back when Imad al-Din Zangi took the city of Edessa, but that part of the Edessan County west of the Euphrates River remained in Christian hands. The city was re-captured by Christian forces in 1146 when Zangi died but was quickly retaken by the Muslims. Meanwhile, partly in response to this Muslim incursion, the Second Crusade had been proclaimed back in Europe, and a great expedition was gathering, to be led by Louis VII, king of France, and the German king, Conrad III. That story awaits in chapter 9.

Not only were the kingdoms sustained by a very small number of resident men-at-arms; even when their noncombatant relatives are added in, "there can only have been from two to three thousand adult members of the Frankish upper classes"[14] in the kingdoms. Even so, many of them had come as pilgrims after the conquest of Jerusalem, and many others were *pullani*—the children or grandchildren of crusaders.[15] As time passed, even many of the original crusaders began to think of themselves as easterners (Orientals). Fulcher of Chartres, who had served as chaplain to Baldwin of Boulogne, wrote in about 1124: "For we who were Occidentals have now become Orientals. He who was a Roman or a Frank has in this land been made into a Galilean or a Palestinian. He who was of Rheims or Chartres has now become a citizen of Tyre or Antioch. We have already forgotten our places of birth; already these are unknown to many of us or not mentioned any more."[16] Fulcher went on to note that they now all spoke Greek and many spoke Arabic as well, and that they were often married to Eastern Christians.

Although many attempts were made to attract settlers from Europe, few came, and so people of Western backgrounds always were only a small minority of residents of the kingdom. A substantial number of residents were Eastern Christians, not only Greek Orthodox but also Jacobites, Maronites, Nestorians, Copts, and Armenians.[17] Many other residents were Jews, but the majority were Muslims, split between Sunnis and Shiites. Of course, the proportions of these various groups differed by area.[18]

Although, as noted, there were enclaves of Muslims who continued to rob and attack Christians, most Muslims in the kingdom were peasants who reportedly were quite content under Christian rule. For one thing, there were no land-hungry Christians eager to confiscate their fields or animals. For another, taxes were lower in the kingdom than in neighboring Muslim countries. Fully as important, the Christian rulers tolerated the Muslims' religion and made no effort to convert them.[19] (So much for modern claims that the crusaders went in search of converts and new religious "markets.") Finally, the Christians "administered justice fairly."[20]

Thus, a Muslim pilgrim who passed through the kingdom while returning from Mecca to Spain wrote that Muslims "live in great comfort under the Franks; may Allah preserve us from such a temptation . . . [Muslims] are masters of their dwellings, and govern themselves as they wish. This is the case in all the territory occupied by the Franks."[21]

CRUSADER COLONIES?

Colonialism refers to the exploitation of one society by another, by which the stronger society forces the weaker society into an unfair economic arrangement and thus enriches itself at the expense of the weaker society. The stronger nation achieves this by exerting direct political control over its colony; hence colonialism involves a resident ruling class of persons from the colonizing society (the colonials).[22] This is the definition of *colonialism* assumed by many modern writers who identify the crusader kingdoms as Western colonies.

However, many historians of the Crusades who routinely refer to the crusader kingdoms as "colonies" and the Christians who remained in the Holy Land as "colonists" seem unaware of the negative, political implications of these words. In their usage these terms seem synonymous with *settlements* and *settlers*. In fact, although Joshua Prawer (1917–1990) is regarded as the major proponent of the crusader colonialism thesis, he nowhere suggests that these were colonies as that term is defined here and as it is used in modern economic and political discourse.[23] All Prawer seems to have meant by *colonialism* is that the crusader kingdoms were ruled by people having a culture different from that of the previous rulers and many of the residents—that the rulers were westerners whereas most residents were easterners or Muslims. If that suffices to define a colony, then all conquests are colonies, and the crusaders merely seized a colony from the Turks (since they, too, were a ruling minority).

In any event, to identify the crusader kingdoms as colonies in the usual sense is absurd, as Prawer clearly understood. In terms of political control, the kingdoms were fully independent of any European state. In terms of economic exploitation, it would be more apt to identify Europe as a colony of the Holy Land, since the very substantial flow of wealth and resources was from the West to the East!

THE MILITARY ORDERS

Given the many unsuppressed Muslim strongholds, the kingdom remained a dangerous place, especially the roads over which pilgrims had to pass in order to reach Jerusalem. According to a Norse pilgrim, the road from the port of Jaffa to Jerusalem was "very dangerous. For the Saracens, always laying snares for Christians, lie hidden in the hollow places of the mountains, and the caves and rocks, watching day and night, and always on the look out for those whom they can attack on account of the fewness of their party, or those who have lagged behind . . . On that road not only the poor and the weak, but even the rich and the strong are in danger."[24] The prior of a Russian monastery agreed that along this road "the Saracens issue and massacre the pilgrims on their way."[25]

Hence, the chronic problem: an acute shortage of military manpower. It was this situation of "endemic insecurity"[26] that prompted the rise of a new kind of monastic order: military monks.

KNIGHTS TEMPLARS

At Easter 1119, a group of pilgrims was set upon by Muslims from Tyre. Three hundred were murdered, and sixty were taken into slavery.[27] Perhaps in direct response to this massacre, two veterans of the First Crusade, the Frankish knights Hugues de Payens and his relative Godfrey de Saint-Omer, proposed the creation of a monastic order for the protection of pilgrims. That may be how the Knights Templars began. But another account has it that "Hou[g] de Payn" led thirty knights to Jerusalem at the start of the reign of Baldwin II, having sworn to fight for the kingdom for three years and then to take holy orders. He and his knights proved to be such superb fighters that, after the Easter disaster, Baldwin talked them out of taking holy orders and into helping defend the pilgrim routes. Baldwin gave them a wing of his palace known as the House of Solomon (sited where Solomon's Temple was believed to have stood) for their residence and the taxes of some villages for their support.

What is certain is that Hugues de Payens and his knights—numbering from nine to thirty, depending on the account—did enter Baldwin's service around 1119 and were not yet a religious order, military or otherwise. Apparently, it was not long before Hugues de Payens and his knights began to consider themselves an order and to refer to their domicile as the Temple. But they had no Rule and no official standing, although they already had begun to acquire funding: in 1121 Count Fulk V of Anjou seems to have given them "an annual subsidy of 30 Angevin livres."[28] References to other substantial gifts and subsidies made at this time also are known. Then in 1126, Hugues de Payens left Jerusalem and went back to Europe to seek new recruits and, more urgently, to seek official standing for an order embracing the seemingly contradictory concepts of the warrior monk.

Fortunately for him, he was able to secure the support of the most powerful man in Europe: Bernard of Clairvaux,[29] head of the rapidly growing Cistercian order, the most respected theologian of the day, and so highly revered that he was able to publicly rebuke archbishops, popes, and kings without any fear of reprisal. In fact, he wrote a long treatise to specify the duties of the pope.[30]

Bernard was born into the nobility and raised to be a knight, but at age twenty he entered the Church. His knightly background was clearly reflected in the military structure he created for the Cistercians. Bernard also was an early and compelling advocate of chivalry, and many have suggested that he served as the model for the legendary Sir Galahad.[31] Perhaps no one in Europe would have responded more favorably to the proposal to create an order of knightly monks, and he quickly did the two things that needed to be done. First, he wrote a Rule for the order. It consisted of seventy-two articles (or paragraphs), and, as with the rule for most orders, it was quite detailed. Not only did it prescribe the schedule for prayers and worship and commit the members to chastity, but it prohibited "reminiscences about past sexual conquests."[32] It also dealt with menus (meat could be served three times a week), with dress (the knights would wear white robes; the red cross on the robes came later), and with modesty (there could be no gold or silver decorations on their armor), and it even limited each knight to three horses and a squire. In addition to writing the Rule, Bernard arranged in 1128 for a Church council to be convened at Troyes were the Rule was accepted and official Church recognition was given to the Order of the Poor Knights of Christ and the Temple of Solomon—soon to be known as the Knights Templars.

Unlike the conventional religious orders, the Templars did not permit young recruits; only mature, qualified knights need apply.[33] They did, however, accept many lacking noble birth and knightly training to serve in many subsidiary roles. First among these were the *sergeants,* some of whom also were mounted, but most of whom served as infantry. Sergeants could not wear the white robes of the knights and were not expected to fight with the same degree of bravery.[34] In addition were the *squires,* who were the personal servants of the knights, each knight having a squire to care for his horses and his armor. Squires sometimes served as infantry in battles. Beyond sergeants and squires were the *serving brothers*, a huge array of servants and support staff, from blacksmiths to cooks. Consequently, those who qualified as knights made up a very small proportion of any Templar garrison. By the middle of the twelfth century, the largest Templar garrisons in the kingdom "consisted of perhaps 50–60 knights, with as many as 400–500 other members."[35] The Templar garrison at Le Chastellet in 1178, when it was destroyed by Saladin, consisted of 80 knights and 750 sergeants.[36] In fact, some castles were entirely manned by sergeants and servants.

In addition to members of the order, the Templars' military forces often were augmented by temporary volunteers and by mercenaries. Apparently, serving with the Templars struck many European fighting men as very appealing, and it also brought them prestige upon their return, so a steady flow of men "volunteered for temporary membership."[37] In addition, the Templars often hired troops to expand their ranks. Not only were a large number of their crossbowmen mercenaries; they also hired knights and sergeants as well. Even so, the number of fighting men available to the Templars in the Holy Land was relatively modest; there were seldom more than three hundred knights and several thousand sergeants, scattered in many small garrisons.[38] The reason their numbers remained small was the need to retain large numbers of members in Europe to staff the huge establishment that soon developed there.

In the immediate aftermath of the Council of Troyes, the order "underwent a rapid expansion throughout Europe,"[39] some of these recruits having been motivated by Bernard's eloquent treatise *In Praise of the New Chivalry* (1128), which stressed that anyone who served in "Christ's Knighthood" was certain to be saved; hence: "Whether we live or die, we are the Lord's . . . Rejoice, brave fighter, if you live and conquer in the Lord; but rather exult and glory, if you die and are joined to the Lord."[40] That was directed to fighting men, but the "glamour" of the order was sufficient to also attract large numbers of lay brothers as well. The total enrollment of the order at its height is unknown, but it is quite credibly estimated that during their two centuries of existence almost twenty thousand Templars (knights and sergeants) died in combat.[41]

A huge wave of contributions also began at this time, some of it in precious metals, but most of it in land, forests, and estates: by 1150 the Templars owned more than forty castles and preceptories in Europe.[42] It is estimated that eventually the Templars possessed nine thousand estates in England and France.[43] Thus did the Templars quickly become immensely rich, but at the cost of needing to station large numbers of their members in Europe in order to manage these huge holdings. And because they sent large amounts of their income east to the kingdom of Jerusalem, they became experts in storing and moving wealth. In addition, they soon found that they could greatly add to their incomes by lending money, especially to nobility and other religious orders, at interest rates varying from 33 to 50 percent a year, although they often used a variety of means for disguising interest lest they be accused of usury. And so the Templars became, if not the central financial institution of Europe, at least a serious competitor to the international Italian banks.[44] Consider but a few examples of their wealth and influence.

The Templar house in London has been characterized as the "medieval precursor of the Bank of England"[45] and began holding the royal treasure in about 1185. In 1204, King John placed the crown jewels in the vault of the London Templars. Many others in England also placed large deposits of precious metals and jewels with the Templars, confident that there they would be safe from robbers, if not from the king: in 1263 King Edward confiscated the huge sum of ten thousand livres that had been deposited with the Templars by barons who had revolted against him.

The Templars also often served as middlemen in affairs of state: In 1158 the king of England arranged a marriage of his son to the daughter of the king of France. To ensure there was no cheating on paying the promised dowry, "some castles were given to the Templars"[46] by the king of France, and in return the Templars paid the king of England the dowry after the marriage had taken place.

Because of their immense wealth, the Templars soon were "amongst the greatest money-lenders of Christendom."[47] Not only did the Templars lend to kings and nobles; they also undertook to manage their financial affairs. This management function rapidly expanded to such an extent that the Templars began to collect the nobility's rents and taxes for them and either place the receipts on deposit or accept them as payment against previous loans. Indeed, the Templars became financially "indispensible to the French throne . . . the Paris Temple was literally the centre of financial administration in France. It offered a complete financial service, administering finances and collecting taxes, transmitting money, controlling debts, and paying pensions."[48]

As Eleanor Ferris summed up: "In the unwarlike atmosphere of the counting-room, the soldiers of the Temple, for over a century, handled much of the capital of western Europe, becoming expert accountants, judicious administrators, and pioneers in that development of credit and its instruments, which was destined to revolutionize the methods of commerce and finance."[49] Not surprisingly, the Templars soon were extremely influential in political life: Grand Masters were routinely consulted on pending decisions of state, both in Europe (especially in England and France) and in the Holy Land.

What seems most remarkable is that, despite their many duties and financial functions, the Templars remained focused on their basic mission to defend the Holy Land, financially and with their arms. Consider the immense outlays involved in building and sustaining castles in Palestine. When they rebuilt the castle at Safad in the 1240s, even when the income from the nearby villages is subtracted, the cost ran to 1.1 million Saracen besants. A knight could be hired as a mercenary (furnishing his own horses and squire) for 120 besants a year; thus the initial cost of refurbishing this castle would have paid about 9,100 knights for a year. The best estimate is that it would have cost another 40,000 besants a year to maintain the castle, or 333 knights' salaries. At this time the Templars had seven castles in Palestine, and the Hospitallers had three.[50] Castles served as secure strongholds from which an area could be controlled. The military orders needed exceptionally strong castles that could be defended by very small garrisons because they always were so short of men.

Clearly, the military orders needed huge European incomes in order to sustain their commitments in the East. So long as that mission was sustained, their immense wealth and power in Europe went unchallenged. But in 1291, with the fall of the last Christian foothold in Palestine and the massacres that ensued, the Templars no longer had an unquestionable mandate and soon became vulnerable to those who coveted their wealth and resented their power—most particularly King Phillip of France, who had Grand Master Jacques de Molay and other leading Templars burned as heretics on March 18, 1314.

KNIGHTS HOSPITALLERS

It all began with a hospital founded around 1070 to nurse wounded and sick pilgrims in Jerusalem. Initially, those staffing the hospital were not members of a recognized religious order, although they may have worn distinctive clothing and might have taken "some sort of religious vows."[51] At some point they began referring to theirs as the Hospital of St. John, but there is very little known of its early days—although elaborate myths were later generated to help with fund-raising. Following the crusader conquest of Jerusalem, reliable references to the hospital begin to appear. It was an enormous undertaking, open to everyone, and able to accommodate about two thousand patients. Not only that; it accommodated its patients, including the desperately poor, in luxury that not even many of the rich enjoyed: a separate feather bed for everyone, and lavish meals.[52] Soon those in charge became as concerned about escorting pilgrims safely on the way from the coast to Jerusalem as they were with treating the wounded who made it to the city. Another military order was born.

How the transformation took place "remains a mystery."[53] All we know is that they began to take over castles and provide them with garrisons, to wear black robes with a white cross on their breasts, and to otherwise appear as rivals to the Templars during the 1120s. Their participation in the major battles of the era also was noted, and it is estimated that they soon had as many knights in the Holy Land as did the Templars, albeit this amounted to only about three hundred men.[54] Officially known as the Order of St. John, the Knights Hospitallers also equaled the Templars in terms of their fighting abilities and the casualties they suffered. But when driven from the Holy Land, the Hospitallers did not withdraw to Europe, but only to Rhodes, whence they continued to fight the Muslims. And when driven from Rhodes, they took over Malta and there repelled repeated Muslim attacks—despite being outnumbered by as much as forty thousand to six hundred.

Also like the Templars, the Hospitallers assembled a vast amount of property in Europe and thereby became involved in financial affairs and money lending, although on a far smaller scale than the Templars. That they continued to be engaged in military resistance to Islam gave them a protective legitimacy that prevented the political conspiracy that overwhelmed the Templars. Indeed, now known as the Knights of Malta, the Hospitallers still exist.[55]

CONCLUSION

The raison d'être of the military orders was the defense of the kingdom of Jerusalem, and they played a leading role in that task. That part of their stories is best told as a facet of the more general effort to protect the kingdom—an effort that also involved the secular knights of the kingdom and the periodic arrival of new crusading armies from Europe.

Chapter Nine

THE STRUGGLE TO
DEFEND THE KINGDOMS

Although Europe continued to send additional crusading armies to the
Holy Land, the burden of defense fell mainly on the knightly orders as
commemorated in the marble tomb of a Knight Templar in London.
His large shield indicates that he fought as an infantryman.
© Foto Marburg / Art Resource, NY

THE CRUSADER KINGDOMS were never at peace, nor could they have been. As Jonathan Riley-Smith explained, "for ideological reasons, peace with the Muslim world was unattainable."[1] Temporary treaties were possible, but, given the doctrine of jihad (holy war), no lasting peace could be achieved except by surrender.

In keeping with jihad, at all times there were raids from Muslim-garrisoned cities within the crusader kingdoms and frequent probing attacks from the Muslim rulers across their borders. For more than forty years these threats were successfully repelled with the help of the military orders and the constant flow of knightly pilgrims, many of whom stayed on to fight for a time—sometimes for as long as several years. But this standoff was too good to last.

In the autumn of 1144, Count Joscelin II, ruler of the county of Edessa, formed an alliance with the Ortoqid Turks and led his army east to campaign against the Seljuk Turks led by Imad al-Din Zengi. But Zengi outmaneuvered them and attacked the city of Edessa, now poorly defended. On Christmas Eve, Zengi's troops broke into the city, and those inhabitants who were not slain were sold into slavery. In the wake of this disaster, Count Joscelin fled to Turbessel, from where he was able initially to hold that portion of his realm west of the Euphrates. In 1150, on a journey to Antioch, Joscelin got separated from his escort and fell into Muslim hands. Zengi had Joscelin's eyes put out and locked him in a dungeon, where he died nine years later.

THE SECOND CRUSADE

News of the fall of Edessa reached the West in early 1145 via returning pilgrims and came "as a terrible shock" to Christians in Europe. "For the first time they realized that things were not well in the East."[2] Consequently, Pope Eugene III issued a bull, *Quantum praesecessores,* calling for a new Crusade. The pope's message aroused little interest. However, the pope soon had the wisdom to recruit Bernard of Clairvaux to his cause, and when the most powerful, persuasive, and revered man in Europe began to preach a Second Crusade, things began to happen.

One thing that happened was that Bernard convened a gathering of the French nobility at Vézelay in Burgundy. "The news that Saint Bernard was going to preach brought visitors from all over France . . . Very soon the audience was under his spell. Men began to cry for Crosses" to sew on their chests.[3] Bernard was prepared for this and had brought many woolen crosses. The decisions to take the cross were not spontaneous; the people "knew why they were there."[4] Even so, Bernard ran out of crosses and tore up his cloak to make more.

Among those who volunteered that day was King Louis VII of France. He had long been planning a pilgrimage to Jerusalem, but Bernard convinced him he should lead an army of crusaders. Consequently, Louis, together with his queen, Eleanor of Aquitaine, and a select group of princes and nobles, prostrated themselves at Bernard's feet and accepted the cross. Louis was twenty-five at this time and was only beginning his "long career of energetic ineffectiveness," as Christopher Tyerman so aptly put it.[5]

Next, Bernard went to Germany, where he convinced King Conrad III and his nephew Frederick Barbarossa to take the cross. Unlike Louis, Conrad was in his early fifties and had considerable military experience. In fact, he had twice previously campaigned in the Holy Land. As in France, the German nobility flocked to hear Bernard, and again there was a public show of taking the cross by men who already had agreed to go.

Just as the First Crusaders were drawn from a closely knit network of family ties, the same was true of those who took the cross this time as well—especially among the French. Not only were most of the volunteers related to many other volunteers, but there were dense family ties to those who had gone on the First Crusade; the majority of the nobles who went had "crusading forefathers."[6]

Unfortunately, as enthusiasm for a new Crusade spread across Germany, it reignited the same anti-Semitism that had caused a rash of attacks on the Rhineland Jews at the start of the First Crusade. As pointed out in chapter 6, these attacks had been the work of a few, but they had set a pattern by directing attention to the issue of continuing to permit Jews to reject Jesus in a context where religious conformity was of growing concern. Even a few churchmen succumbed to this temptation. Abbé Pierre of the French monastery at Cluny pointed out, "What good is the good of going to the end of the world at great loss of men and money, to fight Saracens, when we permit among us other infidels who are a thousand times more guilty toward Christ than are the Mohammedans?"[7]

Nevertheless, it was not in France, but only in the Rhine Valley, that massacres of Jews took place—once again in Cologne, Mainz, Metz, Worms, and Speyer.[8] In this instance, a Monk named Radulph helped stir up the anti-Semitic outbursts. But the death toll would have been far higher had it not been for the intervention of Bernard of Clairvaux. When word reached him about the attacks on Jews, Bernard rode as rapidly as he could to the Rhine Valley and ordered an end to the killings—and they ceased! His intervention was reported by Ephraim of Bonn, a Jewish chronicler:

Then the Lord heard our sigh . . . He sent after the evil priest a decent priest, a great man . . . His name was Abbot Bernard, from the city of Clairvaux . . . [who] said to them[,] "It is fitting that you go forth against Muslims. However, anyone who attacks a Jew and tries to kill him it is as though he attacks Jesus himself. My pupil Radulph who advised destroying them did not advise properly. For in the book of Psalms is written concerning the Jews, 'Kill them not, lest my people forget.'" Everyone esteemed this priest as one of their saints . . . Were it not for the mercies of our Creator Who sent the aforesaid abbot . . . there would not have been a remnant or survivor among the Jews.[9]

Historians have tended to skip the Second Crusade.[10] Jonathan Phillips's 2007 book is the first "full treatment"[11] since Bernhard Kugler's monograph, published in 1866. This neglect is nothing new. Otto of Freising, the respected historian who commanded a major German contingent that was annihilated during the Second Crusade, wrote that "since the outcome of the expedition, because of our sins, is known to all, we . . . leave this to be related by others elsewhere."[12] Consequently, while all of the general histories of the Crusades give extensive coverage to the Battle of Dorylaeum in 1097, the second Battle of Dorylaeum in 1147 receives only a few sentences despite the fact that it was a far bloodier and much more decisive engagement.

It is a mistake to neglect the Second Crusade, because of two very important consequences: It gave a serious and long-lasting blow to the crusading movement in the West, undermining both confidence and commitment. And it restored Muslim confidence; after decades of defeats, usually by far smaller Christian forces, they now believed they could measure up.

The brief account that follows ignores the various "sideshows" to the Second Crusade involving the campaign against the Slavs and the conquest of Lisbon.

As a result of Bernard's effective efforts, it had been agreed that the two most powerful monarchs of Europe would lead two great armies to the Holy Land, setting forth at about Easter 1147. As would be expected, the departures were delayed, and the Germans left in May, the French following in June. As might not have been expected, the two monarchs chose to follow the same route to Constantinople, going overland across Hungary and Bulgaria. Having been in the lead, the Germans reached the Byzantine capital on September 10. That arrival date reflected an army so burdened with camp followers and "substantial contingents of unarmed pilgrims taking advantage of the protection afforded by the military expedition" that it had traveled at less than ten miles a day—far slower than the armies of the First Crusade.[13]

When the Germans reached Constantinople, they found they were not very welcome; had it been up to the Byzantines, there would not have been a Second Crusade. Indeed, just prior to the departure of the crusaders from Europe, the Byzantine emperor Manuel Comnenus had concluded a twelve-year treaty with the Seljuk sultan of Konya (Iconium), who would soon be at war with the crusaders. When the Europeans learned of this arrangement, it added to their already deep suspicions and antagonism towards the "perfidious Greeks."[14] For his part, Manuel was deeply disturbed at having such a large and potentially unruly force camped near his capital. So, just as the emperor Alexius had pressured the First Crusaders to cross into Asia Minor, so, too, the emperor Manuel pressed the Germans to cross the Bosporus—adding substantially to the distrust and dislike the Europeans felt toward the Byzantines. Having crossed over, Conrad decided not to wait for the French but to push on to recover Edessa.

Given the size of his army—perhaps as many as thirty thousand bearing arms[15]—this was not a rash decision. Moreover, Conrad probably hoped that, once free to plunder the countryside, he could somewhat overcome his dire shortages of food and fodder; Emperor Manuel had promised supplies but failed to deliver them. So Conrad marched his army and a huge contingent of noncombatants to Nicaea. There he split his expedition, placing most of the noncombatants under the leadership of Otto, bishop of Freising, who followed the more westerly road through Philadelphia and on to the port of Adalia (whence they sailed to Tyre). Swarms of noncombatants—many of them elderly, most of them poor—were always a stressful drain and hindrance to the crusaders. Despite strenuous efforts to persuade them not to come, large numbers always showed up and had to be fed and protected, while greatly slowing the pace of the advance.[16]

Meanwhile, moving along the same route followed by the First Crusaders, Conrad's army marched down the road to Dorylaeum (see map 7.1, page 143). Although the emperor had not sent any supplies, he did provide Conrad with a group of experienced Byzantine guides, whose purpose may have been to lead the crusaders to their destruction. Some modern historians doubt the claims by the crusaders that they had been betrayed by their guides, but no one challenges that the Byzantine guides did disappear during the night just prior to the Muslim ambush of the Germans.

In desperate need of provisions and especially short of water, the German crusaders reached the small Bathys River near Dorylaeum on October 25. The weary and thirsty troops broke ranks and scattered along the river to drink, and the knights dismounted and led their horses to the stream. At that moment "the whole Seldjuk army fell upon them . . . It was a massacre rather than a battle."[17] Most of the German crusaders were killed, and Conrad was wounded. The king did manage to rally a remnant of perhaps two thousand troops and retreat to Nicaea, where the Greeks confronted them with "exorbitant prices for food."[18] Then the French arrived and Conrad merged his small force with theirs, but he soon fell ill and was evacuated back to Constantinople.

The French had been greeted with an even more hostile reception from the Byzantines than had the Germans—so much so that they briefly entertained the idea of an attack on Constantinople. To avoid the dreadful route south that had helped defeat the Germans, Louis led his French army west toward the port of Ephesus with expectations that by remaining within Byzantine territory he would find the locals cooperative and receive supplies by sea from Emperor Manuel. But the locals were of no help, and no supplies came. Not surprisingly, the army became increasingly disorderly. To restore discipline to the march, Louis placed a Knight Templar in command of each unit of fifty. This paid big dividends when, despite the crusaders' being in Byzantine territory, the Seljuk Turks, allied though they were to the emperor, attacked just beyond Ephesus. Some historians suggest that the emperor had conspired with the Turks;[19] in any event, the Muslims were routed by the French.

At this point Louis turned his forces eastward and headed for the port of Adalia, where he had been promised they would be met by a Byzantine fleet that would ferry them to a landing just west of Antioch. Of course, the fleet sent by the emperor was much too small to accommodate more than a fraction of the army. Some recent historians take this as additional evidence that Manuel "connived at their [the crusaders'] destruction."[20]

After making the best preparations he could, Louis sent the bulk of his army overland to Antioch while he, his court, and as many troops as could be accommodated boarded the ships. The overland march was hopeless. When it began, the horses already were dying by the hundreds and everyone faced starvation. Muslims harassed them along the way, killing all stragglers and foragers. Only a handful of those who set out reached Antioch.

Having sailed safely to Antioch, Louis went to Jerusalem to fulfill his vow for a pilgrimage. Conrad had recovered from his wounds and illness and was already in the Holy City, as were leaders of forces newly arrived from the West. A council of war was held in Acre during which the visiting Europeans and Baldwin III, king of the crusader kingdom of Jerusalem, agreed to attack Damascus. (No representatives of Antioch, Edessa, or Tripoli attended.) The plan had an excellent strategic basis but was tactically ill advised. After an abortive attempt at a siege, and having suffered substantial losses, the Christian forces gave up the attempt.

The Second Crusade was over. Boarding ships provided by the Normans from Sicily, the French king and his entourage headed for home—only to suffer a narrow escape when attacked by a Byzantine fleet. (The Normans and the Byzantines still were fighting over possession of southern Italy.) Of course, this further inflamed Western antagonism toward the Byzantines.

INTERLUDE

In the wake of the Second Crusade, there was a burst of castle-building in the kingdoms, most of the structures financed, and their construction supervised, by the knightly orders. In 1166 there were at least fifty main castles and citadels (a fortification inside a city's walls) scattered across the kingdom of Jerusalem,[21] and hundreds of crusader castles and defensive towers have been mapped by modern archeologists.[22] They were very strongly built and based on European rather than Byzantine designs. Given that survey instruments did not exist, the castles are remarkably well sited, taking advantage of even slight elevations in the landscape. Many of them are within view of another castle, and it long was thought that signals were passed from one to the next. But there is little evidence of any signaling.[23] Nor were the castles and towers designed as a defensive "line": they were not a continuous wall.[24] Instead, the castles were used to house military forces who would sally forth to fight an enemy in the field or, when too outnumbered, would wait secure behind their walls until a field army arrived to attack the enemy.

The failure of the Second Crusade to attempt to regain Edessa, and the abortive siege of Damascus, cost Countess Beatrice the remainder of the county of Edessa in 1150, soon after her husband, Joscelin, was taken captive. Having successfully defended her fortress at Turbessel against Muslim attack but aware that she could not withstand another onslaught that was bound to come, she received a message from the Byzantine emperor Manuel. He offered not to march to her defense, but to buy her remaining territory. After consulting with rulers of the other kingdoms, Beatrice agreed, although both she and the others "were loath to hand over territory to a hated Greek."[25] Manuel sent many bags of gold to the countess, who then turned over her fortresses to Byzantine troops, who proceeded to lose the entire territory to the Muslims a year later.

The losses in the north did not reflect military weakness of the kingdom of Jerusalem. Hence, in January 1153 King Baldwin III of Jerusalem led a powerful army south against the Egyptian stronghold of Ascalon. Known as the Bride of Syria, the city had long sheltered Muslim raiders who preyed upon pilgrims and Christian villages. Marching against Ascalon, Baldwin was accompanied by the Grand Masters of both the Templars and the Hospitallers and their best knights and sergeants. A long siege ensued. Then, in July, the Templars forced a breach in the wall. As too often happened, the Templars then crossed the line separating bravery from foolhardiness and, despite numbering only forty knights, refused reinforcements while they entered the city. When the Muslim defenders realized how few Templars were attacking them, they rallied, killed them all, secured the breach, and dangled the Templars' corpses from the city walls.

But by mid-August the Muslims realized they could not hold out much longer. A surrender agreement was reached allowing all inhabitants of the city to leave in safety with all their movable goods—which they did. Lordship of the city was given to Baldwin's brother, the Count of Jaffa, and the great mosque was consecrated as the Cathedral of Saint Paul. Baldwin III died in 1162 at age thirty-three; it was widely but probably erroneously believed that he had been poisoned by a Syrian physician. He was succeeded by his brother Amalric, Count of Jaffa and Ascalon.

Meanwhile, in Egypt the decadent Fatimid Caliphate had fallen apart. Nasr, the son of the vizier Abbas, murdered the caliph, and Abbas then murdered the caliph's brothers and placed a five-year-old boy on the throne. When the army turned against them, father and son were forced to flee north, only to encounter Templars, who routed their escort—during which action Abbas was killed and Nasr was captured. The Templars sold Nasr back to the caliph's court in Cairo for the huge sum of sixty thousand dinars, whereupon "the late Caliph's four widows personally mutilated him."[26] Then he was hanged above the main city gate, and his remains dangled there for two years. In 1160 the boy caliph died and was succeeded by his nine-year-old cousin, and the constant court intrigues continued.

Seeing this confusion as an opportunity to secure his southern flank, in 1163 Amalric led an army into Egypt. He took Cairo and Alexandria but eventually became alarmed by troubles up north, particularly a threat to Tripoli, and signed a treaty designating that the Egyptians pay him an annual tribute of one hundred thousand pieces of gold. In 1167, Amalric led his army back into Egypt and laid siege to Alexandria. Again the Egyptians negotiated and agreed to a huge tribute payment, and again Amalric returned to

Jerusalem. But the next year he attacked again, supported by the Knights Hospitallers. The Knights Templars, however, refused to march with him, saying Amalric's cause had nothing to do with their mission. In October, Amalric's army seized Bilbeis, just north of Cairo, and massacred or enslaved the inhabitants. This time the Egyptians paid him 2 million pieces of gold to leave. In 1169 Amalric came again, supported by a Byzantine fleet, and laid siege to Damietta, at the very mouth of the Nile. The siege was marred by conflict between Amalric and the Byzantines, which led to a truce between the Christian forces and the new sultan of Egypt, Salah ad-Din, known in the West as Saladin.

SALADIN AND THE FALL OF JERUSALEM

Saladin was a Kurd, the nephew of Shirkuh, who conquered Egypt in 1169 for the Fatimid ruler of Syria, Nur ad-Din, who campaigned many times against the crusader kingdoms. As a reward, Shirkuh was appointed vizier of Egypt, but he died after only two months in office, and Saladin succeeded him. Because Saladin was not yet quite thirty, his promotion did not sit well with many older veterans. But he smoothed over their discontents and soon was the real ruler of Egypt, although he remained careful to preserve the appearance of Nur ad-Din's rule, even while he obviously went his own way. For example, in 1171 he suppressed the Egyptian Fatimids and united Egypt with the Abbasid Caliphate. In addition, Saladin refused to join Nur ad-Din in two invasions of the kingdom of Jerusalem—one in 1171 and a second in 1173, both of which were unsuccessful. Eventually Nur ad-Din realized he had an enemy in Egypt and in 1174 began assembling an army to march against Saladin. However, he developed an abscess and died at age fifty-nine. Although Nur ad-Din's son was recognized as the legitimate heir to the throne, Saladin quickly married Nur ad-Din's forty-five-year-old widow[27] and seized the throne. Thus were Syria and Egypt brought under a single rule.

Although the continuing success of crusader forces against larger Muslim armies was remarkable, it also was contingent to some extent on Muslim disunity—there being obvious limits to the numerical odds that the Christians could overcome. Had the kingdoms been surrounded by a united enemy, not only would they have faced far larger invading armies, but they could have been threatened from all three land sides at once. When Saladin became sultan of Egypt, that eventually became his strategy.

Saladin's chances of success were greatly increased by the incompetent leadership of Emperor Manuel, which brought disaster to the Byzantine army in 1176 when he led an expedition against Sultan Kilij Arslan's capital of Iconium (Konya). Pursuing his Turkish enemies into a mountain pass at Myriokephalon, the emperor allowed his troops to get strung out along a narrow road. The Turks had hidden large forces above the road and suddenly attacked downhill, whereupon Manuel's courage failed and he fled. When his troops broke ranks and tried to flee as well, the whole army was destroyed. "It would take many years to rebuild it; and indeed it was never rebuilt. There were enough troops left to defend the frontiers . . . But nevermore would the Emperor be able to march into Syria . . . Nor was anything left of his prestige."[28] Thus, Muslims facing the crusader kingdoms from the north no longer need worry about a threat to their rear from Constantinople. Worse yet, the Byzantines proceeded to conspire with Saladin against the kingdoms, as will be seen.

Meanwhile, following the death of Amalric in 1174 at the age of thirty-eight, his thirteen-year-old son was crowned as Baldwin IV, king of Jerusalem. Two years later he came of age and took control. Despite suffering from leprosy since boyhood, which soon made him unable to mount his horse unaided and afflicted him with rapidly failing sight, Baldwin lived far longer than expected and, in 1177, at Montgisard, led his far smaller army to a brilliant and bloody victory over a large Egyptian army led by Saladin, that being the latter's first attack on the Christians. While Baldwin IV lived (he died in 1185), Saladin's attempts against the kingdom continued to fail: he launched major efforts in 1183 and 1184.[29]

Initially, Saladin had much better luck against his Muslim neighbors. Soon after coming to power in Egypt, he seized the throne of Syria, taking Damascus in 1174. Later he conquered the former province of Edessa by taking Aleppo in 1183 and Mayyafariqin in 1185. The Christian kingdoms were now surrounded on three sides, with their backs to the Mediterranean Sea. This situation was noted at length by Archbishop William of Tyre in his *History of Deeds Done Beyond the Sea,* written before Saladin began his attacks on the kingdoms: "In former times almost every [Muslim] city had its own ruler . . . not dependent on one another . . . who feared their own allies not less than the Christians [and] could not or would not readily unite to repulse the common danger or arm themselves for our destruction. But now . . . all the kingdoms adjacent to us have been brought under the power of one man."[30]

Also in 1185, the Byzantine emperor initiated negotiations with Saladin, and after several years of talks and frequent exchanges of huge gifts, they signed a treaty to join forces against Western Christians in the Holy Land and any new Crusades.

Even so, the Christians were not in dire straits, still having a sizable field army of well-trained, well-armed troops, including Knights Templars and Hospitallers—altogether numbering perhaps twelve hundred knights and twenty thousand infantry. Given the qualitative differences, they should not have felt especially threatened when, in 1187, Saladin gathered an army of about thirty thousand in Syria to come against them.

In an effort to draw the Christians into battle at their disadvantage, Saladin sent some of his troops to attack the city of Tiberias.

As expected, the outmanned residents withdrew into the city's citadel, having dispatched messengers begging for help. Initially, the Christian leaders met in conference and decided against marching to the relief of Tiberias. But several sought out King Guy of Jerusalem later and convinced him to reverse that decision. So the next morning the Christian army began to march—constantly exposed to harassing strikes against its flanks and rear guard. It was an arid terrain, and soon the troops, and especially the horses, were suffering from thirst. By the next morning the suffering was acute, and the army headed for the nearest source of water at Hattin; Saladin's main army was between them and Lake Tiberius, from which the Muslims had plentiful water.

Then, as the sun rose and with the wind at their backs, Saladin's forces set fire to large collections of brush, and the smoke made it difficult for the Christians to keep track of their units. Soon the infantry began to break their formations and head for water, leaving the cavalry on their own. At this auspicious moment, Saladin's troops charged against the disorganized Christians, and a brutal battle ensued. Several times thundering charges by the Christian knights nearly turned the tide, but eventually chaos reigned and the slaughter began. Thousands died in battle, and all of the Templars and Hospitallers taken captive were beheaded; the other captives were enslaved.

With the crusader field army destroyed, the kingdoms were at Saladin's mercy and were quickly overrun. Most of the cities and fortresses surrendered without a fight, having few defenders. Jaffa did hold out and had to be taken by storm, which resulted in the entire population of survivors being sold into slavery. Within two months there remained only Tyre, Antioch, Tripoli, "a few isolated castles[,] and the Holy City of Jerusalem."[31]

Jerusalem was crowded with refugees from other cities already fallen to the Muslims: "[f]or every man there were fifty women and children."[32] There were only two knights in Jerusalem. So, arms were distributed to every able-bodied man—although most knew little or nothing about how to use them. In late September, Saladin's army arrived and surrounded the city. After several days of preparation the Muslims attacked the walls and met furious resistance from the tiny band of untrained defenders. Repeated attacks brought repeated failures, but after five days a breach had been made in the wall. Some of the Christian fighters wanted to charge out through the breach and fight to the death. But cooler heads prevailed, noting that only by surrender could they prevent all the women and children from becoming slaves. So they asked Saladin for surrender terms. He demanded a ransom of ten gold pieces for each man to be spared (with two women or ten children counted as one man). As for the poor, Saladin agreed to free seven thousand of them in return for thirty thousand besants.[33] That left thousands without hope. If, in the end, there was no massacre, about half of the city's Latin Christian residents were marched away to the slave markets.

There is an aspect of the fall of Jerusalem that is very seldom mentioned by historians. The Greek residents of the city, fully aware that an alliance was being formed between the Byzantine emperor and Saladin, "were ready to betray the city" by opening the gates. In return for their support, Saladin had all the Christian churches in the Holy Land converted from the Latin to the Greek Orthodox rite, in keeping with the treaty he signed in 1189 with Emperor Isaac.[34]

"GLORIFYING" SALADIN

As Robert Irwin pointed out, "In Britain, there ha[s] been a long tradition of disparaging the Crusaders as barbaric and bigoted warmongers and of praising the Saracens as paladins of chivalry.

Indeed, it is widely believed that chivalry originated in the Muslim East. The most perfect example of Muslim chivalry was, of course, the twelfth-century Ayyubid Sultan Saladin."[35]

This view of the chivalrous Saladin is rampant among historians. In his esteemed study *The Kingdom of the Crusaders*, Dana Carleton Munro put it this way: "When we contrast with this [the crusader conquest of Jerusalem] the conduct of Saladin when he captured Jerusalem from the Christians in 1187, we have a striking illustration of the difference between the two civilizations and realize what the Christians might learn from contact with the Saracens in the Holy Land."[36] (Notice the present tense.) In similar fashion, the distinguished Samuel Hugh Moffett noted that Saladin "was unusually merciful for his time. He allowed the Crusaders, who had entered it [Jerusalem] in a bloodbath, to leave the city in peace."[37] It was in this same spirit that, in 1898, Germany's Kaiser Wilhelm visited Damascus and placed a bronze laurel wreath on Saladin's tomb. The wreath was inscribed to "the Hero Sultan Saladin . . . From one great emperor to another."[38]

Admiration for Saladin is not a recent invention. Since the Enlightenment, Saladin has "bizarrely" been portrayed "as a rational and civilized figure in juxtaposition to credulous barbaric crusaders."[39] Even Edward Gibbon, writing in 1788, noted, "Of some writers it is a favourite and invidious theme to compare the humanity of Saladin with the massacre of the first crusade . . . but we should not forget that the Christians offered to capitulate, and that the Mahometans of Jerusalem sustained the last extremities of an assault and storm."[40] There we have it, one of the primary rules of warfare at that time: cities were spared if they did not force their opponents to take them by storm; they were massacred as an object lesson to other cities if they had to be stormed, since this usually inflicted heavy casualties on the attackers. This rule did not require cities to surrender quickly: long sieges were acceptable, but only

until the attackers had completed all of the preparations needed
to storm the walls. Of course, cities often did not surrender at this
point because they believed the attack could be defeated.

Not only have Saladin's modern fans ignored this rule of war;
they have carefully ignored the fact, acknowledged by Muslim writers, that Jerusalem was an exception to Saladin's usual butchery of
his enemies. Saladin had looked forward to massacring the Christians in Jerusalem, but he offered about half of them a safe conduct in exchange for their surrender of Jerusalem without further
resistance. In most other instances Saladin was quite unchivalrous.
Following the Battle of Hattin, for example, he personally partici-
pated in butchering some of the captured Knights Templars and
Hospitallers and then sat back and enjoyed watching the execution
of the rest of them. As told by Saladin's secretary, Imad ed-Din:
"He [Saladin] ordered that they should be beheaded, choosing to
have them dead rather than in prison. With him was a whole band
of scholars and Sufis and a certain number of devout men and ascetics; each begged to be allowed to kill one of them, and drew his
sword and rolled back his sleeve. Saladin, his face joyful, was sit-
ting on his dais; the unbelievers showed black despair."[41] It seems
fitting that during one of his amazing World War I adventures
leading irregular Arab forces against the Turks, T. E. Lawrence
"liberated" the kaiser's bronze wreath from Saladin's tomb, and it
now resides in the Imperial War Museum in London.

A WASTED VICTORY

Saladin blundered when he failed to move quickly to fully occupy
the kingdoms in the wake of the catastrophic crusader losses at
Hattin. He seems to have assumed there was no need to hurry.
After all, the Christian cities were desperately short of armed defenders: they had been stripped to form their now-defeated army.

But the cities were strongly fortified, and Saladin's mostly cavalry forces "had no taste for attacking fortifications."[42] In addition, loaded down with booty, much of Saladin's army had drifted away. Consequently, Saladin not only moved rather slowly but found it in his interest "to buy" the surrender of cities "by allowing the inhabitants to go free."[43]

But where could they go? Of course, the Muslim residents of the surrendered cities had no need to go anywhere, and many of the Greek Christians were allowed to stay as well; Saladin was on the verge of signing a treaty with Emperor Isaac. But the European Christians had no choice but to flock to their last unconquered cities: Antioch, Tyre, and Tripoli.

The arrival of so many refugees strained the food supplies of these enclaves, especially at Tyre, where the majority of noble refugees gathered, but they also added substantial numbers of defenders—some survivors from Hattin, many fighting men who had formed the small garrisons left behind in the castles and cities when the rest marched to Hattin, and large numbers of able-bodied males who could be armed. Moreover, since the Christian enclaves were centered on port cities, they could be supplied and reinforced by sea. And they were.

Perhaps no single event had as much impact on saving the crusader kingdoms as did the arrival at Tyre of a ship carrying Conrad of Montferrat. Conrad had been in Constantinople on his way to join his father, William V, the Marquess of Montferrat, who had gone to the Holy Land in 1183 and taken command of the major castle of Saint Elias, just north of the Dead Sea. When Conrad learned of Saladin's latest invasion, he immediately set sail for Acre with a small band of knights. As his ship entered the harbor, the bells that always announced the arrival of a ship did not ring, so Conrad became suspicious and did not anchor. When a harbor official came out in a boat to see who they were, Conrad learned that the city had fallen to Saladin, and he promptly sailed north to Tyre.[44]

Conrad arrived in Tyre to discover that its leaders were considering surrender. But they took heart at the arrival of Conrad and his companions and placed him in command to prepare the city for a defiant defense. Eventually, Saladin arrived and began a siege of the city. But the walls were stout and the defenders were obviously well armed and determined, and the Muslims could not prevent traffic in and out of Tyre's harbor. So Saladin soon took his army elsewhere in search of easier pickings. But in November, finally having fully realized the importance of this Christian seaport, Saladin returned to Tyre, this time with two new plans for conquest. First of all, he brought with him Conrad's father, who, although quite elderly, had fought at Hattin and been taken captive. Marching the old man out into full view from the walls of Tyre, Saladin had a crier inform Conrad that his father would be killed unless he surrendered the city. According to Arab sources, Conrad was "a devil"[45] who shouted back that his father had lived long enough. Beaming with pride at his son's steadfastness, William V was marched away and eventually released.[46]

Saladin's second plan to take Tyre was far more dangerous to the city. For the past decade, Saladin had been building an Egyptian navy.[47] It had recently proved its worth in skirmishes with several small fleets trading with the kingdoms. Now he sent ten of his galleys to blockade Tyre's harbor, setting up an effective siege. Conrad met this threat by sending Tyre's galleys to launch a dawn attack on Saladin's blockaders. Finding the Muslim crews asleep and without lookouts, the attackers met with total success: five Egyptian galleys were captured, and the other five went aground when, with Christian galleys in close pursuit, their crews jumped overboard.[48] While this naval debacle was under way, Saladin massed his troops and attacked the city, assuming that at that moment Conrad's attention would be on the harbor. But when Saladin's troops approached, Conrad led his knights charging out of the gates and surprised and routed Saladin's entire army. Setting fire to his siege engines to keep them out of Christian hands, Saladin marched away.

Tyre was safe. Soon thereafter a large Norman fleet from Sicily arrived to resupply and greatly reinforce Tripoli and Antioch. It would be another century before the Muslims could again push the crusaders to the water's edge.

Conrad's stunning victories over Saladin made him famous all over Europe and would eventually result in his selection as king of Jerusalem. Meanwhile, he dispatched emissaries to Europe to urge another Crusade. The delegation was headed by Joscius, the new archbishop of Tyre. (Joscius had replaced the historian William of Tyre.) In January 1189 the archbishop gained an audience with King Henry II of England and King Philip II of France, who were meeting to discuss their territorial disputes. "So eloquent was his appeal for aid for the Holy Land that both kings, the count of Flanders, and many other lords took the cross, and agreed to begin preparations for a new crusade."[49] Meanwhile, the new pope, Clement III, managed to convince Germany's Holy Roman Emperor, Frederick Barbarossa, to take the cross once more. (Frederick had accompanied his uncle Conrad III on the Second Crusade.)

THE THIRD CRUSADE

The new Crusade began in disjointed fashion. The English and the French had first to settle several bitter disputes. Then Henry II died and his son Richard (already known as the Lionhearted) was crowned king of England. Richard had also taken the cross, so the English commitment to the Crusade remained. But because the English crown still had huge holdings in France (the entire Atlantic coast was theirs), he and Philip II had much to negotiate before they could head east. Meanwhile, Frederick Barbarossa began marching to the Holy Land.

FREDERICK'S CAMPAIGN

On May 11, 1189—twenty-three months after the Battle of Hattin—the emperor Frederick led his army out of Regensburg (Ratisbon) into Hungary and then through Serbia and on toward Constantinople. As always, it is very difficult to say how many troops Frederick had enlisted, but all sources agree that it was a large number. Many historians have settled on one hundred thousand,[50] but that seems rather high. More likely is the estimate that Frederick had assembled three thousand knights,[51] and it was usual for there to be about five or six times as many infantry as knights, which would have amounted to around twenty thousand first-line fighting men. Of course, there must have been the usual contingents of camp followers and commoners, so there might have been one hundred thousand people on the march. Whatever the actual number, it was sufficient so that news of the Germans marching toward him caused Saladin considerable worry, and he exerted himself in trying to raise an army able to meet them. In addition, Saladin had a Byzantine card to play.

After several years of negotiations and the exchange of piles of expensive gifts, in 1189 the Byzantine emperor Isaac entered into a mutual defense treaty with Saladin, committing the Byzantine army against all Western forces attempting to reach the Holy Land. Consequently, when in advance of his march to the Holy Land Emperor Frederick sent the bishop of Münster and other distinguished Germans to the Byzantine court to arrange passage, Isaac imprisoned them and gave their horses and equipment to Saladin's representatives.[52] Then, contrary to the usual failure of the Byzantines to live up to their agreements when it might prove costly to do so, when Frederick's army crossed into Byzantine territory, Isaac caused irregular forces to harass him along the way and then dispatched his main army to stop the Germans at Philippopolis. But Frederick's crusaders simply swept the Byzantines aside, inflicting immense casualties. Then, in order to force the release of the bishop and his retinue, Frederick devastated a substantial area in Thrace as he moved toward Constantinople.

At this point, Isaac wrote an astonishing letter to Saladin claiming to have rendered Frederick's forces harmless: "[T]hey have lost a great number of soldiers, and it was with great difficulty that they escaped my brave troops. They were so exhausted that they cannot reach your dominions; and even if they should succeed in reaching them, they could be of no assistance to their fellows, nor could they inflict any injury on your excellency."[53] Nevertheless, Isaac wished Saladin to send him troops. None came.

Meanwhile, Frederick's powerful forces marched onward, seized Adrianople, and "even planned a siege of Constantinople."[54] So, in February 1190, Emperor Isaac surrendered and signed the Treaty of Adrianople, which ceded Frederick free passage and supplies, and gave him distinguished hostages to ensure that the treaty was fulfilled.

During this time, several Greek Orthodox bishops "who favored Saladin out of hatred for [Latin Christians]"[55] kept him abreast of what really was going on—of Frederick's easy passage through Byzantium and of his successful storming of the Muslim-held fortress city of Iconium (Konya) with only slight losses. Moving on toward Antioch with no substantial forces in his way, Frederick fell from his horse while fording the Saleph River and drowned. Frederick's death ended the German Crusade. He had been adored and trusted by all his subordinates, and although he was replaced by his son Frederick, the Duke of Swabia, the army was devastated by the emperor's death. Over the next several days huge numbers simply turned around and went home. Ten days later, when young Frederick reached Antioch, his army may have shrunk to five thousand effectives, and when he reached the coastal area of the kingdom of Jerusalem he had only about three hundred knights.[56] Saladin breathed a great sigh of relief.[57]

A NAVAL CRUSADE

Meanwhile, Richard the Lionhearted and Philip Augustus of France were gathering their forces, raising huge sums to meet the costs of crusading, and getting ready to set out. But they had no intentions of following the overland route through Byzantium. They planned to sail to the Holy Land, taking full advantage of Saladin's failure to capture all of the Christian ports.

But long before Richard and Philip Augustus embarked, the Christian cause was greatly strengthened by the arrival of "a series of crusading fleets [from] the ports of northwestern Europe. They bore Danes, Frisians, North Germans, Flemings, English, Bretons, and men of Northern France."[58] It is impossible to know how many new crusaders were involved, but "there is no doubt that by New Year 1190 hundreds of Christian ships of all types were either beached or anchored around [Acre]."[59] These newcomers joined King Guy of Jerusalem in laying siege to the city. Saladin met this threat by bringing up his army, and, by surrounding the area, he placed the Christian siege under siege.

A stalemate ensued because Saladin could not persuade his troops to attack the crusader ranks. In the restricted ground on which the city of Acre stood, the Muslims could not use their hit-and-run tactics and scatter to safety if charged by heavy cavalry. Nor were they willing to attack the ranks of solid infantry, for "the crossbows of the crusaders outranged their bows, and the solid line of spears formed an almost impossible obstacle."[60] With the Christians being resupplied by sea, a standoff began. In an effort to perfect his siege, Saladin placed a fleet of fifty galleys in the harbor at Acre to prevent resupplies from coming in. This seems not to have been adequate, and so in June 1190 he sent the remainder of his new Egyptian navy to fight its way into the harbor at Acre.[61] It is not clear that the Christians resisted this move since it was greatly to their benefit. For one thing, this allowed the Christian fleets uncontested passage up and down the coast. More important, powerful crusader fleets soon blockaded the Acre harbor, trapping Saladin's entire navy.

In March 1191, Philip Augustus and his French flotilla arrived at Tyre and from there went south and joined the siege of Acre. Meanwhile, Richard stopped in Cyprus, where his treasure ship had gone aground during a storm. This island was under the control of a Byzantine rebel, Isaac Comnenus, who had seized the English treasure and held the crew and troops aboard, although he released the civilian passengers, including Richard's new fiancée, Berengaria of Navarre. Initially, Isaac also agreed to return both treasure and troops. Then, thinking he was secure in his great fortress at Famagusta, he broke his word and issued orders for Richard to leave the island. Enraged, Richard and his English forces quickly overran the island, much to the pleasure of the local population; apparently Isaac was a tyrant, given to raping virgins and torturing rich citizens. He surrendered without a fight when Richard promised not to put him into irons; Richard "kept" his word by locking him up in silver chains. After his release in 1194, Isaac returned to Constantinople, where he was poisoned in 1195.

The conquest of Cyprus gave the crusaders an extremely important naval base from which they could support and supply the kingdoms so long as they held any port cities. From Cyprus, Richard sailed his army to join the siege at Acre, arriving in June. Soon after the English landed, the crusaders were further reinforced by a fleet from Genoa. These new forces quickly swept aside the encircling outer Muslim lines and advanced to the gates of the city. The Muslim garrison surrendered—without Saladin's permission. Saladin's entire navy surrendered as well; many crews simply jumped overboard and swam ashore.

With Acre secure, it was time to begin the recovery of the kingdoms, but without the king of France. At this moment Philip Augustus withdrew and went home. He had long been very ill with dysentery, but the main reason he left was to settle urgent political disputes that had arisen back in France. However, Philip did leave behind several thousand troops, and the funds to pay them.

Now the Third Crusade came down to a match between Richard the Lionhearted and Saladin.

RICHARD AND SALADIN

Richard was a complex character: "As a soldier he was little short of mad, incredibly reckless and foolhardy, but as a commander he was intelligent, cautious, and calculating. He would risk his own life with complete nonchalance, but nothing could persuade him to endanger his troops more than was absolutely necessary."[62] Troops adore such a commander.

In August 1191, Richard organized his crusader army and began to march south from Acre along the coast in the direction of Jerusalem. His force consisted of about four thousand knights, fourteen thousand infantry, and two thousand Turcopoles—light infantry, most of them hired locally. The infantry included a substantial number of crossbow teams. Because of the summer heat, the crusaders marched only during the mornings, and Richard was careful to situate his camps where there was adequate water; he was not about to be forced to fight at a disadvantage simply because of thirst. The fleet followed the army down the coast, resupplying them so they were independent of local sources. The fleet also took aboard those wounded by Saladin's hit-and-run mounted archers, who lurked wherever there was cover.

Unfortunately for the Muslims, their constant harassment failed to goad the crusaders into breaking their solid formation— the heavy cavalry on the ocean side shielded by an impregnable column of infantry and crossbow teams. So, reluctantly, and at the urging of his emirs who still basked in the glow of Hattin, Saladin decided to risk a pitched battle. He chose a spot where his army's northern flank was protected by the forest of Arsuf (or Arsur), with wooded hills to the south. On September 7, 1191, the Muslims attacked, using their standard tactic of rush in and then retreat, hoping to get the crusaders to break ranks and pursue them. But with Richard riding up and down the formation, the crusaders stood firm[63] while their "crossbowmen took a heavy toll."[64] At this point, the Muslims launched a more determined attack. Once they were committed, the crusader heavy cavalry passed through the ranks of the infantry and launched a massive charge against Saladin's forces. They not only inflicted heavy losses but did not scatter in pursuit of the enemy—as Christian heavy cavalry had so often done in the past. Instead, Richard was able to keep the knights under control and lead them back to form up again. When the Muslims attacked again, they were slammed by another cavalry charge. And then another. Having suffered huge losses—including more than thirty emirs—Saladin's forces fled the field.

"But more important . . . Saladin's troops became convinced that they could not win in the open field, and lost all interest in attempting pitched battles. The battle of Arsuf was the last [Muslim] attempt to destroy king Richard's host."[65] In fact Saladin's army became increasingly reluctant to face crusaders under any circumstances. A year after their defeat at Arsuf, a substantial army sent by Saladin to recapture Jaffa confronted Richard and a tiny force of fifty knights (only six of them mounted) and several hundred crossbowmen. Although they very greatly outnumbered Richard's force, the Muslims did not prevail—partly from unwillingness to press their attack.[66] Even so, they suffered terrible losses. This was the last significant engagement of the Third Crusade; both sides were more than ready for diplomacy.

It often is suggested that because Richard failed to reconquer Jerusalem, Saladin prevailed in denying the West that most important measure of the success of the Third Crusade. In truth, Richard made no attempt to retake the Holy City, and Saladin held it only by default. Richard knew that Jerusalem was of immense symbolic importance in Europe but recognized that it was a military liability—that to protect Jerusalem from Muslim attacks would require a large garrison and a safe corridor to the sea. But once his army went home, the kingdom of Jerusalem would lack the resources needed to meet either requirement. Better that the kingdom have secure borders that maximized the effectiveness of its armed forces than that Jerusalem itself be returned briefly to Christian control. Instead, Richard included a clause in the Treaty of Ramla he signed with Saladin in 1192 that allowed unarmed Christian pilgrims access to the city.

Saladin may have signed that agreement in good faith, but he died a year later, at age fifty-five. Only six years after Saladin's death, Richard died from a crossbow wound suffered while putting down a revolt in part of his French territory. He was forty-one.

Unfortunately, few back in Europe saw the inevitability and the wisdom in Richard's unwillingness to retake Jerusalem. Thus, a year before Richard died, Pope Innocent III had begun to call for a new Crusade.

THE FOURTH CRUSADE

Because the Fourth Crusade culminated in the crusaders' sacking Constantinople, it has long served as a primary "proof" that the Crusades were a shameful episode in the greedy history of the West. Only six years after the world had learned of the Nazi death camps and the extent of the Holocaust, the distinguished Cambridge historian Steven Runciman could write: "There was never a greater crime against humanity than the Fourth Crusade."[67] Runciman certainly knew that many other cities of this era not only had been sacked but had had their populations massacred to the last resident, compared with probably fewer than two thousand deaths[68] during the crusader sack of Constantinople, a city of about 150,000.[69] So why this uniquely extreme condemnation? Ah, but the others were just dreary medieval cities; this was *the* "great city . . . filled with works of art that had survived from ancient Greece and with the masterpieces of its own exquisite craftsmen."[70] Indeed, admiration for the sophisticated city is a standard theme in the outrage against the Fourth Crusade. As Speros Vryonis put it, "The Latin soldiery subjected the greatest city in Europe to an indescribable sack . . . Constantinople had become a veritable museum of ancient and Byzantine art."[71] Or, in the words of Will Durant, the crusaders "now—in Easter week—subjected the rich city to such spoliation as Rome had never suffered from Vandals or Goths."[72] There even is a whole school of scholars who, in addition to lamenting the damage to the city, claim that the Fourth Crusade was from the start nothing but a diabolical Venetian plot to eliminate Byzantine commercial competition.[73]

These bitter condemnations of the Fourth Crusade led Pope John Paul II, in 2001, to apologize to the Greek Orthodox Church: "It is tragic that the assailants, who set out to secure free access for

Christians in the Holy Land, turned against their brothers in the faith. That they were Latin Christians fills Catholics with deep regret."[74]

Nothing here about the prior sacks of the city by Byzantines themselves during political coups: in 1081 Alexius Comnenus "allowed his foreign mercenaries to plunder the capital for three days."[75] Nor is there a word to acknowledge the centuries of Orthodox brutalities against Latin Christians: in 1182 the emperor incited mobs to attack all Western residents of Constantinople, during which "[t]housands, including women, children, and the aged, were massacred"[76]—many more deaths than are thought to have occurred during the city's sack by the crusaders.[77] Not a word about the instances of Byzantine treachery that occurred during each of the first three Crusades and that cost tens of thousands of crusaders their lives. Surely it is not surprising that these many acts of betrayal built up substantial animosity toward Byzantium. Then, in 1204, those who had journeyed east as members of the Fourth Crusade also were deceived by a Byzantine emperor who, after the crusaders helped restore him to the throne, broke his glittering promises and launched fire ships against the crusader fleet. Meanwhile, the Latin residents of Constantinople fled the city in fear of their lives—recalling the massacre of 1182—and took refuge in the crusader camp. This left the crusaders "without food or money,"[78] stranded on a hostile shore. That's when they attacked Constantinople.

Now for the details.

Pope Innocent's initial call for the new Crusade was ignored. The Germans were on the outs with Rome, while the French and English were at war again. But just as the lethargic response to the Second Crusade was overcome by the efforts of Saint Bernard of Clairvaux, the Fourth Crusade was in response to the exertions of Fulk of Neuilly—a French cleric who accepted the pope's request to preach a new Crusade. The climax came during a tournament held by Count Thibaut of Champagne in 1199. In the midst of the usual dangers and injuries involved in jousting matches, concerns over the Muslim occupation of Jerusalem arose, and Count Thibaut ended up leading a group of his friends and relatives in taking the cross.[79] From there, enthusiasm for a new Crusade spread and the planning began.

Once again it was agreed that the crusaders would go east by sea, but with a brilliant change in destination. Why fight peripheral battles in the Holy Land when Egypt was the aggressive power? So the original plan was to sail an irresistible army to the mouth of the Nile and put the enemy out of business for good. It made a great deal of sense.

Of course, those organizing the new Crusade had no navy. So they sent a delegation to Venice, then the primary naval power in the Mediterranean. The Venetians agreed to transport forty-five hundred knights with their horses, nine thousand squires, and twenty thousand infantry, plus food for nine months and an escort of fifty fighting galleys for the price of ninety-one thousand marks.[80] To meet this enormous obligation the Venetians had to suspend nearly all of their foreign trade and devote a year to the rapid construction of boats.

In June 1202 the promised Venetian fleet was ready. Unfortunately, the crusaders had gathered only about a third of the force they had planned on. And since they were expecting to pay the Venetians by charging each crusader for his passage, the shortfall in numbers left them about thirty-one thousand marks short of the sum promised to the Venetians, even after the leaders borrowed all they could from moneylenders.[81] At this point the doge of Venice offered a solution.

Doge Enrico Dandolo was well into his eighties and blind, but he remained a brilliant, inspirational, and extremely energetic leader.[82] What he proposed was that the Venetians join the Crusade and that payment of the remaining balance be postponed. In return, on their way to Egypt the flotilla would stop and conquer Zara (or Zadar), a city on the Dalmatian coast across the Adriatic Sea from Venice, which had recently rebelled against Venetian rule.

So, on October 1, 1202, the crusader fleet of more than two hundred ships, including sixty war galleys, left Venice with about fifteen thousand fighting men and thousands of horses aboard, bound for Zara.[83] In late November, Zara surrendered without resistance, and soon thereafter the crusader fleet sailed on south to Corfu to winter.

At this point an exiled Byzantine prince, Alexius, the son of deposed emperor Isaac II and himself a claimant to the throne, made the crusaders a remarkable proposal. In return for their aid in recovering the throne, Alexius would pay them two hundred thousand silver marks, supply all provisions for their expedition against Egypt, reinforce the expedition with ten thousand Byzantine troops, submit the Greek Church to Rome, and then permanently station five hundred knights to augment the forces of the Christian kingdoms in the Holy Land.[84] Not only was the offer of immense, immediate benefit; perhaps more important, it proposed a longed-for solution to the problem of sustaining the kingdoms. It always had been obvious that the kingdoms were in permanent jeopardy so long as their security was dependent on Europe. But if the primary responsibility could be shifted to Byzantium, help would be much closer and far more dependable—especially if threats from Egypt were eliminated. And so the fleet rounded Greece and set sail for Constantinople.

On July 5, 1203, the crusader fleet landed at Galata, across from Constantinople, and the Venetians broke the chain blocking the entrance to the Golden Horn and then sailed into the city's harbor. The current Byzantine emperor had so utterly neglected Constantinople's defense that the few rotting galleys that the Greeks could send against the Venetians were sunk in moments. Then, on July 17 came the attack on the city. With the blind old doge waving the banner of Saint Mark in the lead galley and "shouting at his forces,"[85] some Venetians landed. When his forces seemed hesitant to scale the walls, the doge demanded to be set ashore, and, as "Dandolo had calculated, [the men] were shamed by the old man's bravery; they could not abandon their venerable leader and rushed to join him."[86] The walls were scaled, gates were forced, and the Venetians occupied a portion of the city. Meanwhile, the crusader army marched toward the city from the other side. When the Greeks marched out a huge army to confront them, the crusaders formed solid ranks and awaited their attack. None came; the Greeks decided to withdraw instead. That night the emperor deserted, whereupon the Byzantines opened the remaining city gates and accepted Alexius IV as their new emperor. In response, the crusaders marched out of the city and camped across the Golden Horn at Pera.

At first things went well. Although he found little money in the treasury, Alexius IV began to pay installments on his debt of two hundred thousand marks. But he faced unflinching hostility from his subjects; the priests and upper classes hated Latins and held them in contempt. As tensions grew, "the remaining resident Latins," to escape what seemed to be an impending massacre, "took their families and as much as they could of their property and crossed the harbor to join the crusaders."[87] Shortly thereafter, Emperor Alexius shifted with the political wind and ceased making payments on his debt. War became imminent.

Twice the Greeks sent fire ships against the Venetian fleet; the formula for Greek fire seems already to have been lost. The attacks failed. Meanwhile, inside the city a palace coup placed another member of the royal family—known as Mourtzouphlus because he had bushy eyebrows that met—on the throne. He strangled

Alexius IV with a bowstring and murdered other possible royal claimants. The new emperor immediately began to strengthen the defenses and sent troops to cut off all supplies to the crusaders.

As the esteemed French historian Jean Richard explained, "The situation of the crusaders became impossible . . . [they] were without food or money, far from the theatre of operations they wished to reach. The Venetians were no better placed; they too had counted on the subsidies promised by Alexius IV."[88]

So the leaders gathered and evaluated the possibilities. Their diversion to put a new emperor favorable to the West on the Byzantine throne had been costly in time, money, and lives. Whatever the state of the emperor's treasury, Constantinople was bursting with immense wealth. They decided to sack the city, and an agreement was reached as to how the booty would be gathered up and divided. Unfortunately, the group also decided to put the throne of Byzantium firmly in Western hands by instituting a new dynasty.

The crusader plan was to assault the walls and towers from flying bridges extended from the masts of the largest transport boats, meanwhile landing additional troops and cavalry on the shore. On April 9 the attack began and eventually failed—partly because an unfavorable wind forced the fleet offshore. On April 12, with a strong wind at their back, the Venetians were able to grapple their flying bridges to some of the towers, crusaders drove the defenders from that section of the wall, and some descended and broke down gates from inside. Mounted knights rode into the city. By nightfall the crusaders held a section of the city several hundred yards in from the walls. They slept in their ranks, expecting fierce resistance in the morning. Instead, Mourtzouphlus fled during the night and all resistance collapsed; most of the upper classes had already fled.[89]

For three days the crusaders sacked the city. Most accounts stress rape and murder rather than the looting. No doubt such brutalities occurred, but the estimated death rate was low (as noted), while the booty was immense; to speak of "sacking" a city is in reference to soldiers stuffing sacks full of valuables. The commanders ordered that all booty be turned in for division. Of course, much was held out—especially small valuables such as jewels. Even so, what was turned in eventually yielded four hundred thousand marks as well as ten thousand suits of armor.[90]

With the city at their feet, the Europeans went ahead with their plans for a new dynasty. Thus, Baldwin of Flanders was installed as the new emperor of Byzantium. As might have been expected, his successful rule required the presence and backing of a Western army. When they placed Baldwin on the throne, the crusaders had pledged to remain to defend him until 1205; all plans for an attack on Egypt had been discarded. When that date was reached, the Fourth Crusade was officially ended, and about seven thousand fighting men boarded Venetian ships and sailed home. Without their backing, huge hunks of the empire soon broke away, and by 1225 there was little left under Western rule, although a Western emperor held on in Constantinople until 1261.

CONCLUSION

The conquest of Constantinople was very badly received in the West; the pope was especially angry. For one thing, the initial retaking of Zara encouraged the conclusion that the entire enterprise had been nothing more than Venetian opportunism. In addition, the attacks had all been on Christians—albeit of the Eastern variety. But most important was the fact that nothing had been done to recapture Jerusalem or to drive the Egyptians out of the Holy Land. That was unacceptable to Pope Innocent III. There must be a Fifth Crusade.

Chapter Ten

CRUSADES
AGAINST EGYPT

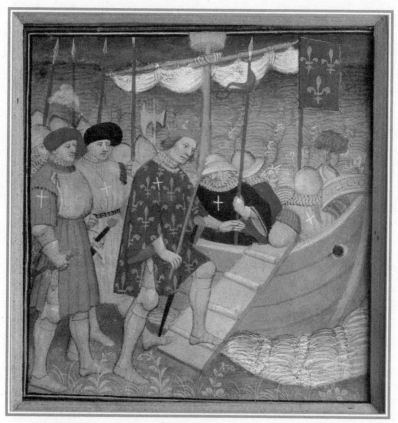

King Louis IX of France boards a ship in Cyprus on his way to Egypt
at the head of a great army. Although both of the Crusades he led
failed (he died during the second), he was so admired that twenty-seven
years after his death he was canonized as Saint Louis.

AFTER THE THIRD CRUSADE, it had become obvious to Western leaders that the Holy Land could never be secure if its defense continued to depend upon emergency expeditions from Europe. It was pointless to keep sending forces to rescue Tyre, Antioch, and Acre when the major threat to the kingdoms was in Egypt. But if Western forces conquered and ruled Egypt, most of the Muslim pressure against the Holy Land would be removed and major Christian-controlled forces would be available close by to offer any needed protection. That became the new strategy.

Of course, the Fourth Crusade had set out to impose just that solution but ultimately had not made any effort to do so. Saladin's heirs still ruled Egypt, Jerusalem was still in Muslim hands, and the security of the kingdoms was as imperiled as ever. Worse yet, there was growing opposition in Europe to the immense costs of crusading. So, fully aware of what was at stake, in 1213 Pope Innocent III began calling for a Fifth Crusade.

THE FIFTH CRUSADE

Things got off to a bad start. Innocent died suddenly in 1216, and many of the leading nobles had already crusaded once and did not wish to go again; Philip II still ruled France. Many of the nobility also were embroiled in local conflicts, and some in the "Crusade" against the Albigensians. Nevertheless, Pope Honorius III managed to get Duke Leopold VI of Austria and King Andrew II of Hungary to agree to lead armies. They arranged to march their troops (some sailed) to Spalato (Split) on the Dalmatian coast and there to board Venetian ships in August 1217.

This may have been the largest force yet to be assembled for a Crusade—perhaps ten thousand mounted knights and an appropriate infantry force.[1] Keep in mind, however, that statistics from this era are estimates based on shaky evidence. In any event, the troops far outnumbered the capacity of the ships that had been hired, and they had to be transported in waves to Acre; the passage took about three weeks in each direction. In Acre they were further reinforced by troops from Cyprus led by King Hugh I and joined by forces from the kingdoms and by contingents from the knightly orders.

Before the crusaders could embark to attack Egypt, their plans were delayed when King Andrew of Hungary decided to go home instead. He had been ill; quite likely he had been poisoned by relatives who regarded him as a usurper of the throne. In January 1218 he gathered his forces and headed home.[2] Andrew made many stops along the way, most of them to attend weddings. His departure so reduced the forces available that the decision was made to await the arrival of many additional contingents known to be on the way from Germany and Friesland.[3] These forces began to arrive by sea in April 1218. Consequently, in May the crusader fleet began to arrive in the harbor of Damietta (Dumyât); the attack on Egypt had begun.

Damietta is located at the very mouth of the main branch of the Nile, about two miles inland, and backs on Lake Manzala. The city was heavily fortified, having a triple wall and many towers. On an island in the river, just opposite the city, was a very formidable tower, constructed of seventy tiers, from which a huge chain was suspended that, when attached to the city's walls, blocked ships from sailing up the Nile.[4]

The crusaders established their camp on the west bank of the Nile, just across from Damietta. It was a fine defensive site with access to the sea. But it was not ideal for offensive purposes: the crusaders would have to attack across the Nile. On June 23 they did, "in 70 or 80 ships."[5] The attack was driven off. A week later they failed again. Then, at the end of August, the crusaders lashed two large ships together and on this base constructed a "a miniature castle"[6] from which extended a massive ramp. The crusaders sailed this contraption against the tower in the Nile. Troopers stormed over the ramp, forced the garrison to surrender, and then cut the massive chain blocking passage up the Nile. It was a remarkable achievement in all respects, and the Muslims in Damietta were stunned by it all and expected the city to fall forthwith—which it probably would have had the crusaders made a serious effort.[7] Instead, the crusaders decided to wait until the river receded and more reinforcements arrived. (Very little was ever done promptly during this entire campaign.)

By the end of September substantial reinforcements did arrive. Unfortunately, so did Cardinal Pelagius of Albano, sent by the pope to unify the crusader command. Pelagius was a Spaniard, "a man of great industry and administrative experience, but singularly lacking in tact."[8] He proceeded to threaten excommunication of all who disagreed with him and, mistaking stubbornness for determination, brought about the failure of the Fifth Crusade. It happened this way.

While the crusaders dallied after taking the great tower, the Muslims gathered their forces, and in October they attacked the crusader camp. Although greatly outnumbered, the crusaders not only repelled the attack but killed nearly all of the attackers. Again, though, they were content to enjoy their victory rather than go on the offensive. However, the sultan of Egypt was so convinced that it would be necessary to surrender Jerusalem to the Christians that he ordered that the Holy City be ruined. Demolition of the walls began late in March, and (Greek) Christian homes were sacked.[9]

Meanwhile, in February 1219 the crusaders finally were ready to attack Damietta again. At this same moment a succession conspiracy so frightened Al-Kāmil, sultan of Egypt, that he mounted his horse and deserted his army during the night. At dawn, when the troops discovered they had been abandoned by their leader, they panicked and fled, many abandoning their weapons. But rather than storm Damietta, which could have had only a very small garrison by this time, the crusaders merely encircled the city, setting up a new camp there.

Now the Muslims wanted a settlement. They proposed to surrender all portions of the kingdom of Jerusalem, including the city itself, and sign a thirty-year truce if the crusaders would leave Egypt. The military leaders wanted to accept the offer. Count Pelagius said no. The Muslims then offered to pay thirty thousand bezants in addition to the previous terms. Again Pelagius turned them down. In doing so, he ignored two essential facts: his army was shrinking as various crusader contingents left for home, and the Egyptian army was being reinforced from Syria and other Islamic powers. In May 1219 the Muslims attacked the crusader encampment. An unmovable crusader infantry inflicted huge losses on them. Two weeks later the Muslims attacked again, and once again their corpses littered the field of battle.

Not content to keep on smashing Muslim attacks, Pelagius now turned tactician and ordered an attempt to storm Damietta. But the attack made no headway. Nor did a second, two days later. Another attack on July 13 and yet another on July 31 also failed. These defeats weakened the crusader forces and undermined their resolve while at the same time restoring some confidence to the Muslims. At the end of August the crusader army fell into an ambush and suffered a bloody defeat—losing perhaps as many as forty-three hundred men.[10] Even so, they remained a large and dangerous opponent.

At this point the Egyptians once again sought a treaty. Unfortunately for them, as the new treaty offer was being discussed among the Crusade leaders who might have accepted it despite Pelagius's opposition, some Christian sentries facing Damietta noticed a lack of activity in the nearest tower, got a long ladder, climbed up, and discovered that the tower and a whole section of wall had been abandoned. More troops were quickly summoned, and Damietta was taken without opposition. Although the various Arab chroniclers claim that the crusaders then proceeded to massacre all the inhabitants, far more consistent with the abandonment of the walls is the crusader claim that they found a city nearly deserted except for many dead and dying, presumably victims of some dread disease.[11]

Now in possession of Damietta, Pelagius took such complete control that King John of Palestine boarded his ships and sailed back to Acre. And in the spring (1220) many other crusaders did so, too. However, the defectors were replaced by many contingents of Italian troops led by various archbishops and bishops. Not only did these churchmen prove to be inept military leaders; they couldn't even impose discipline at Damietta: the contemporary documents report widespread drunkenness and disorder. Nor could the clergy convince the army to march against the Egyptians.

A year passed, during which the Muslims constructed strong fortifications at El Mansûra to replace Damietta as a barrier to crusader penetration farther south. Then, with the arrival of more Germans and the return of King John of Jerusalem, Pelagius was able to mount a new campaign. While the troops marched south, a huge fleet of perhaps six hundred ships, galleys, and boats followed on the Nile. When they reached El Mansûra it was clear that a long siege would be required to take it. But rather than bypass the Muslim encampment, Pelagius began to construct a fortified camp facing El Mansûra. It was a dangerously vulnerable position. Worse yet, it did not isolate El Mansûra, and thousands of fresh Muslim troops flowed into their encampment. Pelagius and the clergy were warned repeatedly by the experienced military men as well as by Alice, the dowager queen of Cypress. Unfortunately, as Oliver of Paderborn, who was present, noted in his superb history of the Fifth Crusade, "[N]ow, for our sins, all sound judgment departed from our leaders."[12] At this point the Muslims placed substantial forces to the north, where they began to attack and sink supply boats coming from Damietta. Soon the Muslim forces were positioned not only to block supplies from coming south but to endanger any crusader retreat. Finally recognizing the danger, Pelagius led a withdrawal of his now disorganized forces, whereupon the Muslims destroyed some dikes and allowed the Nile to flood over the only land route north from the crusader encampment.

Trapped and lacking supplies, even Pelagius realized it was time for a peace settlement; the Muslims were unwilling to press too hard because the crusaders were still a lethal battle force, and both sides knew that substantial new German crusader contingents were expected at Damietta any moment. So, on August 30, 1221, an eight-year armistice was accepted, the crusaders agreed to the complete evacuation of Egypt, and both sides released their prisoners. Missing was the Muslim evacuation of the Holy Land that had been offered in their previous efforts to achieve peace.

As it turned out, the expected German reinforcements did not arrive until eight years later, when Frederick II, the Holy Roman Emperor, after twice being excommunicated for failure to keep his vow to crusade, finally led a small force to Acre in 1229. Lacking the forces needed to accomplish much, Frederick nevertheless managed to negotiate a treaty with Al-Kamil, the sultan of Egypt, that returned

Jerusalem, Bethlehem, and Nazareth to Christian rule. As a reward, Pope Gregory IX withdrew Frederick's excommunication.

Jerusalem remained in Christian hands for fifteen years. Then, on August 23, 1244, the Khwarazmians—Turkish nomads newly arrived from Asia and allied with the sultan of Egypt—swept over the "feeble defences" of Jerusalem, "killing any Franks they found and desecrating the Christian Holy Places."[13] Next the Khwarazmians rode south to join up with an Egyptian army, and the combined force set out to drive the Christians into the sea. The kingdoms and the knightly orders quickly assembled all their forces and met the Muslim host at Gaza, where the Christian army was annihilated. The only reason crusaders were able to hang on to their port cities was because civil war broke out between the Turks and the Egyptians.

SAINT LOUIS'S MAGNIFICENT FAILURE

Within several weeks of the disaster, the bishop of Beirut sailed from Acre "to tell the princes of the West . . . that reinforcements must be sent if the whole kingdom were not to perish."[14] Fortunately for the kingdom, this appeal coincided with the king of France's having taken the cross subsequent to having made an unexpected recovery from a severe illness. He may well have taken the cross before word of the latest disaster in the kingdoms reached the West; in any event, Louis IX was long revered for his crusading expeditions as well as his holiness: he was canonized as Saint Louis in 1297, only twenty-seven years after his death.

The Crusade led by Saint Louis probably was the best organized, best financed, and best planned of all the Crusades, and this was mainly due to the ability and rectitude of its leader.[15] Louis began by convening a group of nobles in Paris in October 1245.

At his urging, most took the cross. At the same time he imposed a very substantial tax to pay for a Crusade.

Once again the plan was to attack Egypt—landing at Damietta and marching to Cairo. This time the campaign would avoid the flooding season of the Nile that had led to the catastrophe of 1221. As he made his preparations, Louis attempted to enlist other European kings but could not do so. He was especially disappointed to have been unable to recruit King Haakon of Norway, since he could have supplied the needed fleet. Consequently, Louis arranged for ships from many different places including England and Scotland, but mostly from Genoa.

By 1248, after many delays, Louis finally set sail for Cyprus, arriving on September 17. The crusaders spent the winter there. Meanwhile, a request came from Bohemond V, Prince of Antioch, for aid in repelling attacks by Khwarazmian Turks, and Louis sent him five hundred knights.[16] At the end of May 1249 the crusaders reboarded their ships and set sail for the Egyptian coast. They probably numbered "2,500 to 2,800 knights, 5,000 crossbowmen and about 15,000 other combatants."[17] They landed on the beach at Damietta and were immediately attacked by Egyptian cavalry. But the Muslim charges were unavailing against a solid wall of infantry spears (even the Christian knights fought on foot), and, after suffering heavy losses, the Muslims withdrew. Not just from the beach, but from the city—and the civilian population fled behind them. Damietta had fallen in only a few hours.[18]

Unfortunately, this quick victory upset the entire timetable. Louis had expected to spend the summer taking Damietta and to move on up the Nile in the fall, after the level of the river had fallen back to normal. To head south now would be to campaign during the flood stages of the Nile, an action that had brought the Fifth Crusade to grief. So Louis had his forces settle down and wait. This was never an easy undertaking. Camps were always disorderly and prone to high death rates from disease and disputes. As the summer passed, Louis's forces slowly dwindled; some contingents even went home.

Finally, on November 20, Louis led his crusaders against the fortress of El Mansûra, which had been built to oppose Pelagius's forces in 1220. It had been greatly strengthened during the interim. To reach El Mansûra, the crusaders had to cross the Nile. They were unable to build an adequate bridge, but they bribed a local Copt to show them a fordable spot.[19] It was a difficult crossing, and some knights drowned. Worse yet, despite firm orders to form up on the opposite bank, the advance guard attacked Egyptian troops camped outside the walls without waiting for the rest of the army. When the Egyptians fled, the hotheaded advance guard chased after them despite furious efforts by the Grand Master of the Templars to halt them, and soon the crusaders were engaged in street fighting within El Mansûra. Here the Muslims rallied, and the greatly outnumbered advance guard was slaughtered. However, the rest of the army arrived and drove the Egyptians from the fortress. El Mansûra was theirs.

At that point the crusaders probably should have withdrawn back to Damietta. But victory gave them confidence to begin negotiations to trade Damietta for the Holy Land. As the talks dragged on, the Muslims began successfully to interfere with the passage of crusader supply boats up the Nile, and the army began to succumb to its very unhealthy location on a swampy shore. Soon, of about 2,700 knights who had marched south, only about 450 remained in fighting condition.[20] Finally, Louis ordered his troops back to Damietta—but along the way all discipline fell apart, and through a misunderstanding the crusaders surrendered. The Muslims quickly killed all stragglers and all of the sick and wounded aboard crusader boats on the Nile. Many others were given the choice of death or conversion to Islam—and many chose death. Although he, too, was a prisoner, Louis was not faced with that dire alternative. Instead, an enormous ransom was negotiated (it was brought by the Templars), and Louis and his principal barons were freed.

Louis did not return to France for another four years. Instead, he went to the Holy Land and spent large sums strengthening and rebuilding the defenses at Acre and Jaffa. When he finally went back to France in 1254, he left a garrison of one hundred French knights and a substantial number of infantry to defend Acre; it cost Louis about ten thousand pounds a year to pay their wages and expenses, which amounted to about 4 percent of the crown's annual income.[21]

The failure of Louis to lead a successful Crusade disillusioned many Europeans and contributed greatly to their growing opposition to crusading. Indirectly, it had even more dire effects in Egypt: the sultan was murdered by his father's Mamluk slaves (see below), thus ending the reign of Saladin's dynasty. The Mamluks ruled Egypt for the next 267 years.

BAIBARS ASSAULTS THE KINGDOMS

One of the Egyptian commanders who helped defeat Saint Louis was a Mamluk named Baibars (Baybars). Ten years later the first Mamluk sultan of Egypt was assassinated, and Baibars seized the throne. He was a very effective, if brutal, ruler.

Mamluk was not an ethnic or tribal identity. In Arabic, the word means "to be owned."[22] All Mamluks were slaves who were kidnapped or purchased as children—often from villages in the Caucasus, so it was not unusual that Baibars had blue eyes and was very tall. These young Caucasian boys were raised as Muslims and trained as slave warriors dedicated to the sultan.

Having come to power in 1260, Baibars spent the first two years of his reign consolidating his power, reorganizing the army, and building a new navy.[23] By 1263 he was ready to venture into the Holy Land. He began by sacking Nazareth and destroying its famous church. Then he led his troops to Acre but found it far too well fortified and defended—the garrison included the knights and infantry endowed by Louis IX—so he settled for sacking the area around the city and then returned to Egypt.

In 1265 he came with a far larger force and with lethal intentions. His first target was the small port town of Caesarea. It fell with little resistance. Next Baibars led his forces up the coast to Haifa. "Those inhabitants that were warned in time fled to boats in the anchorage, abandoning both the town and the citadel, which were destroyed; and the inhabitants that had remained there were massacred."[24] Then Baibars attacked the large Templar castle at Athlit. He was able to burn the village outside the walls but could make no headway against the fortress. So, toward the end of March, he continued south along the coast to the small port town of Arsuf (also Arsur or Apollonia). It was defended by 270 Hospitallers who fought "with superb courage."[25] The lower town fell to Baibars at the end of April, but the citadel continued to hold. Baibars proposed surrender terms allowing all the knights to go free. They surrendered, whereupon Baibars broke his word and enslaved them all. Then, fearing that the crusaders might someday recover this outpost, Baibars had citadel and town razed so completely that the site has never been resettled. Then once again it was Acre's turn, and once again Baibars found it much too strong and so led his army back to Egypt.

In 1266 Baibars turned his attention to the islands of resistance that remained inland. First, he led his troops to the great castle of Montfort—but saw at once that it was too strong. So he led his troops to the great Templar castle at Safed, in the Galilean uplands. The garrison consisted of some Templars and a substantial number of

Syrian mercenaries. With the arrival of Baibars, the Syrians began to desert, and soon it was impossible for the Templars to adequately man the walls. Baibars offered the Templars terms: to hand over the fortress and to withdraw without harm to Acre. The Templars opened the gates and marched out. The Muslims seized them and beheaded each and every one.[26] Next, Baibars turned his attention to the Christian village of Qara, massacring all the adults and enslaving the children. That fall he sent an army to attack Antioch, but his generals decided not to make the attempt.

The next spring (1267), Baibars once again paraded his troops before Acre and this time made an attack on the walls, which was turned back in a bloody defeat. Baibars compensated for this by scouring the countryside for Christians, or suspected Christians, and surrounded Acre with their headless bodies. To no avail.

In 1268 Baibars conquered Jaffa and slaughtered the inhabitants. Then in May he launched his army against Antioch. The garrison lacked sufficient numbers to fully man the walls, but they were able to beat back the first attack. The knights knew that Baibars had failed to keep the surrender terms at Safed and Arsuf, so negotiations led nowhere. The second Muslim attack on Antioch burst through the walls. What followed was "the single greatest massacre of the entire crusading era"[27]—a massacre that even shocked Muslim chroniclers.[28] The gates were closed and guarded, and an orgy of torture, killing, and desecration ensued—fully acting out the descriptions that Pope Urban II has used to arouse the crowd in the meadow at Clermont nearly two centuries earlier. Should there be any doubt, Baibars himself bragged about the massacre of Antioch in detail.

Since Count Bohemond VI, ruler of Antioch, was away when this disaster befell his city, Baibars sent him a letter telling him what he had missed: "You would have seen your knights prostrate beneath the horses' hooves, your houses stormed by pillagers . . . You would have seen your Muslim enemy trampling on the place where you celebrate Mass, cutting the throats of monks, priests and deacons upon the altars, bringing sudden death to the Patriarchs and slavery to the royal princes. You would have seen fire running through your palaces, your dead burned in this world before going down to the fires of the next."[29] Granted, the city had resisted; but since Baibars's surrender agreements had proved worthless in the past, what option was there?

Sad to say, it is no surprise that the massacre of Antioch is barely reported in many recent Western histories of the Crusades. Steven Runciman gave it eight lines,[30] Hans Eberhard Mayer gave it one,[31] and Christopher Tyerman, who devoted several pages to lurid details of the massacre of Jerusalem during the First Crusade, dismissed the massacre of Antioch in four words.[32] Karen Armstrong devoted twelve words to reporting this massacre, which she then blamed on the crusaders since it was their dire threat that had created a "new Islam" with a "desperate determination to survive." Armstrong also noted that because Baibars was a patron of the arts, he "was not simply a destroyer . . . [but also] a great builder."[33]

With the fall of Antioch, the Christian kingdoms in the East consisted of only a very narrow fringe surrounding a few ports along the coast: Acre, Tyre, Sidon, Beirut, and Alexandretta, the latter being a tiny coastal enclave in what had been the kingdom of Antioch.[34] Baibars chose not to attempt to take these last strongholds, partly because of their imposing fortifications and skillful defenders, and partly because their access to the sea made it impossible to put them under an effective siege. He had an additional worry as well. Word was spreading that Louis IX was organizing another Crusade.

SAINT LOUIS'S BLUES

Now in his fifties and somewhat frail, Saint Louis still longed to save the kingdoms and reconquer Jerusalem. After discussions with Pope Clement IV, in 1267 Louis took the cross once more, as did his three sons and two brothers—Charles of Anjou and Alphonse of Poitiers. But outside France, only King Henry III of England and King James I of Aragon agreed to join him.

This new Crusade was about as carefully planned and organized as its recent predecessor—which is why it took nearly three years to get rolling. It was, of course, another naval Crusade, and Louis chartered a fleet from Genoa to augment the ships available to him in Marseille. Again, the initial target was Egypt, and Cagliari in southern Sardinia was chosen as the assembly point. Louis arrived there in June 1270. But the fleet from Aragon was so badly damaged by a storm that it never arrived, the survivors having returned home to reorganize. In England, Henry III had decided not to go but sent his son Edward in his stead, which delayed the departure of the English fleet until August. So Louis decided to move without the others and led his troops almost due south to the African coast, landing at Tunis on July 18, 1270. The French quickly seized a fortress on the site of ancient Carthage and established a secure camp.[35]

It has long been debated why Louis sailed to Tunis rather than to Egypt or even Acre. The consensus is that he believed that Muhammad I, the emir of Tunis, was ready to convert to Christianity if he had the protection of a strong Christian army.[36] Only after the landing was it discovered that this was a false rumor. Although the city was only weakly defended, Louis decided to avoid stirring up trouble while he waited for the arrival of Aragonese and English crusaders. But what the local Muslim forces were too weak to do, the climate accomplished. "The summer heat beat down on the crusaders and nurtured an outbreak of deadly diseases in the camp. Soldiers began to die in great numbers."[37] Soon Louis fell ill, too. On August 25, 1270, King Louis IX died. His body was returned to France. His magnificent tomb at Saint-Denis was destroyed during the French Wars of Religion, and his remains disappeared.

Soon after Louis died, Prince Edward arrived with his English forces and was stunned to find the French forces preparing to sail home. His force was far too small to attempt an attack on Baibars in Egypt, but rather than simply throw in his hand, the prince sailed on to Acre, where he landed in May 1271 with two to three hundred knights and perhaps six hundred infantry.[38] Although the troops available to him were insufficient to reclaim any of the lost territory, they made Acre virtually invulnerable. This allowed Edward to negotiate a ten-year peace treaty with Baibars. Then he went home, to discover his father had died and that he now was King Edward I.

Meanwhile, in 1271 Baibars sent his new navy to attack Cyprus. Even with the advantage of surprise it was no contest: by nightfall there was no Egyptian fleet. At about this same time, Baibars's forces were able to conquer the huge Hospitaller fortress of Krak des Chevaliers, which gave the Muslims control of the approaches to Tripoli. But then Baibars agreed to the ten-year treaty with Prince Edward, ending his threat to the last Christian strongholds. On July 1, 1277, Baibars died. There are several traditions concerning his cause of death, but it is generally believed that he poisoned the drink of an Ayubite prince and then carelessly drank it himself.[39]

CONCLUSION

The crusading spirit did not die with Saint Louis, but the doubts that had long been building up were greatly encouraged by his failures. If such well-funded and well-organized Crusades, led by a skilled and saintly leader, could not prevail, what could? Moreover, even Louis had faced widespread opposition—especially by the clergy—to the taxes necessary to fund these undertakings. In the wake of Louis's defeat and death, angry opposition to crusader taxes grew louder, and many prominent people began to condemn the continuing defense of the Holy Land as a useless, misguided, and perhaps wicked "quagmire."

Conclusion

MISSION ABANDONED

This nineteenth-century painting of the return home of an elderly crusader is symbolic of the end of the crusading era, which fell victim to the unwillingness of Europeans to continue to pay taxes in support of the crusader kingdom.
© *Erich Lessing / Art Resource, NY*

S o long as the costs of the Crusades were born by the crusaders and their families, there were few who objected to the repeated efforts to free and preserve the Holy Land. But when kings began to lead, the expense of crusading soon was being imposed on everyone, including the clergy and the religious orders, in the form of crusader taxes. Grumbling began at once. The grumbling grew increasingly louder when bloody "crusades" began against "heretics" in Europe: thousands of Cathars, Waldensians, Beghards, and Beguines were condemned by the Church and killed in battle or hunted down and massacred. In the midst of all this, a medieval version of an antiwar movement eventually prevailed; after two centuries of support, the kingdoms in the Holy Land were abandoned.

CRUSADER TAXES

Having been the first king to lead a Crusade, Louis VII of France was the first, in 1146, to impose a tax to fund his venture to the Holy Land. This tax seems to have been levied only on the clergy, especially the monastic orders; in any case, the abbot of Ferrières was the first to complain that the tax was unfair and too severe. His was hardly a lone voice. The abbot of Saint-Benoît-sur-Loire protested that he would need to melt down some sacred silver and gold altar furnishings in order to raise the sum demanded.[1] The abbot of Mont-Saint-Michel not only complained bitterly that the tax involved "the spoliation" of the church, but "ascribed the failure of the expedition to a divine judgment."[2] It is unknown how much was raised by Louis's tax, but it was not enough. He also borrowed substantial sums and wrote several times to his head tax collector asking for advances and loans.

Then King Henry II of England and King Philip Augustus of France imposed a far heavier tax in 1166, and this time on the laity as well as the clergy. The rate in England was placed at two pence of each pound sterling of income for the first year, and one penny in each of the next four years. Equivalent rates were charged in France. This may have been the first time in Europe that a tax was imposed on income rather than on property.[3] This tax seems to have aroused little antagonism. But that was not the case in 1188, when another income tax was imposed in England and France to support what came to be the Third Crusade. Hence, this tax was known as the Saladin Tithe, and it stirred up intense anger.

The Saladin Tithe was first initiated by Henry II of England and embraced by Philip Augustus. It required a payment of 10 percent (a tithe) on all revenues and movable properties by everyone who was not going to go crusading. What really distressed the king's subjects was that prior taxes had been left to conscience: a person was assumed to have paid the correct amount. This time a Templar and a Hospitaller were appointed as collectors in each parish, joined by a priest and two parishioners. This collection team was empowered to investigate suspicious cases and to imprison offenders until they paid up.[4] Many ecclesiastics predicted that the Crusade would come to a bad end because of this abusive taxation. One French troubadour even sang of "tyrants who have taken up the cross so they may tax clerks, citizens, and soldiers . . . more have taken the cross out of greed than faith."[5]

On July 6, 1189, Henry II died and was succeeded by his son Richard the Lionhearted. Because of the Saladin Tithe, Richard inherited a bursting treasury, containing at least one hundred thousand marks despite the fact that just before his death Henry had given thirty thousand marks to the Templars and Hospitallers to spend on the defense of Tyre.[6] Even though Richard turned out to be a prodigious spender, he always had the money to spend.

At the close of the twelfth century the tax burden shifted from the crowns to the papacy: in 1199 Innocent III imposed a tax of 2.5 percent a year on all clerical incomes to support the Fourth Crusade. This led to many incidents of open rebellion and non-payment.

Crusade taxes peaked during the reign of Saint Louis. It has been calculated that from 1247 to 1257, Louis spent 1.5 million livres on crusading, or more than six times his royal revenues. The difference was made up by "gifts" and special taxes. As for "gifts," in 1248, eighty-two towns in northern France were ordered to "give" large sums "to help the overseas journey."[7] They gave about 275,000 livres. In addition, huge sums came from taxes on the churches: the "French clergy offered a tenth over five years," which may have added up to almost a million livres.[8] Even so, many of the leading nobles paid their own way as well as that of their contingents; crusading was hugely expensive.

GRUMBLES

From the start, some Christian theologians had condemned the doctrine that crusading earned forgiveness for sins and was the moral equivalent of taking monastic vows. These criticisms increased as the Crusades failed to accomplish their goals, encouraging claims that God did not sanction these wars. Worse yet, "many Christians began to blaspheme,"[9] claiming that God was favoring the Muslims. A well-known troubadour asked, "God, why did you bring this misfortune upon our French king . . . It is with good reason that we cease to believe in God and worship Muhammad."[10] Even more damaging was a poem by a Knight Templar, written in despair after the massacre or enslavement of the knights at Arsuf by Baibars:

> *My heart is so full of grief that it would take little more to make me kill myself at once or tear off this cross which I took in honor of Him who was crucified. For neither cross nor my faith protects and guides against the cursed Turks. Rather it seems, as anyone can see, that to our hurt God wishes to protect them . . . Thus he is mad who seeks to fight the Turks since Jesus Christ does not deny them anything.*[11]

To counter such objections, leading churchmen argued that God permitted these defeats because of the sins of the crusaders.[12] The crusaders themselves often adopted this explanation and staged many elaborate displays of contrition; recall the three-day fast and then the barefoot march around the walls of Jerusalem in 1099. Of course, contrition had its limits, and the whores were never banished from the encampments.[13] In any event, claims that God did not support the Crusades grew increasingly loud and popular—especially among those paying the most in taxes.

Finally, when the Church held a council at Lyon in 1274, the pope asked the esteemed Humbert of Romans, Master General of the Dominican order, to report on current opposition to crusading. It was a masterful summing-up.

Humbert began by noting how the Muslims had provoked the Crusades. For more than six hundred years they had been attacking Christendom. Once the whole of North Africa had been a flourishing Christian region; now only one Christian bishopric remained, in Morocco. They had invaded Spain, Sicily, and Italy. Worst of all, they had taken and profaned the Holy Land. Without question the Crusades were a Christian duty. Why then did so many shirk from going?

Some failed to go because they were sunk into sin and self-indulgence. More failed to go because they were afraid. And afraid not merely of combat: many otherwise brave knights were terrified of going to sea. (It was common knowledge that many battle-hardened veterans backed out of their vow to take the cross when it came time to board a ship.) Others failed to go because they were too concerned about their own affairs. Still others because of family obligations; women had often been very vocal opponents of crusading, albeit some had ridden east with their husbands, sons, and lovers.

But the truly important reason that an increasing number would not go crusading was the attacks being heaped on it by so many critics. Some of these were pacifists who held it to be a sin to kill anyone. Some objected that it made more sense to leave the Muslims in peace unless they invaded Europe: "[w]hen we conquer and kill them we send them to hell, which is contrary to Christian charity."[14] Others condemned the Crusades for wasting the lives and energy of the best and brightest. Many asked how much more useful Louis IX could have been had he remained in France and lived to an old age. Some of the most persuasive critics attacked crusading as futile: there were too many Muslims, and Palestine was too far away. And always it came back to taxes. Crusading was too expensive.

It also was becoming too disruptive. Some of the most vociferous critics of crusading were equally vociferous in criticizing the Catholic Church on other grounds as well. The Cathars (Albigensians) condemned all killing, including capital punishment, and aimed specific condemnations against the Crusades. The Waldensians likewise opposed killing and extended this to condemnations of all crusading. These views probably helped kindle opposition to both groups, but the launching of military attacks on both—these also justified as "Crusades" by the Church—played a far more important role in generating opposition to all crusading. The campaigns against the Cathars and the Waldensians were brutal wars of extermination that devastated parts of Europe, damaged the economy, and led to great bitterness in many European communities.

The result of all these factors was that after Edward I sailed back to England in 1272, no more large crusading groups ever came to the Holy Land—although several very small contingents did appear, including one led by Countess Alice of Blois in 1287 and another under Odo of Grandson in 1290.

THE KINGDOM FALLS

In February 1289 Saif al-Din Qalawun (or Kalavun), the Mamluk sultan of Egypt, marched a huge army north and laid siege to Tripoli, one of the five remaining crusader ports in the Holy Land. When warned by the Templars that the Egyptians were coming, at first no one in Tripoli believed it. And, confident of the immense strength of their fortifications, they made no special preparations until the enemy was literally at the gates. Much to their surprise, not only was the Muslim army much larger than anyone in Tripoli had thought possible; this Muslim force brought immense siege engines able to smash the city's walls. As the bombardment ensued, members of the Venetian merchant community within Tripoli decided that the city could not be held and sailed away with their most precious possessions. This alarmed the Genoese merchants, and so they, too, scrambled aboard their ships and left. This threw the city into disorder just as the Muslims launched a general assault on the breaches in the walls. As hordes of Egyptian troopers swarmed into the city, some Christians were able to flee to the last boats in the harbor. As for the rest, the men were slaughtered, and the women and children were marched away to the slave markets.

Then "Qalawun had the city razed to the ground, lest the Franks, with their command of the sea, might try to recapture it."[15] He also founded new Tripoli a few miles inland, where it could not be reached by sea.

That left Acre, Tyre, Beirut, and Haifa.

On his deathbed, Qalawun had his son and heir, al-Ashraf, swear he would conquer Acre. So in April 1291, al-Ashraf arrived at Acre with an even larger army than his father had marched to Tripoli and with even more powerful siege machines. The defenders fought bravely and with great skill; several times they sallied out the gates and attacked the Muslim camp. But all the while their fortifications were being reduced to rubble by the huge stones hurled by the siege engines, although supplies continued to arrive by sea from Cyprus and some civilians were evacuated on the return voyages. In May, a month after the siege began, reinforcements consisting of one hundred mounted knights and two thousand infantry came from Cyprus. But they were too few.

Soon the battle was being fought in the streets, and many civilians were crowding aboard rowboats to reach the galleys out in the harbor. But most people were unable to leave, and "[s]oon the Moslem soldiers penetrated right through the city, slaying everyone, old men, women and children alike."[16] By May 8, all of Acre was in Muslim hands except for the castle of the Templars, which jutted out into the sea. Boats from Cyprus continued to board refugees from the castle while the Templars, joined by other surviving fighting men, held the walls. At this point al-Ashraf offered favorable terms of surrender, the Templars accepted, and a contingent of Mamluks was admitted to supervise the handover. Unfortunately, they got out of hand. As the Muslim chronicler Abu'l-Mahasin admitted, the Mamluk contingent "began to pillage and to lay hands on the women and children."[17] Furious, the Templars killed them all and got ready to fight on. The next day, fully aware of what had gone wrong, al-Ashraf offered the same favorable terms once again. The commander of the Templars and some companions accepted a safe-conduct to arrange the surrender, but when they reached the sultan's tent they were seized and beheaded. Seeing that from the walls, the remaining Templars decided to fight to the death. And they did.

Less than a month later this huge Muslim army arrived at Tyre. The garrison was far too small to attempt a defense and sailed away to Cyprus without a fight. Next, the Muslims marched to Beirut. Here, too, resistance was beyond the means of the garrison, and they, too, sailed to Cyprus. Haifa also fell without opposition; the monks on Mount Carmel were slaughtered and their monasteries burned. The last Christian enclave was now the Templars' fortress island of Ruad, two miles off the coast. The Templars held out there until 1303, leaving then only because of the suppression of their order by the king of France and the pope. After the fall of Acre, the Hospitallers gathered on Cyprus and then, in 1310, seized the island of Rhodes from the Byzantines. There they built a superior navy and played an important role in defending Western shipping in the East.

And so it ended. It should be kept in mind that the kingdoms had survived, at least along the coast, for nearly as long as the United States has been a nation.

MUSLIM MEMORIES

Karen Armstrong is one of the many who would have us believe that the Crusades are "one of the direct causes of the conflict in the Middle East today."[18] That may be so, but not because the Muslim world has been harboring bitterness over the Crusades for the past many centuries. As Jonathan Riley-Smith explained: "One often reads that Muslims have inherited from their medieval ancestors bitter memories of the violence of the crusaders. Nothing could be further from the truth. Before the end of the nineteenth century Muslims had not shown much interest in the crusades . . . [looking] back on [them] with indifference and complacency."[19] Even at the time they took place, Muslim chroniclers paid very little attention to the Crusades, regarding them as invasions by "a primitive, unlearned, impoverished, and un-Muslim people, about whom Muslim rulers and scholars knew and cared little."[20] Moreover, most Arabs dismissed the Crusades as having been attacks upon the hated Turks, and therefore of little interest.[21] Indeed, in the account written by Ibn Zafir at the end of the twelfth century, it was said that it was better that the Franks occupied the kingdom of Jerusalem as this prevented "the spread of the influence of the Turks to the lands of Egypt."[22]

Muslim interest in the Crusades seems to have begun in the nineteenth century, when the term itself[23] was introduced by Christian Arabs who translated French histories into Arabic—for it was in the West that the Crusades first came back into vogue during the nineteenth century. In Europe and the United States "the romance of the crusades and crusading" became a very popular literary theme, as in the many popular novels of Sir Walter Scott.[24] Not surprisingly, this development required that, at least in Britain and America, the Crusades be "de-Catholicized."[25] In part this was done by emphasizing the conflict between the Knights Templars and the pope, transforming the former into an order of valiant anti-Catholic heroes. In addition, there developed a strong linkage between the European imperial impulse and the romantic imagery of the Crusades "to such an extent that, by World War One, war campaigns and war heroes were regularly lauded as crusaders in the popular press, from the pulpit, and in the official propaganda of the British war machine."[26]

Meanwhile in the East, the Ottoman Empire was fully revealed as "the sick man of Europe," a decrepit relic unable to produce any of the arms needed for its defense, which highlighted the general backwardness of Islamic culture and prompted "seething anger"[27] against the West among Muslim intellectuals, eventually leading them to focus on the Crusades.

Thus, current Muslim memories and anger about the Crusades are a twentieth-century creation,[28] prompted in part by "post–World War I British and French imperialism and the post–World War II creation of the state of Israel."[29] It was the last sultan of the Ottoman Empire to rule with absolute authority, Abdülhamīd II (r. 1876–1909), who began to refer to European Crusades. This prompted the first Muslim history of the Crusades, published in 1899. In the introduction, its author, Sayyid Ali al-Hariri, noted: "The sovereigns of Europe nowadays attack our Sublime Empire in a manner bearing great resemblance to the deeds of those people in bygone times [the crusaders]. Our most glorious sultan, Abdulhamid II, has rightly remarked that Europe is now carrying out a Crusade against us."[30]

This theme was eagerly picked up by Muslim nationalists. "Only Muslim unity could oppose these new crusades, some argued, and the crusading threat became an important theme in the writings of the pan-Islamic movement"[31] Even within the context of Muslim weakness in the face the modern West, Islamic triumphalism flourished; many proposed that through the Crusades the "savage West . . . benefited by absorbing [Islam's] civilized values." As for crusader effects on Islam, "how could Islam benefit from contacts established with an inferior, backward civilization?"[32]

Eventually, the image of the brutal, colonizing crusader proved to have such polemical power that it drowned out nearly everything else in the ideological lexicon of Muslim antagonism toward the West—except, of course, for Israel and paranoid tales about the worldwide Jewish conspiracy.

CONCLUSION

The thrust of the preceding chapters can be summarized very briefly. The Crusades were not unprovoked. They were not the first round of European colonialism. They were not conducted for land, loot, or converts. The crusaders were not barbarians who victimized the cultivated Muslims. They sincerely believed that they served in God's battalions.

BIBLIOGRAPHY

Abulafia, Anna Sapir. 1985. "Invectives Against Christianity in the Hebrew Chronicles of the First Crusade." In Edbury 1985, 66–72.

Abun-Nasr, Jamil. 1971. *A History of the Maghrib*. Cambridge: Cambridge Univ. Press.

Afsaruddin, Asma. 1990. "The Great Library at Alexandria." *American Journal of Economics and Sociology* 49:291–92.

Ahmad, Aziz. 1975. *A History of Islamic Sicily*. Edinburgh: Edinburgh Univ. Press.

Ajram, Dr. K. 1992. *The Miracle of Islamic Science*. Cedar Rapids, IA: Knowledge House.

Alroy, Gil Carl. 1975. *Behind the Middle East Conflict: The Real Impasse Between Arabs and Jews*. New York: G. P. Putnam's Sons.

Andrea, A. J. 2003. "The Crusades in Perspective: The Crusades in Modern Islamic Perspective." *History Compass* 1:1–4.

Anonymous. [c. 1102] 1962. *Gesta Francorum: The Deeds of the Franks and Other Pilgrims to Jerusalem*. Translated by Rosalind Hill. Oxford: Clarendon Press.

Armstrong, Karen. [1991] 2001. *Holy War: The Crusades and Their Impact on Today's World*. 2nd ed. New York: Random House.

Asbridge, Thomas. 2004. *The First Crusade: A New History*. Oxford: Oxford Univ. Press.

Atiya, Aziz S. 1968. *History of Eastern Christianity*. Notre Dame: Univ. of Notre Dame Press.

———. 1966. *Crusade, Commerce and Culture*. New York: John Wiley & Sons.

Bachrach, Bernard S. 1985. "On the Origins of William the Conqueror's Horse Transports." *Technology and Culture* 26:505–31.

Bairoch, Paul. 1988. *Cities and Economic Development: From the Dawn of History to the Present*. Chicago: Univ. of Chicago Press.

Baldwin, Marshall W., ed. 1969. *A History of the Crusades*. Vol. 1, *The First Hundred Years*. Madison: Univ. of Wisconsin Press.

Baldwin, Summerfield. 1937. *Business in the Middle Ages*. New York: Henry Holt.

Barber, Malcolm. 1994. *The New Knighthood: A History of the Order of the Temple*. Cambridge: Cambridge Univ. Press.

Baron, Salo Wittmayer. 1957. *A Social and Religious History of the Jews*. Vols. 3, 4, and 5. New York: Columbia Univ. Press.

Becker, Carl Heinrich. [1909] 2006. *Christianity and Islam*. Boston: IndyPublish.

Bibliography

———. 1926a. "The Expansion of the Saracens—the East." In *The Cambridge Medieval History,* ed. J. B. Bury, H. M. Gwatkin, and J. P. Whitney, 2:329–65. Cambridge: Cambridge Univ. Press.

———. 1926b. "The Expansion of the Saracens—Africa and Europe." In *The Cambridge Medieval History,* ed. J. B. Bury, H. M. Gwatkin, and J. P. Whitney, 2:366–90. Cambridge: Cambridge Univ. Press.

Bédier, Joseph, and Pierre Aubry. 1909. *Chansons de Croisade.* Honoré Champion: Paris.

Beeching, Jack. 1982. *The Galleys at Lepanto.* New York: Charles Scribner's Sons.

Berry, Virginia G. 1969. "The Second Crusade." In Baldwin 1969, 463–512.

Biddle, Martin. 1999. *The Tomb of Christ.* Thrupp, UK: Sutton Publishing.

Bloom, Jonathan. 2007. "Islam on the Temple." *Times Literary Supplement,* December 7, 7–8.

Boas, Adrian J. 1998. "The Frankish Period: A Unique Medieval Society Emerges." *Near Eastern Archaeology* 61:138–73.

Boorstin, Daniel J. 1983. *The Discoverers.* New York: Random House.

Bramhall, Edith Clementine. 1901. "The Origin of the Temporal Privileges of Crusaders." *American Journal of Theology* 5:279–92.

Brand, Charles M. 1962. "The Byzantines and Saladin, 1185–1192: Opponents of the Third Crusade." *Speculum* 37:167–81.

Brent, Michael, and Elizabeth Fentress. 1996. *The Berbers.* Oxford: Blackwells.

Brickman, William W. 1961. "The Meeting of East and West in Educational History." *Comparative Education Review* 5:82–98.

Brown, Gordon S. 2003. *The Norman Conquest of Southern Italy and Sicily.* Jefferson, NC: McFarland & Co.

Brundage, James A. 1985. "Prostitution, Miscegenation and Sexual Purity in the First Crusade." In Edbury 1985, 57–65.

Bull, Marcus. 1993. *Knightly Piety and the Lay Response to the First Crusade: The Limousin and Gascony, c. 970–c. 1130.* Oxford: Clarendon Press.

Bulliet, Richard W. [1975] 1990. *The Camel and the Wheel.* New York: Columbia Univ. Press.

———. 1979a. *Conversion to Islam in the Medieval Period: An Essay in Quantitative History.* Cambridge, MA: Harvard Univ. Press.

———. 1979b. "Conversion to Islam and the Emergence of Muslim Society in Iran." In *Conversion to Islam,* ed. Nehemia Levtzion, 30–51. New York: Holmes & Meier.

Burman, Edward. 1986. *The Templars: Knights of God.* Rochester, VT: Destiny Books.

Butler, Alfred. [1902] 1992. *The Arab Conquest of Egypt.* Brooklyn: A&B Publishers Group.

———. 1884. *Ancient Coptic Churches in Egypt.* Vol. 2. Oxford: Oxford Univ. Press.

Cahen, Claude. 1969. "The Turkish Invasion: The Selchükids." In Baldwin 1969, 135–76.

Cardini, Franco. 2001. *Europe and Islam.* Oxford: Blackwell.

Carroll, James. 2004. *Crusade: Chronicles of an Unjust War.* New York: Metropolitan Books.

Cate, James Lea. 1969. "The Crusade of 1101." In Baldwin 1969, 343–69.

Cazel, Fred A. 1955. "The Tax of 1185 in Aid of the Holy Land." *Speculum* 30: 385–92.

Chandler, Tertius. 1987. *Four Thousand Years of Urban Growth: An Historical Census.* 2nd ed. Lewiston, NY: Edwin Mellen Press.

Charanis, Peter. 1969. "The Byzantine Empire in the Eleventh Century." In Baldwin 1969, 177–219.

Chazan, Robert. 2006. *The Jews of Medieval Western Christendom, 1000–1500.* Cambridge: Cambridge Univ. Press.

———. 1996. *In the Year 1096: The First Crusade and the Jews.* Philadelphia: Jewish Publication Society.

———. 1986. *European Jewry and the First Crusade.* Berkeley: Univ. of California Press.

———, ed. 1980. *Church, State, and Jew in the Middle Ages* (a collection of original sources). West Orange, NJ: Behrman House.

Cheetham, Nicolas. 1983. *Keepers of the Keys: The History of the Popes from St. Peter to John Paul II.* New York: Scribner's.

Cohen, Raymond. 2008. *Saving the Holy Sepulchre.* New York: Oxford Univ. Press.

Cole, Penny J. 1991. *The Preaching of the Crusades to the Holy Land, 1095–1270.* Cambridge, MA: Medieval Academy of America.

Colish, Marcia L. 1997. *Medieval Foundations of the Western Intellectual Tradition: 400–1400.* New Haven, CT: Yale Univ. Press.

Collins, Roger. 1998. *Charlemagne.* Toronto: Univ. of Toronto Press.

Comnena, Anna. [c. 1148] 1969. *The Alexiad.* London: Penguin Classics.

Constable, Giles. 1953. "The Second Crusade as Seen by Contemporaries." *Traditio* 9:213–79.

Curry, Andrew. 2002. "The Crusades, the First Holy War." *U.S. News & World Report,* April 8, 36.

Daniel-Rops, Henri. 1957. *Cathedral and Crusade: Studies of the Medieval Church, 1050–1350.* London: Dent.

Davidson, H. R. Ellis. 1976. *The Viking Road to Byzantium.* London: George Allen & Unwin.

Davis, Paul K. 2001. *100 Decisive Battles from Ancient Times to the Present.* Oxford: Oxford Univ. Press.

Davis, William Stearns, ed. 1913. *Readings in Ancient History: Illustrative Extracts from the Sources.* Vol. 2, *Rome and the West.* Boston: Allyn and Bacon.

Delbrück, Hans. [1920] 1990. *The Barbarian Invasions: History of the Art of War.* Vol. 2. Lincoln: Univ. of Nebraska Press.

Dennet, Daniel C., Jr. 1948. "Pirenne and Muhammad." *Speculum* 23:165–90.

d'Eszlary, Charles. 1958. "Magna Carta and the Assises of Jerusalem." *American Journal of Legal History* 2:189–214.

Dickens, Mark. 1999. "The Church of the East." www.oxuscom.com/ch-of-east.htm.

Donner, Fred McGraw. 1981. *The Early Islamic Conquests.* Princeton, NJ: Princeton Univ. Press.

Duby, Georges. 1994. *The Knight, the Lady, and the Priest.* Chicago: Univ. of Chicago Press.

———. 1977. *The Chivalrous Society.* Berkeley: Univ. of California Press.

Duffy, Eamon. 1997. *Saints and Sinners: A History of the Popes.* New Haven, CT: Yale Univ. Press.

Duncalf, Frederic. 1969a. "The Councils of Piacenza and Clermont." In Baldwin 1969, 220–52.

———. 1969b. "The First Crusade: Clermont to Constantinople." In Baldwin 1969, 253–79.

———. 1921. "The Peasants' Crusade." *American Historical Review* 26:440–53.

Durant, Will. 1950. *The Age of Faith.* New York: Simon and Schuster.

Edbury, Peter. 1999. "Warfare in the Latin East." In *Medieval Warfare: A History*, ed. Maurice Keen, 89–112. Oxford: Oxford Univ. Press.

———, ed. 1985. *Crusade and Settlement* (papers in honor of R. C. Smail.). Cardiff, UK: Univ. College Cardiff Press.

Ehrenkreutz, A. S. 1955. "The Place of Saladin in the Naval History of the Mediterranean Sea in the Middle Ages." *Journal of the American Oriental Society* 75:100–116.

Ekelund, Robert B., Robert F. Hébert, Robert D. Tollison, Gary M. Anderson, and Audrey B. Davidson. 1999. *Sacred Trust: The Medieval Church as an Economic Firm.* New York: Oxford Univ. Press.

Erdmann, Carl. [1935] 1977. *The Origin of the Idea of Crusade.* Princeton, NJ: Princeton Univ. Press.

Erdoes, Richard. 1988. *A.D. 1000: Living on the Brink of the Apocalypse.* New York: Harper and Row.

Fahmy, Aly Mohamed. 1966. *Muslim Sea-Power in the Eastern Mediterranean.* Cairo: National Publication.

Farah, Caesar E. 1994. *Islam: Beliefs and Observations.* 5th ed. Hauppauge, NY: Barron's.

Ferris, Eleanor. 1902. "The Financial Relations of the Knights Templars to the English Crown." *American Historical Review* 8:1–17.

Fink, Harold S. 1969. "The Foundation of the Latin States, 1099–1118." In Baldwin 1969, 368–409.

Fletcher, Richard. 1997. *The Barbarian Conversion: From Paganism to Christianity.* New York: Henry Holt and Company.

———. 1992. *Moorish Spain.* Berkeley: Univ. of California Press.

France, John. 2002. "Patronage and the Appeal of the First Crusade." In *The Crusades: The Essential Readings,* ed. Thomas F. Madden, 195–207. Oxford: Blackwell Publishing.

———. 1999. *Western Warfare in the Age of the Crusades, 1000–1300.* Ithaca, NY: Cornell Univ. Press.

———. 1997. *Victory in the East.* Cambridge: Cambridge Univ. Press.

Fregosi, Paul. 1998. *Jihad in the West: Muslim Conquests from the 7th to the 21st Centuries.* Amherst, NY: Prometheus Books.

Fulcher of Chartres. [c. 1127] 1969. *A History of the Expedition to Jerusalem, 1095–1127.* Knoxville: Univ. of Tennessee Press.

Gabrieli, Francesco. 1964. "Greeks and Arabs in the Central Mediterranean Area." *Dumbarton Oaks Papers* 18:57–65.

Gay, Peter. 1966. *The Enlightenment.* New York: W. W. Norton.

Gibb, Sir Hamilton A. R. 1969. "The Caliphate and the Arab States." In Baldwin 1969, 81–98.

———. 1958. "Arab-Byzantine Relations Under the Umayyad Caliphate." *Dumbarton Oaks Papers* 12:219–33.

Gibbon, Edward. [1776–1788] 1994. *The History of the Decline and Fall of the Roman Empire*. 3 vols. London: Allen Lane / Penguin Press.

Gidal, Nachum T. 1988. *Jews in Germany: From Roman Times to the Weimar Republic*. Cologne: Könemann.

Gies, Frances, and Joseph Gies. 1994. *Cathedral, Forge, and Waterwheel: Technology and Invention in the Middle Ages*. New York: Harper Collins.

Gil, Moshe. 1992. *A History of Palestine, 634–1099*. Cambridge: Cambridge Univ. Press.

Gillingham, John. 1999. "An Age of Expansion: c. 1020–1204." In *Medieval Warfare: A History*, ed. Maurice Keen, 59–88. Oxford: Oxford Univ. Press.

Gimpel, Jean. 1976. *The Medieval Machine: The Industrial Revolution of the Middle Ages*. New York: Penguin Books.

Glubb, Lieutenant-General Sir John Bagot. [1963] 1995. *The Great Arab Conquests*. New York: Barnes and Noble.

Grabar, Oleg. 2006. *The Dome of the Rock*. Cambridge, MA: Belknap Press of the Harvard Univ. Press.

Graetz, Heinrich Hirsh. 1894. *History of the Jews*. Vol. 3. Philadelphia: Jewish Publication Society of America.

Graham, Rose. 1908. "The Taxation of Pope Nicholas IV." *English Historical Review* 23:434–54.

Grosser, Paul E. and Edwin G. Halpern. 1983. *Anti-Semitism: Causes and Effects. An Analysis and Chronology of Nineteen Hundred Years of Anti-Semitic Attitudes and Practices*. New York: Philosophical Library.

Guibert of Nogent. [c. 1106] 1997. *Gesta Dei per Francos (The Deeds of God through the Franks)*. Rochester, NY: Boydell Press.

Hallam, Elizabeth, ed. 2000. *Chronicles of the Crusades: Eyewitness Accounts of the Wars Between Christianity and Islam*. New York: Welcome Rain.

Hamilton, Bernard. 2000. *The Leper King and His Heirs: Baldwin IV and the Crusader Kingdom of Jerusalem*. Cambridge: Cambridge Univ. Press.

Hanson, Victor Davis. 2001. *Carnage and Culture: Landmark Battles and the Rise of Western Power*. New York: Doubleday.

Hill, Donald R. 1993. *Islamic Science and Engineering*. Edinburgh: Edinburgh Univ. Press.

Hillenbrand, Carole. 1999. *The Crusades: Islamic Perspectives*. Edinburgh: Edinburgh Univ. Press.

Hitti, Philip Khuri. 2002. *History of Syria Including Lebanon and Palestine*. Piscataway, NJ: Gorgias Press.

Hodgson, Marshall G. S. 1974. *The Venture of Islam: Conscience and History in a World Civilization*. 3 vols. Chicago: Univ. of Chicago Press.

Holt, P. M. 1983. "Saladin and His Admirers: A Biographical Reassessment." *Bulletin of the School of Oriental and African Studies, University of London* 46:235–39.

Horvath, Ronald J. 1972. "A Definition of Colonialism." *Current Anthropology* 13: 45–57.

Hunt, E. D. 1982. *Holy Land Pilgrimage in the Later Roman Empire, A.D. 312–460.* Oxford: Clarendon Press.

Hussey, Joan M. 1969. "Byzantium and the Crusades." In Wolff and Hazard 1969, 123–51.

Hyland, Ann. 1994. *The Medieval Warhorse: From Byzantium to the Crusades.* London: Grange Books.

Irwin, Robert. 2006. *Dangerous Knowledge: Orientalism and Its Discontents.* New York: Overlook Press.

Issawi, Charles. 1957. "Crusades and Current Crisis in the Near East: A Historical Parallel." *International Affairs* 33:269–79.

Jaki, Stanley. 1986. *Chance or Reality and Other Essays.* Lanham, MD: Univ. Press of America / Intercollegiate Studies Institute.

Jaki, Stanley L. 1986. *Science and Creation.* Edinburgh: Scottish Academic Press.

Jamison, Alan G. 2006. *Faith and Sword: A Short History of Christian-Muslim Conflict.* London: Reaktion Books.

Jamison, Evelyn. [1939] 1969. "Some Notes on the *Anonymi Gesta Francorum.*" In *Studies in French Language and Mediaeval Literature: Presented to Professor Mildred K. Pope by Pupils, Colleagues, and Friends,* 183–208. Freeport, NY: Books for Libraries Press.

Jandora, John Walter. 1990. *The March from Medina: A Revisionist Study of the Arab Conquests.* Clinton, NJ: Kingston Press.

———. 1986. "Developments in Islamic Warfare: The Early Conquests." *Studia Islamica* 64:101–13.

Jenkins, Romilly. [1969] 1987. *Byzantium: The Imperial Centuries, A.D. 610–1071.* Toronto: Univ. of Toronto Press.

Johnson, Edgar N. 1969. "The Crusades of Frederick Barbarossa and Henry VI." In Wolff and Hazard 1969, 87–122.

Kaegi, Walter E. 1992. *Byzantium and the Early Islamic Conquests.* Cambridge: Cambridge Univ. Press.

Karsh, Efraim. 2007. *Islamic Imperialism: A History.* Updated ed. New Haven, CT: Yale Univ. Press.

Kedar, Benjamin Z. [1990] 2002. "The Subjected Muslims of the Frankish Levant." In *The Crusades: The Essential Readings,* ed. Thomas F. Madden, 235–64. Oxford: Blackwell Publishing.

———. 1984. *Crusade and Mission: European Approaches Toward the Muslims.* Princeton, NJ: Princeton Univ. Press.

———. 1974. "The General Tax of 1183 in the Crusading Kingdom of Jerusalem: Innovation or Adaptation?" *English Historical Review* 89:339–45.

Kennedy, Hugh. 2001. *The Armies of the Caliphs.* London: Routledge.

Knobler, Adam. 2006. "Holy Wars, Empires, and the Portability of the Past: The Modern Uses of the Medieval Crusade." *Comparative Studies in Society and History* 48:293–325.

Kollek, Teddy and Moshe Pearlman. 1970. *Pilgrims to the Holy Land.* New York: Harper and Row.

Krey, August C. 1921. *The First Crusade: The Accounts of Eye-Witnesses and Participants.* Princeton, NJ: Princeton Univ. Press.

Krueger, Hilmar C. 1969. "The Italian City States and the Arabs before 1095." In Baldwin 1969, 40–53.

LaMonte, John L. 1932. *Feudal Monarchy in the Latin Kingdom of Jerusalem, 1100–1291.* Cambridge: Harvard Univ. Press.

Lane-Pool, Stanley. [1898] 2002. *Saladin: All-Powerful Sultan and Uniter of Islam.* New York: Cooper Square Press.

Lawrence, C. H. 2000. *Medieval Monasticism.* 3rd ed. London: Longman.

Leighton, Albert C. 1972. *Transportation and Communication in Early Medieval Europe, A.D. 500–1100.* Newton Abbot, UK: David & Charles.

Lewis, Archibald R. 1951. *Naval Power and Trade in the Mediterranean, A.D. 500–1100.* Princeton, NJ: Princeton Univ. Press.

Lewis, Bernard. 2002. *What Went Wrong? Western Impact and Middle East Response.* Oxford: Oxford Univ. Press,

———. [1982] 2001. *The Muslim Discovery of Europe.* New York: W. W. Norton.

———. 1994. *Islam and the West.* Oxford: Oxford Univ. Press.

———. 1987. *The Jews of Islam.* Princeton, NJ: Princeton Univ. Press.

———. 1967. *The Assassins: A Radical Sect in Islam.* London: Weideenfeld & Nicolson.

Lofland, John, and Rodney Stark. 1965. "Becoming a World-Saver: A Theory of Conversion to a Deviant Perspective." *American Sociological Review* 30:862–75.

Lomax, Derek W. 1978. *The Reconquest of Spain.* London: Longman.

Lopez, Robert S. 1976. *The Commercial Revolution of the Middle Ages, 950–1350.* Cambridge: Cambridge Univ. Press.

———. 1969. "The Norman Conquest of Sicily." In Baldwin 1969, 54–67.

Lunt, W. E. 1915. "Papal Taxation in England in the Reign of Edward I." *English Historical Review* 30:398–417.

Maalouf, Amin. 1984. *The Crusades Through Arab Eyes.* New York: Schocken Books.

Mackensen, Ruth Stellhorn. 1936. "Background of the History of Moslem Libraries (Concluded)." *American Journal of Semitic Languages and Literature* 52:104–10.

———. 1935a. "Background of the History of Moslem Libraries." *American Journal of Semitic Languages and Literature* 51:114–25.

———. 1935b. Background of the History of Moslem Libraries (Continued)." *American Journal of Semitic Languages and Literature* 52:22–33.

Madden, Thomas F. 2003. *Enrico Dandolo and the Rise of Venice.* Baltimore: Johns Hopkins Univ. Press.

———. 2002a. "The Real History of the Crusades." *Crisis Magazine,* April 1. Online edition.

———. 2002b. "The Crusades in the Checkout Aisle." *Crisis Magazine* e-letter, April 12.

———. 1999. *A Concise History of the Crusades.* Lanham, MD: Rowman & Littlefield.

Maier, Christoph T. 1994. *Preaching the Crusades.* Cambridge: Cambridge Univ. Press.

Manchester, William. 1993. *World Lit Only by Fire: The Medieval Mind and the Renaissance.* New York: Little, Brown and Company.

Marshall, Christopher. 1994. *Warfare in the Latin East, 1192–1291.* Cambridge: Cambridge Univ. Press.

Matthew, Donald. 1992. *The Norman Kingdom of Sicily.* Cambridge: Cambridge Univ. Press.

Mayer, Hans Eberhard. 1982. "Henry II of England and the Holy Land." *English Historical Review* 97:721–39.

——. 1972. *The Crusades*. Oxford: Oxford Univ. Press.

McLynn, Frank. 2007. *Richard and John: Kings at War*. Cambridge, MA: Da Capo Press.

McNeal, Edgar H., and Robert Lee Wolff. 1969. "The Fourth Crusade." In Wolff and Hazard 1969, 153–85.

Michaud, J. F. 1855. *The History of the Crusades*. New York: Redfield.

Miller, David. 2005. *Richard the Lionheart: The Mighty Crusader*. London: Phoenix.

Mitchell, Lt. Col. Joseph B., and Sir Edward Creasy. 1964. *Twenty Decisive Battles of the World*. New York: Macmillan.

Mitchell, Sydney Cox. 1951. *Taxation in Medieval England*. New Haven, CT: Yale Univ. Press.

Moffett, Samuel Hugh. 1992. *A History of Christianity in Asia*. Vol. 1. San Francisco: HarperSanFrancisco.

Montgomery, Field-Marshall Viscount (Bernard). 1968. *A History of Warfare*. New York: World.

Moore, R. I. 2008: "A Bad Call," *Times Literary Supplement,* April 25, 25.

Munro, Dana Carleton. 1936. *The Kingdom of the Crusaders*. New York: D. Appleton-Century Company.

Nicholson, Helen. 2003. *The Knights Hospitaller*. Woodbridge, UK: Boydell Press.

——. 2001. *The Chronicle of the Third Crusade, a Translation of "The Itinerium Peregrinorum et Gesta Regis Ricardi."* Aldershot, UK: Ashgate.

Nicholson, Robert. 1969. "The Growth of the Latin States, 1118–1144." In Baldwin 1969, 410–47.

Nicolle, David. 2005. *Acre, 1291: Bloody Sunset of the Crusader States*. Oxford: Osprey Publishing.

——. 2004a. *Historical Atlas of the Islamic World*. London: Mercury Books.

——. 2004b. *Crusader Castles in the Holy Land, 1097–1192*. Botley, UK: Osprey.

——. 1993. *Armies of the Muslim Conquest*. Oxford: Osprey.

Norwich, Viscount John Julius. 1991. *Byzantium: The Apogee*. New York: Alfred A. Knopf.

——. 1990. *Byzantium: The Early Centuries*. London: Penguin Books.

O'Callaghan, Joseph F. 2003. *Reconquest and Crusade in Medieval Spain*. Philadelphia: Univ. of Pennsylvania Press.

Olson, Eric W. 1997. *The Battle of Hattin, 1187*. Fort Leavenworth, KS; U.S. Army Command and General Staff College.

Oman, Charles W. 1960. *Art of War in the Middle Ages, A.D. 378–1515*. Ithaca, NY: Cornell Univ. Press.

Ostrogorsky, George. 1969. *History of the Byzantine State*. New Brunswick, NJ: Rutgers Univ. Press.

Painter, Sidney. 1969a. "Western Europe on the Eve of the Crusades." In Baldwin 1969, 3–29.

——. 1969b. "The Third Crusade: Richard the Lionhearted and Philip Augustus." In Wolff and Hazard 1969, 45–85.

Partington, James Riddick. [1960] 1999. *A History of Greek Fire and Gunpowder.* Baltimore: Johns Hopkins Univ. Press.

Patton, General George S. 1947. *War as I Knew It.* Boston: Houghton Mifflin.

Payne, Robert. [1959] 1995. *The History of Islam.* New York: Barnes and Noble.

———. 1984. *The Dream and the Tomb: A History of the Crusades.* New York: Stein & Day.

Payne-Gallwey, Sir Ralph. 2007. *The Crossbow: Its Military and Sporting History, Construction, and Use.* New York: Skyhorse Publishing.

Peters, Edward. 2004. "The *Firanj* Are Coming—Again." *Orbis* (Winter): 3–17.

———. 1998. *The First Crusade: The Chronicle of Fulcher of Chartres and Other Source Materials.* 2nd ed. Philadelphia: Univ. of Pennsylvania Press.

Peters, F. E. 1993. *The Distant Shrine: The Islamic Centuries in Jerusalem.* New York: A.M.S Press.

Phillips, Jonathan. 2007. *The Second Crusade.* New Haven, CT: Yale Univ. Press.

———. 2004. *The Fourth Crusade and the Sack of Constantinople.* New York: Viking.

———. 1996. *Defenders of the Holy Land: Relations Between the Latin East and the West, 1119–1187.* Oxford: Clarendon Press.

———. 1995. "The Latin East, 1098–1291." In Riley-Smith 1995, 112–40.

Pickthall, M. M. 1927. *The Cultural Side of Islam.* New Delhi: Kitab Bhanan.

Pirenne, Henri. 1939. *Medieval Cities: Their Origins and the Revival of Trade.* Princeton, NJ: Princeton Univ. Press.

Poliakov, Léon. 1965. *The History of Anti-Semitism: From the Time of Christ to the Court Jews.* Vol.1. New York: Vanguard Press.

Porges, Walter, 1946. "The Clergy, the Poor, and the Non-Combatants on the First Crusade." *Speculum* 21:1–23.

Prawer, Joshua. 1972. *The Crusaders' Kingdom: European Colonialism in the Middle Ages.* New York: Praeger.

Previté-Orton, C. W. 1966. *The Shorter Cambridge Medieval History.* Vol. 1. Cambridge: Cambridge Univ. Press.

Pringle, R. Denys. 1991. "Survey of Castles in the Crusader Kingdom of Jerusalem, 1989." *Levant* 23:87–91.

Procopius. [c. 560] 1888. *Of the Buildings of Justinian.* London: Adelphi.

Procter, George. [1856] 2007. *History of the Crusades: Their Rise, Progress, and Results.* Whitefish, MT: Kessinger Publishing Co.

Pryor, John H. 1992. *Geography, Technology, and War: Studies in the Maritime History of the Mediterranean, 649–1571.* Cambridge: Cambridge Univ. Press.

Queller, Donald E., Thomas K. Compton, and Donald A. Campbell. 1974. "The Fourth Crusade: The Neglected Majority." *Speculum* 49:441–65.

Queller, Donald E., and Gerald W. Day. 1976. "Some Arguments in Defense of the Venetians and the Fourth Crusade." *American Historical Review* 81:717–37.

Queller, Donald E., and Thomas F. Madden. 1997. *The Fourth Crusade: The Conquest of Constantinople.* 2nd ed. Philadelphia: Univ. of Pennsylvania Press.

Queller, Donald E., and Susan J. Stratton. 1969. "A Century of Controversy on the Fourth Crusade." *Studies in Medieval and Renaissance History* 6:235–77.

Ralph of Caen. [c. 1118] 2005. *The Gesta Tancredi: A History of the Normans on the First Crusade.* Aldershot, UK: Ashgate.

Read, Piers Paul. 1999. *The Templars*. New York: St. Martin's Press.

Regan, Geoffrey. 1998. *Lionhearts: Saladin, Richard I, and the Era of the Third Crusade*. New York: Walker and Co.

Richard, Jean. 1999. *The Crusades, c. 1071–c. 1291*. Cambridge: Cambridge Univ. Press.

Riley-Smith, Jonathan. 2005. *The Crusades: A History*. 2nd ed. London: Continuum.

———. 2003. "Islam and the Crusades in History and Imagination, 8 November 1898– 11 September 2001." *Crusades* 2:151–67.

———. 2002a. "Casualties and the Number of Knights on the First Crusade." *Crusades* 1:13–28.

———. 2002b. "Early Crusaders to the East and the Costs of Crusading, 1095–1130." In *The Crusades: The Essential Readings*, ed. Thomas F. Madden, 156–71. Oxford: Blackwell Publishing.

———. 1999. *Hospitallers: The History of the Order of Saint John*. London: Hambledon Press.

———. 1997. *The First Crusaders, 1095–1131*. Cambridge: Cambridge Univ. Press.

———, ed. 1995. *The Oxford Illustrated History of the Crusades*. Oxford: Oxford Univ. Press.

———, ed. 1991. *The Atlas of the Crusades*. New York: Facts on File.

———. 1986. *The First Crusade and the Idea of Crusading*. Philadelphia: Univ. of Pennsylvania Press.

———. 1983. "The Motives of the Earliest Crusaders and the Settlement of Latin Palestine, 1095–1100." *English Historical Review* 98:721–36.

———. 1978. "Peace Never Established: The Case of the Kingdom of Jerusalem." *Transactions of the Royal Historical Society*, 5th ser., 28:87–112.

———. 1973. *The Feudal Nobility and the Kingdom of Jerusalem, 1174–1277*. New York: Macmillan.

Robert the Monk. [c. 1106] 2005. *History of the First Crusade: Historia Iherosolimitana*. Aldershot, UK: Ashgate.

Rodgers, Admiral William L. [1940] 1996. *Naval Warfare Under Oars, 4th to 16th Centuries*. Annapolis, MD: Naval Institute Press.

Rodinson, Maxime. 1980. *Muhammad*. New York: Random House.

Roland, Alex. 1992. "Secrecy, Technology, and War: Greek Fire and the Defense of Byzantium, 678–1204." *Technology and Culture* 33:655–79.

Rose, Susan. 1999. "Islam Versus Christendom: The Naval Dimension, 1000–1600." *Journal of Military History* 63:561–78.

Runciman, Sir Steven. 1969a. "The Pilgrimages to Palestine Before 1095." In Baldwin 1969, 68–78.

———. 1969b. "The First Crusade: Clermont to Constantinople." In Baldwin 1969, 253–79.

———. 1969c. "The First Crusade: Constantinople to Antioch." In Baldwin 1969, 280–307.

———. 1969d. "The First Crusade: Antioch to Ascalon." In Baldwin 1969, 308–41.

———. 1951. *A History of the Crusades*. 3 vols. Cambridge: Cambridge Univ. Press.

Russell, Josiah Cox, 1972. *Medieval Regions and Their Cities*. Bloomington: Indiana Univ. Press.

———. 1958. *Late Ancient and Medieval Population.* Philadelphia: American Philosophical Society.

Ruthven, Malise. 2004. *Historical Atlas of Islam.* Cambridge, MA: Harvard Univ. Press.

Salahi, M. A. 1995. *Muhammad: Man and Prophet.* Shaftesbury, UK: Element.

Saunders, J. J. 1962. *Aspects of the Crusades.* Christchurch, NZ: Univ. of Canterbury Press.

Siberry, Elizabeth. 1995. "Images of the Crusades in the Nineteenth and Twentieth Centuries." In *The Oxford Illustrated History of the Crusades,* ed. Jonathan Riley-Smith, 365–85. Oxford: Oxford Univ. Press.

———. 1985. *Criticism of Crusading, 1095–1274.* Oxford: Clarendon Press.

Sire, H. J. A. 1996. *The Knights of Malta.* New Haven, CT: Yale Univ. Press.

Sivan, Emmanuel. 1973. *Modern Arab Historiography of the Crusades.* Tel Aviv: Tel Aviv Univ., Shiloah Center for Middle Eastern and African Studies.

Smail, R. C. 1995. *Crusading Warfare, 1097–1193.* 2nd ed. Cambridge: Cambridge Univ. Press.

———. 1951. "Crusaders' Castles of the Twelfth Century." *Cambridge Historical Journal* 10:133–49.

Southern, R. W. 1970. *Western Society and the Church in the Middle Ages.* London: Penguin.

Spielvogel, Jackson J. 2000. *Western Civilization.* 4th ed. Belmont, CA: Wadsworth.

Stark, Rodney. 2007. *Discovering God: The Origins of the Great Religions and the Evolution of Belief.* San Francisco: HarperOne.

———. 2005. *The Victory of Reason: How Christianity Led to Freedom, Capitalism, and Western Success.* New York: Random House.

———. 2003. *For the Glory of God: How Monotheism Led to Reformations, Science, Witch-Hunts, and the End of Slavery.* Princeton, NJ: Princeton Univ. Press.

———. 1996. *The Rise of Christianity.* Princeton, NJ: Princeton Univ. Press.

Stark, Rodney, and Roger Finke. 2000. *Acts of Faith: Explaining the Human Side of Religion.* Berkeley: Univ. of California Press.

Strayer, Joseph R. 1969. "The Crusades of Louis IX." In Wolff and Hazard 1969, 487–518.

Taylor, Joan. 2008. "The Nea Church." *Biblical Archaeology Review* 34 (January/February): 51–59.

Ter-Ghevondian, Aram. 1983. "The Armenian Rebellion of 703 Against the Caliphate." *Armenian Review* 36:59–72.

Throop, Palmer A. 1940. *Criticism of the Crusade: A Study of Public Opinion and Crusade Propaganda.* Amsterdam: N. V. Swets & Zeitlinger.

Turnbull, Stephen. 2004. *The Walls of Constantinople, A.D. 324–1453.* New York: Osprey.

Tyerman, Christopher. 2006. *God's War: A New History of the Crusades.* Cambridge, MA: Belknap Press.

———. 1998. *The Invention of the Crusades.* Toronto: Univ. of Toronto Press.

Usher, Abbot Payson. 1966. *A History of Mechanical Inventions.* Cambridge, MA: Harvard Univ. Press.

Van Cleve, Thomas C. 1969. "The Fifth Crusade." In Wolff and Hazard 1969, 377–428.

Bibliography

Van Houts, Elisabeth. 2000. *The Normans in Europe.* Manchester, UK: Manchester Univ. Press.

Verbruggen, J. F. 2002. *The Art of Warfare in Western Europe During the Middle Ages from the Eighth Century.* Rochester, NY: Boydell Press.

Vryonis, Speros. 1967. *Byzantium and Europe.* New York: Harcourt, Brace, and World.

Webb, Diana. 2001. *Pilgrims and Pilgrimage in the Medieval West.* London: I. B. Tauris.

Wheeler, Benjamin W. 1969. "The Reconquest of Spain Before 1095." In Baldwin 1969, 30–39.

White, Lynn, Jr. 1962. *Medieval Technology and Social Change.* Oxford: Oxford Univ. Press.

———. 1940. "Technology and Invention in the Middle Ages." *Speculum* 15:141–56.

William of Tyre. [1180] 1943. *A History of Deeds Done Beyond the Sea.* 2 vols. New York: Columbia Univ. Press.

Wolff, Robert Lee. 1969. "The Latin Empire of Constantinople." In Wolff and Hazard 1969, 187–233.

Wolff, Robert Lee, and Harry W. Hazard, eds. 1969. *A History of the Crusades.* Vol. 2, *The Later Crusades, 1189–1311.* Madison: Univ. of Wisconsin Press.

Ye'or, Bat. 1996. *The Decline of Eastern Christianity Under Islam: From Jihad to Dhimmitude.* Rutherford, NJ: Fairleigh Dickinson Univ. Press.

———. 1985. *The Dhimmi: Jews and Christians Under Islam.* Rutherford, NJ: Fairleigh Dickinson Univ. Press.

Ziada, Mustafa M. 1969. "The Mamluk Sultans to 1293." In Wolff and Hazard 1969, 735–58.

NOTES

INTRODUCTION:
GREEDY BARBARIANS IN ARMOR?

1. Payne 1984, 28–29.
2. There are four versions of the pope's speech, all of them written several years later. They differ considerably, although there is substantial overlap. In addition, there are several, somewhat different translations of each into English.
3. Version of Robert of Rheims; document in Peters 1998, 27.
4. Quoted in Michaud 1855, 51.
5. Armstrong [1991] 2001; Prawer 1972.
6. Ekelund et al.. 1996.
7. Quote from Madden 2002a.
8. Quoted in Curry 2002, 36.
9. June 20, 1999, sec. 4, p. 15.
10. Ontario Consultants on Religious Tolerance, www.religioustolerance.org/chr_cru1.htm.
11. Armstrong [1999] 2001, 4.
12. Carroll 2004, 5.
13. Quoted in Richard 1999, 475.
14. Hume 1761, 1:209.
15. Quoted in Richard 1999, 475.
16. Riley-Smith 2003, 154.
17. Quoted in Saunders 1962, 11.
18. Quoted in Saunders 1962, 11–12.
19. Gibbon [1776–1788] 1994, bk. 6, chap. 58.
20. Duby 1977; France 1997; Mayer 1972.
21. In Riley-Smith 2003, 159.
22. Armstrong [1991] 2001, xii.
23. Mayer 1972, 22–25.
24. Ekelund et al. 1996. This is one of the most inept and uninformed efforts at trying to apply economic principles by analogy that I have ever encountered.
25. Spielvogel 2000, 259.
26. See Tyerman 1998.

27. To list them would take most of a page. Some will be mentioned in the text; the rest will fill the endnotes.

CHAPTER ONE:
MUSLIM INVADERS

1. Quoted in Karsh 2007, 4.
2. Rodinson 1980, 273.
3. Becker [1909] 2006, 2.
4. Becker 1926a, 329.
5. Kennedy 2001, 6.
6. Donner 1981, 221.
7. Glubb [1963] 1995, 125.
8. Becker 1926a, 345.
9. Jandora 1990, 1986.
10. Jandora 1990.
11. Gil 1992, 61–64.
12. Gil 1992, 54.
13. Gil 1992, 70.
14. Glubb [1963] 1995, 230.
15. Glubb [1963] 1995, 238
16. Glubb [1963] 1995, 240.
17. Second only to Constantinople (Chandler 1987).
18. Glubb [1963] 1995, 241.
19. Glubb [1963] 1995, 284.
20. Abun-Nasr 1971.
21. Brent and Fentress 1996.
22. Brent and Fentress 1996.
23. Ye'or 1996, 48.
24. Becker 1926a, 370.
25. Fregosi 1998, 94
26. Fregosi 1998, 96.
27. Fregosi 1998, 132.
28. Jamison 2006, 16.
29. Quoted in Jandora 1990, 105.
30. Kennedy 2001, chap. 7.
31. Kaegi 1992.
32. Kennedy 2001; Nicolle 1993.
33. Glubb [1963] 1995, 25.
34. Donner 1981; Glubb [1963] 1995; Kennedy 2001.
35. Kaegi 1992, 39–40.
36. Donner 1981, 225.
37. Saunders 1962, 29.
38. Kennedy 2001, 7.
39. Hodgson 1974, vol. 1.
40. Hodgson 1974, 1:268.

41. Payne [1959] 1995, 105.
42. Hodgson 1974; Payne [1959] 1995.
43. Ter-Ghevondian 1983.
44. Stark 2007, chap. 8.
45. Stark 2001, 133.
46. Capponi 2006.
47. Hodgson 1974, 1:308.
48. Lofland and Stark 1965; Stark and Finke 2000.
49. Bulliet 1979a.
50. Armstrong [1999] 2001, 4.
51. Lomax 1978, 58–59.

CHAPTER TWO: CHRISTENDOM STRIKES BACK

1. Norwich 1990, 324.
2. Jenkins [1966] 1987, 42.
3. Ostrogorsky 1969, 125.
4. Norwich 1990, 325.
5. Kennedy 2001, 12.
6. Turnbull 2004.
7. Roland 1992.
8. Partington [1969] 1999, 12–13.
9. Roland 1992.
10. Partington [1960] 1999.
11. Partington [1960] 1999.
12. Fregosi 1998.
13. Davis 2001, 105.
14. Hanson 2001, 141.
15. Cowley and Parker 2001, xiii.
16. Davis 1913, 362.
17. Quoted in Mitchell and Creasy 1964, 111.
18. Hanson 2001; Montgomery 1968.
19. Both quotations from Mitchell and Creasy 1964, 110–11.
20. Davis 1913, 363.
21. Quoted in Mitchell and Creasy 1964, 112.
22. White 1962; White 1940.
23. Mitchell and Creasy 1964.
24. Gibbon [1776–1788] 1994, bk. 5, chap. 52, p. 336.
25. Delbrück [1920] 1990, 441.
26. Hitti 2002, 469.
27. Cardini 2001, 9
28. Lewis [1982] 2001, 19.
29. Lewis [1982] 2001, 59–60.
30. Hanson 2001.
31. Lomax 1978, 32.

32. Collins 1998; Lomax 1978.

33. Lomax 1978, 32.

34. Wheeler 1969, 34.

35. Quoted in O'Callaghan 2003, 26.

36. Quoted in O'Callaghan 2003, 25.

37. O'Callaghan 2003, 27.

38. Lomax 1978, 65.

39. Lomax 1978, 74.

40. Norwich 1991.

41. Norwich 1991, 93.

42. Norwich 1991, 284.

43. Brown 2003, 36.

44. Brown 2003, 36.

45. Brown 2003, 37.

46. Norwich 1991, 285.

47. Norwich 1991, 285.

48. Brown 2003, 42.

49. In Van Houts 2000, 243.

50. Comnena [c. 1148] 1969, 54.

51. Matthew 1992.

52. Pirenne 1939, 25.

53. Gabrieli 1964; Gibb 1958.

54. Dennet 1948 listed six objections to Pirenne's thesis, none of them involving their naval ability to close off European access to the Mediterranean.

55. Quoted in Pryor 1992, 103.

56. Lewis 1951, 69.

57. Lewis 1951, 72.

58. Norwich 1991, 94.

59. Lewis 1951, 71.

60. Stark 2005.

61. Krueger 1969, 40.

CHAPTER THREE:
WESTERN "IGNORANCE" VERSUS
EASTERN "CULTURE"

1. Lewis 2002, 6.

2. Lewis 2002, 7.

3. Lewis 2002, 6.

4. Moffett 1992, 344.

5. Hodgson 1974:1:298.

6. Hodgson 1974:1:298.

7. Butler [1902] 2005, 114.

8. Jandora 1986, 112.

9. Jamieson 2006, 23; Lewis 1951, 64.

Notes

10. Aly Mohamed Fahmy's fine book on Muslim sea-power (1966) depends almost entirely on Byzantine and other Western sources.
11. Lewis 1951, 66–67.
12. Davis 2001, 257; also Beeching 1982, 192.
13. Beeching 1982, 192.
14. Davis 2001, 260.
15. Kollek and Pearlman 1970, 59.
16. Gil 1992, 94.
17. Hill 1993, 10.
18. Bloom 2007, 7.
19. Nasr 1993, 135–36.
20. Nasr 1993, 136.
21. Ajram 1992.
22. Quoted in Brickman 1961, 85.
23. Dickens 1999, 8.
24. Brickman 1961, 84.
25. In Peters 1993, 90.
26. Gil 1992, 470.
27. Quoted in Gil 1992, 470.
28. Pickthall 1927.
29. Farah 1994, 199.
30. Jaki 1986, 208.
31. See Colish 1997; Stark 2003, chap. 2.
32. Butler 1884, 239.
33. Mackensen 1936, 106.
34. Mackensen 1936, 110.
35. For a summary, see Butler [1902] 2005 and Mackensen 1935a.
36. Quoted in Mackensen 1935a, 117.
37. Afsaruddin 1990, 292.
38. Mackensen 1935a
39. Moffett 1992, 355.
40. Mackensen 1935a, 122.
41. *Works* XII.
42. Quoted in Gay 1966.
43. Gibbon [1776–1788] 1994, bk. 6, chap. 71.
44. Boorstin 1983, 100.
45. Manchester 1993, 3, 5.
46. Stark 2005; 2003.
47. Gimpel 1976, viii, 1.
48. White 1940, 151.
49. Ajram 1992, app. B.
50. Ajram 1992, app. B.
51. Bulliet [1975] 1990.
52. Leighton 1972, 112.
53. Bulliet [1975] 1990, 20.

54. Leighton 1972, 107.
55. Usher 1966, 184.
56. Leighton 1972, 74–75.
57. France 1994, 91.
58. Lopez 1976, 44.
59. Bairoch 1988, 125; Gimpel 1976, 43.
60. Gies and Gies 1994; Gimpel 1976; White 1962.
61. Stark 2005, chap. 2.
62. White 1940.
63. Hyland 1994, 114.
64. France 1999, 17.
65. France 1994, 149.
66. Smail 1995, 81.
67. Quoted in France 1994, 149.
68. Payne-Gallwey 2007, 3.
69. Marshall 1994, 59–60.
70. Payne-Gallwey 2007, 20.
71. Payne-Gallwey 2007, 4.
72. Comnena [c. 1148] 1969, 327.
73. Verbruggen 2002.
74. Marshall 1994, 172–73.
75. Marshall 1994, 172.
76. Rose 1999, 569.
77. Pryor 1992, 30.
78. Bachrach 1985.

CHAPTER FOUR:
PILGRIMAGE AND PERSECUTION

1. John puts him in Jerusalem more frequently than do the other Gospels.
2. Gil 1992, 483.
3. Quoted in Runciman 1969, 69.
4. Hunt 1982, 4.
5. Eusebius, *Life of Constantine*, quoted in Peters 1993, 26–27.
6. Kollek and Pearlman 1970, 38.
7. In Peters 1993, 33.
8. Runciman 1969, 69–70.
9. Quoted in Hunt 1982, 150.
10. Hunt 1982, 34.
11. Hunt 1982, 56.
12. Runciman 1969, 69.
13. Russell 1958, 101.
14. Kollek and Pearlman 1970, 51.
15. Kollek and Pearlman 1970, 52.
16. Procopius [c. 560] 1888.
17. Procopius [c. 560] 1888, 138.

18. Taylor 2008.
19. Gil 1992, 54.
20. Gil 1992, 58.
21. Gil 1992, 69.
22. Peters 1993, 31.
23. Rodinson 1980.
24. Gil 1992, 471.
25. Gil 1992, 472.
26. Salahi 1995, 170–71.
27. Grabar 2006.
28. Kollek and Pearlman 1970, 67.
29. Runciman, 1951, 1:29.
30. Cohen 2008.
31. Runciman 1969, 77.
32. All based on Runciman 1969.
33. Runciman 1969, 73.
34. Kollek and Pearlman 1970, 1.
35. Riley-Smith 1997, 28.
36. Erdoes 1988, 26.
37. Riley-Smith 1997, 28.
38. Painter 1969, 15.
39. In Webb 2001, 35.
40. Runciman 1969, 76.
41. Gil 1992, 487.
42. Davidson 1976, chap. 5.
43. Runciman 1951, 1:47.
44. Lopez 1969, 61.
45. Davidson 1976, 254.
46. Hodgson 1974, 2:26.
47. See Atiya 1968; Gil 1992; Hodgson 1974; Runciman 1951, vol. 1.
48. Runciman 1951, 1:35.
49. In Biddle 1999, 72.
50. Kollek and Pearlman 1970, 82.
51. Runciman 1951, 1:49.
52. Taylor 2008.
53. All four examples from Riley-Smith 1997, 37–38.
54. Stark 2001, chap. 2.
55. Cahen 1969, 138.
56. Norwich 1991, 340.
57. Norwich 1991, 341.
58. Quoted in Norwich 1991, 343.
59. Charanis 1969, 192.
60. Quoted in Norwich 1991, 356.
61. Gil 1992, 410.
62. Gil 1992, 412.
63. Runciman 1969, 78.

64. Gil 1992, 488.
65. Runciman 1951, 1:79.

CHAPTER FIVE:
ENLISTING CRUSADERS

1. Duncalf 1969a, 234.
2. Baldric in Peters 1998, 28.
3. Fletcher 1997, 19.
4. Duffy 1997, 27.
5. Fletcher 1997, 38.
6. For a summary, see Stark 2003.
7. Cheetham 1983, 84.
8. Stark 2004, 56.
9. Cole 1991, 6.
10. Stark and Finke 2000, chap. 3.
11. Duby 1994; Lawrence 2000.
12. Bull 1993, 117.
13. Riley-Smith 2005, 4.
14. Chandler 1987, 159.
15. Bull 1993.
16. Porges 1946, 4.
17. Document in Peters 1998, 11–12.
18. Painter 1969a, 15.
19. Document in Peters 1998, 12–13.
20. Erdmann [1935] 1977.
21. Cole 1991, 3.
22. Document in Peters 1998, 37.
23. Document in Peters 1998, 44.
24. Riley-Smith 2005, 9.
25. Riley-Smith 1997, 63.
26. Riley-Smith 1997, 62.
27. Constable 1953.
28. Riley-Smith 1997, 2.
29. Riley-Smith 1997.
30. Stark 2007, 2005.
31. Riley-Smith 1997, chap. 4.
32. Munro 1911, 497.
33. Riley-Smith 1997, 110.
34. Riley-Smith 1986, 43.
35. Lloyd 1995, 55.
36. Riley-Smith 1986, 117.
37. Riley-Smith 1997, 129.
38. Lloyd 1995, 55.
39. Calculation based on Munro 1911.
40. Runciman 1969b, 276.

41. Duncalf 1969b, 267.
42. Stark 2005.
43. Riley-Smith 1997, 116.
44. France 1994, 86.
45. Riley-Smith 1997, 118.
46. Riley-Smith 1997, 119.
47. Riley-Smith 2005, 23.
48. Robert of Reims version; document in Peters 1998, 29.
49. Brundage 1985; Porges 1946.
50. Runciman 1951, 1:113.
51. Comnena [c. 1148] 1969, 309.
52. Document in Peters 1998, 108–9.
53. Document in Peters 1998, 103.
54. Runciman 1951, 1:114.
55. Chandler 1987, 15.
56. Document in Peters 1998, 104–7.
57. Albert of Aachen; document in Peters 1998, 104–7.
58. Riley-Smith 1997, 49.
59. Brundage 1985.
60. Quoted in Riley-Smith 1997, 72.

CHAPTER SIX:
GOING EAST

1. Fulcher of Chartres [c. 1127] 1969, 81.
2. Russell 1958.
3. Comnena [c. 1148] 1969, 311.
4. Runciman 1951, 1:123; Tyerman 2006, 99.
5. Runciman 1951, 1:336.
6. Riley-Smith 1991, 28.
7. Brundage 1985.
8. Runciman 1951, 1:339–40.
9. France 1994.
10. Summary in Duncalf 1921, 452.
11. Mayer 1972.
12. Duncalf 1969b, 256; Duncalf 1921, 452; France 1994, 86; Gillingham 1999, 59.
13. Duncalf 1921.
14. Asbridge 2004, 82.
15. Mayer 1972, 40.
16. Quoted in Duncalf 1921, 441.
17. Document in Peters 1998, 104.
18. Document in Krey 1921, 49.
19. Duncalf 1921, 444–45.
20. Document in Krey 1921, 51.
21. Tyerman 2006, 98.
22. Tyerman 2006.

23. Duncalf 1969b, 260.
24. Baron 1957; Chazan 2006; Chazan 1996; Chazan 1986; Chazan 1980; Graetz 1894; Grosser and Halpern 1983; Poliakov 1965; Runciman 1951, vol. 1; Stark 2001.
25. Poliakov 1965, 45.
26. Madden 1999, 20.
27. Runciman 1951, 1:141.
28. Runciman 1951, 1:142.
29. Comnena [c. 1148] 1969, 313–14.
30. Runciman 1951, 1:144.
31. Runciman 1951, 1:149.
32. Runciman 1951, 1:152.
33. Comnena [c. 1148] 1969, 422.
34. France 1994, 116.
35. Anonymous [c. 1102] 1962, 6, 10.
36. France 1994, 118.
37. France 1994, 135.
38. Jamison [1939] 1969, 208.

CHAPTER SEVEN:
BLOODY VICTORIES

1. Runciman 1969c, 289.
2. Runciman 1951, 1:179.
3. Anonymous [c. 1102] 1962, 15.
4. Anonymous [c. 1102] 1962, 17.
5. Anonymous [c. 1102] 1962, 17.
6. France 1994, 122.
7. France 1994, 170–75.
8. Fulcher of Chartres [c. 1127] 1969, 84.
9. Anonymous [c. 1102] 1962, 20.
10. Runciman 1951, 1:186.
11. Runciman 1951, 1:187.
12. Anonymous [c. 1102] 1962, 23.
13. Runciman 1951, 1:192.
14. Anonymous [c. 1102] 1962, 27.
15. Chandler 1987.
16. Runciman 1951, 1:216.
17. Runciman 1951, 1:214–15.
18. Anonymous [c. 1102] 1962, 35.
19. France 1994, 301.
20. Anonymous [c. 1102] 1962, 37.
21. France 1994, 286.
22. France 1994, 279.
23. Anonymous [c. 1102] 1962, 69.
24. Runciman 1951, 1:256.
25. Riley-Smith 1986, 67.

26. Riley-Smith 1986, 66.
27. France 1994, 287; Riley-Smith 1986, 66.
28. Runciman 1969d, 329.
29. Runciman 1951, 1:279.
30. Runciman 1951, 1:339–40.
31. France 1994, 327.
32. Runciman 1951, 1:284.
33. France 1994, 351.
34. Guibert of Nogent [c. 1106] 1997, 131.
35. Guibert of Nogent [c. 1106] 1997, 132.
36. Document in Peters 1998, 256–61.
37. France 1994, 355.
38. Stark 2001.
39. France 1994, 343.
40. Gil 1992, 828.
41. Document reprinted in Peters 1998, 264–68.
42. Tyerman 2006, 160.
43. Runciman 1951, 1:297.

CHAPTER EIGHT:
THE CRUSADER KINGDOMS

1. William of Tyre [c. 1180] 1943, bk. 9, chap. 9.
2. Russell 1972, 201–5.
3. Riley-Smith 1983, 733.
4. Fink 1969, 370.
5. Fulcher of Chartres [c. 1127] 1969, 150.
6. Riley-Smith 1983, 732.
7. Riley-Smith 1983, 734.
8. Boas 1998, 152.
9. Prawer 1972, 73.
10. Chandler 1987, 471.
11. Fink 1969, 385.
12. Munro 1936.
13. Munro 1936, 86.
14. Runciman 1951, 2:291–92.
15. Boas 1998, 142.
16. Fulcher of Chartres [c. 1127] 1969, 271.
17. Boas 1998, 139.
18. Kedar [1990] 2002, 244–45.
19. Kedar 1984.
20. Kedar [1990] 2002, 254.
21. Quoted in Munro 1936, 106–7.
22. See Horvath 1972.
23. Prawer 1972.
24. Quoted in Burman 1986, 15–16.

25. Quoted in Burman 1986, 16.

26. Burman 1986, 14.

27. Burman 1986, 19.

28. Burman 1986, 23.

29. Bernard was canonized in 1174, only twenty-one years after his death. His reputation has been so enduring that in 1953, the eight hundredth anniversary of his death, Pope Pius XII devoted an encyclical to recommending his virtues to all.

30. Southern 1970.

31. Daniel-Rops 1957.

32. Barber 1994, 17.

33. Barber 1994, 16.

34. Marshall 1994, 57.

35. Prawer 1972, 261.

36. Marshall 1994, 45.

37. Marshall 1994, 57.

38. Prawer 1972, 261.

39. Burman 1986, 33.

40. Bernard of Clairvaux, *De Laude Novae Militiae*, vol. 1.

41. *Catholic Encyclopedia*, s.v. "The Knights Templars."

42. Barber 1994, 22.

43. *Catholic Encyclopedia*, s.v. "The Knights Templars."

44. Stark 2005.

45. Baldwin 1937, 96.

46. Burman 1986, 82.

47. Burman 1986, 83.

48. Burman 1986, 88.

49. Ferris 1902, 1.

50. Riley-Smith 2005, 81.

51. Nicholson 2003, 3.

52. Riley-Smith 1999, 25.

53. Riley-Smith 1999, 33.

54. Nicholson 2003, 13.

55. See Sire 1996.

CHAPTER NINE:
THE STRUGGLE TO DEFEND THE KINGDOMS

1. Riley-Smith 1978, 99.

2. Runciman 1951, 2:238.

3. Runciman 1951, 2:253.

4. Tyerman 2006, 279.

5. Tyerman 2006, 275.

6. Phillips 2007, 99–101.

7. In Poliakov 1965, 48.

8. Stark 2001, chap. 3.

9. In Chazen 1980, 107–8.

10. Berry 1969, 463.
11. Moore 2008, 28.
12. In Phillips 2007, xxiii–xxiv.
13. Tyerman 2006, 318.
14. Procter [1856] 2007, 220.
15. Phillips 2007, 169.
16. Siberry 1985, 25.
17. Runciman 1951, 2:268.
18. Phillips 2007, 180.
19. Phillips 2007, 206.
20. Riley-Smith 2005, 128.
21. Nicolle 2004b, 50.
22. Pringle 1991.
23. Riley-Smith 1991, 56.
24. Smail 1951.
25. Runciman 1951, 2:329.
26. Runciman 1951, 2:366.
27. Lane-Poole [1898] 2002, 372.
28. Runciman 1951, 2:414.
29. Hamilton 2000.
30. William of Tyre [c. 1180] 1943, 2:407.
31. Runciman 1951, 2:462.
32. Runciman 1951, 2:464.
33. Lane-Poole [1898] 2002, 229.
34. Brand 1962, 170.
35. Irwin 2006, 213.
36. Munro 1935, 56.
37. Moffett 1992, 391.
38. Riley-Smith 2005, 305; Siberry 1995, 368.
39. Tyerman 2006, 351.
40. Gibbon [1776–1788] 1994, bk. 6, chap. 59.
41. Quoted in Madden 1999, 78.
42. Painter 1969b, 46.
43. Painter 1969b, 47.
44. Lane-Poole [1898] 2002, 221.
45. Ibn-el-Athir, quoted in Lane-Poole [1898] 2002, 222.
46. Lane-Poole [1898] 2002, 222; Runciman 1951, 2:472.
47. Ehrenkreutz 1955.
48. Ehrenkreutz 1955, 111.
49. Painter 1969b, 47.
50. Runciman 1959, 3:11.
51. Painter 1969b, 57.
52. Brand 1962, 173.
53. Quoted in Brand 1962, 175.
54. Brand 1962, 175.
55. Brand 1962, 177.

56. Painter 1969, 50.
57. Runciman 1951, 3:16.
58. Painter 1969b, 50.
59. Pryor 1992, 129.
60. Painter 1969b, 52.
61. Pryor 1992, 129.
62. Painter 1969b, 73.
63. Smail 1995, 164.
64. Painter 1969b, 74.
65. Painter 1969b, 75.
66. McLynn 2007, 214–15.
67. Runciman 1951, 3:130.
68. Durant 1950, 605; Tyerman 2006, 553.
69. Chandler 1987.
70. Runciman 1951, 3:123.
71. Vryonis 1967, 152.
72. Durant 1950, 605.
73. For a fine summary, see Queller and Stratton 1969.
74. Quoted in Phillips 2004, xiii.
75. Queller and Madden 1997, 135.
76. Queller and Madden 1997, 135.
77. Carroll 1993, 157, 131; Durant 1950, 605; Tyerman 2006, 553.
78. Richard 1999, 250.
79. McNeal and Wolff 1969, 159.
80. McNeal and Wolf 1969, 162.
81. McNeal and Wolff 1969, 167.
82. Madden 2003.
83. McNeal and Wolff 1969, 173.
84. Richard 1999, 247–48.
85. McNeal and Wolff 1969, 179.
86. Phillips 2004, 175.
87. McNeal and Wolff 1969, 181.
88. Richard 1999, 250.
89. Wolff 1969, 189.
90. McNeal and Wolff 1969, 185.

CHAPTER TEN:
CRUSADES AGAINST EGYPT

1. Van Cleve 1969, 388.
2. Van Cleve 1969, 393.
3. Van Cleve 1969, 394.
4. Runciman 1951, 3:152; Van Cleve 1969, 398–99.
5. Van Cleve 1969, 399.
6. Van Cleve 1969, 400.
7. Runciman 1951, 3:154.

8. Runciman 1951, 3:155.
9. Runciman 1951, 3:158.
10. Van Cleve 1969, 414.
11. Runciman 1951, 3:162; Van Cleve 1969, 418.
12. Quoted in Hallam 2000, 254.
13. Tyerman 2006, 771.
14. Runciman 1951, 3:256.
15. Strayer 1969, 487.
16. Richard 1999, 345.
17. Richard 1999, 345.
18. Runciman 1951, 3:262.
19. Runciman 1951, 3:266
20. Richard 1999, 348.
21. Riley-Smith 2005, 208.
22. Ziada 1969, 735.
23. Ziada 1969.
24. Runciman 1951, 3:318.
25. Runciman 1951, 3:318.
26. Madden 1999, 181.
27. Madden 1999, 181.
28. Runciman 1951, 3:325.
29. Madden 1999, 181–82.
30. Runciman 1951, 3:325.
31. Mayer 1972, 281.
32. Tyerman 2006, 810.
33. Armstrong [1991] 2001, 448.
34. Riley-Smith 1991, 115.
35. Madden 1999, 184; Riley-Smith 2005, 210.
36. Riley-Smith 2005, 210.
37. Madden 1999, 185.
38. Madden 1999, 211.
39. Runciman 1951, 3:348.

CONCLUSION:
MISSION ABANDONED

1. Siberry 1985, 118.
2. Siberry 1985, 119.
3. Siberry 1985, 120.
4. Cazel 1955, 385.
5. Bédier and Aubry 1909, 45.
6. Painter 1969, 55.
7. Tyerman 2006, 779.
8. Tyerman 2006, 779.
9. Siberry 1985, 194.
10. Siberry 1985, 194.

11. Quoted in Throop 1940, 178.
12. Siberry 1985, 69.
13. Brundage 1985.
14. Quoted in Throop 1940, 169.
15. Runciman 1951, 3:407.
16. Runciman 1951, 3:419.
17. Quoted in Nicolle 2005, 83.
18. Armstrong [1991] 2001, xiv.
19. Riley-Smith 2003, 160–61.
20. Peters 2003, 6.
21. Hillenbrand 1999, 4–5.
22. In Hillenbrand 1999, 45.
23. There was no Arabic term for "crusaders." They had merely been referred to as "Franks."
24. Knobler 2006, 310.
25. Knobler 2006, 310.
26. Knobler 2006, 310.
27. Lewis 2002, 3.
28. Peters 2003; Riley-Smith 2003.
29. Andrea 2003, 2.
30. Sivan 1973, 12.
31. Knobler 2006, 320.
32. Various Muslims quoted by Riley-Smith 2003, 162.